The Newer Eve

Also by Christine Collette

FOR LABOUR AND FOR WOMEN: THE WOMEN'S LABOUR LEAGUE, 1906–1918

THE INTERNATIONAL FAITH: Labour's Attitudes to European Socialism, 1918–1939

EUROPEAN WOMEN'S HISTORY: A Reader (*With Fiona Montgomery*)

INTO THE MELTING POT: Teaching Women's Studies in the New Millennium (*With Fiona Montgomery*)

MODERN BRITAIN SINCE 1979 (*With Keith Laybourn*)

JEWS, LABOUR AND THE LEFT (*Edited With Stephen Bird*)

The Newer Eve

Women, Feminists and the Labour Party

Christine Collette

First published 2009 by
PALGRAVE MACMILLAN

Palgrave Macmillan in the UK is an imprint of Macmillan Publishers Limited, registered in England, company number 785998, of Houndmills, Basingstoke, Hampshire RG21 6XS.

Palgrave Macmillan in the US is a division of St Martin's Press LLC, 175 Fifth Avenue, New York, NY 10010.

Palgrave Macmillan is the global academic imprint of the above companies and has companies and representatives throughout the world.

Palgrave® and Macmillan® are registered trademarks in the United States, the United Kingdom, Europe and other countries.

ISBN-13: 978–0–230–22214–4 hardback
ISBN-10: 0–230–22214–5 hardback

This book is printed on paper suitable for recycling and made from fully managed and sustained forest sources. Logging, pulping and manufacturing processes are expected to conform to the environmental regulations of the country of origin.

A catalogue record for this book is available from the British Library.

A catalog record for this book is available from the Library of Congress.

10   9   8   7   6   5   4   3   2   1
18   17   16   15   14   13   12   11   10   09

Printed and bound in Great Britain by
CPI Antony Rowe, Chippenham and Eastbourne

In memoriam Leslie Arthur Collette

Contents

Figures and Tables

Figures

Tables

Acknowledgements

Grateful thanks are due to Hilda Smith, who lent me her National Joint Committee of Working Women's Organizations papers and encouraged me to begin this book. John Grigg and Barbara Humphries of Labour Heritage were most helpful, as was Darren Treadwell of the Labour Party archives and research centre, Manchester. Labour Heritage members over the years have been supportive, and special thanks are due to Irene Wagner and Florence Davy, with whom I worked closely and whose history is indicated in these pages. Stephen Bird's work has been invaluable; from the archives in Labour Party headquarters in the 1980s, he founded Labour Heritage and oversaw the transfer of the archives to Manchester, where he managed them for many years.

In addition to Labour Heritage, the following publishers have given permission to reproduce material: Manchester University Press, Oxford University Press, Edinburgh University Press, Macmillan, Ashgate Publishing and Lawrence & Wishart. Permission was given for use of those quotes from the MacDonald papers in *For Labour and for Women* which are reproduced here; repeated efforts to renew contact have been unavailing. The author and publisher would like to apologise for any inadvertent infringement of copyright and have sought to keep within the Publishers' Fair Dealing Convention guidelines. Reproduced material has been attributed on first citation.

Lesley Mullett typed the book and was central to this project reaching fruition. Finally, Michael Strang and Ruth Ireland at Palgrave saw the final draft through into production.

List of Abbreviations

AEU	Amalgamated Engineering Union
CPGB	Communist Party of Great Britain
EOC	Equal Opportunities Commission
IFTU	International Federation of Trade Unions
IFWW	International Federation of Working Women
ILP	Independent Labour Party
LRC	Labour Representation Committee
LSI	Labour and Socialist International
NAC	National Abortion Campaign
NALGO	National and Local Government Officers' Association
NFWW	National Federation of Working Women
NJC	National Joint Committee of Working Women's Organisations
NLAWC	National Labour Women's Advisory Council
NUDAW	National Union of Distributive and Allied Workers
NUR	National Union of Railwaymen
NUSEC	National Union of Societies for Equal Citizenship
NUWM	National Unemployed Workers' Movement
NUWSS	National Union of Women's Suffrage Societies
SJC	Standing Joint Committee of Working Women's Organisations
TUC	Trades Union Congress
UPW	Union of Post Office Workers
USDAW	Union of Shop, Allied and Distributive Workers
WAC	Women's Action Committee
WCG	Women's Cooperative Guild
WLL	Women's Labour League
WRP	Workers' Revolutionary Party
WSPU	Women's Social and Political Union
WTUL	Women's Trade Union League
WVS	Women's Voluntary Service
YTS	Youth Training Scheme
YWCA	Young Women's Christian Association

Introduction

Daughter of the Ancient Eve
We know the gifts you gave, and give;
Who knows the gifts that you shall give
Daughter of the Newer Eve?
> Mrs K.M. Shailes, Chairing 23rd National Conference of
> Labour Women, 1945

They noted all over the world signs of the change that was coming, and women of the working classes have taken the foremost
place in it. A tremendous transformation was going to take
place on this earth; and the injustices of the ages, the misery
of the oppressed classes, and the sorrow of the poor, and the
tyranny of the wealthy were going to be swept away forever.
Nothing could stop the movement. When the trades union
movement fully realised that all workers, men and women,
youths and maidens, were members one of another, then they
would hear more than the rumble of revolution in the distance;
the revolution would be here.
> Ada Salter, Women's Labour League conference, 1914,
> *Daily Dispatch*, Gertrude Tuckwell Collection, 345/79

Two women, two wars. Expressions of hope and forecasts of change.
Both women steeped in Labour Party women's organizations and both
sure that women had something special to offer, that the future would
be transformed because of women's gifts. This idea of the necessity of
women's contribution to a future world of equality and ease, and the
protest implicit in the second quote, that men in the Labour movement
undervalued this contribution and therefore delayed the revolution,

have remained constant throughout women's involvement in Labour Party politics. Yet is the protest justified? Can the idea that women's special gifts be realized through the agency of the Labour Party be put into practice? Was it ever feasible to expect that the Labour Party, which dedicated itself not to revolution but to representing working people in parliament, would have the ideological space to value, the political space to acknowledge women's special gifts? Can one indeed objectify 'the Labour Party' in this way, giving it a single identity as actor and endowing it with power to act? Claims for women such as those voiced above must be called feminist, although neither of the speakers reported above would have given herself that label. How had such ideas come to be voiced at the rather staid Labour Party women's conferences, even in time of war that encouraged such chiliastic expression? How far has feminism, which is the motor of ideas about women, influenced and been assimilated by women committed to Labour's project, and how far have they been influenced by feminism?[1]

This book attempts to answer such questions by considering three successive phases in the history of women, feminism and the Labour Party. In each phase, a separate women's group affiliated to the Labour Party was active: the Women's Labour League (1906–1918), the Standing Joint Committee of Industrial Women's Organisations (SJC, 1916–1953), and the National Joint Committee of Working Women's Organisations (NJC, 1953–1993). The first part deals with the early twentieth century, when the Women's Labour League was formed and representation, the claim for the enfranchisement of working people and of women, was the overarching political issue both for the Labour Party and for women's groups. The campaign for women's enfranchisement at this time is generally seen as the culmination of the first 'wave' of feminism, dating from Mary Wollstonecraft's 1792 *Vindication of the Rights of Women*. The second part considers the consequences of the First and Second World Wars, and activity in the inter-war period, when international action against the rise of fascism was an important part of Labour and of feminist politics. During this period the Women's Labour League was replaced by the SJC which succeeded the League in advising the Party on 'matters of interest to women' and in arranging the national conference of Labour women. The Labour Party Chief Woman's Officer and the SJC secretary were one and the same person. The third part recounts the activities of the NJC, which succeeded the SJC but lost some of its functions, and the effect of the growth of a second wave of feminism on women in the Labour Party and their contribution to its development. The League and the SJC overlapped, the League ceasing activity in 1918 while the SJC was founded in 1916; however, the last four years of League activity were so dominated by the outbreak of the First World War that their history fits more neatly into the second period. The SJC itself underwent several name changes but remained basically the same organization. These successive groups have been neglected yet are particularly interesting because while intimately connected with the Labour Party, they remained separate from the Party, electing their own officers and deciding their own agenda and practices. All three groups represented political/Party, trades union, and consumer/Cooperative women. Given that feminism, like socialism, is a global term applied to whole ranges of, sometimes contradictory, theory and practice, which change over time, feminist ideas then current are considered in each of the three parts. Factual chapters are interspersed with short biographical and autobiographical accounts that illustrate how individual women related to the themes of the day.

Some of the activities described are constant themes throughout the three phases, for instance the interest in children's wellbeing, education and employment, and in equal pay. Others are period specific, such as suffrage and support for mining communities in times of strike action. In dealing with these activities, recognizing priorities, it soon becomes apparent that there are external, major and related factors affecting how women participate in the Labour Party: women's position in the workforce; the general political climate; war or peace. Change in women's labour market position, more employment and better conditions and pay directly affects women's relationship to the labour movement; unemployed women are not represented by trades unions and low paid, part-time workers have low status in the labour market which is reflected in their status in political movements. Thus the First and Second World Wars, drastically changing women's labour force participation, affected also their labour movement participation. The political climate is important in encouraging or hindering social change and in determining whether there is a Labour government or strong opposition which women can lobby; in the premierships or oppositions of Harold Wilson or James Callaghan it was easier to address and influence government than it was under Margaret Thatcher's rule. This is a useful reminder that ideas such as socialism and feminism are expressed and understood against political practices.

The history of women in the Party – as far as political women went, often the same SJC individuals – is a different history to the one given here because, as part and parcel of the Party, they were less able to act autonomously as women. Some, but not all, were incorporated into women's groups and councils at local, district, and regional level. As such, they had success and, as Matthew Worley found in his study of five counties between the wars, 'proved able to ensure party support and discussion of "non-traditional" male concerns, such as child welfare clinics'.[2] However, local and regional parties, and the national Party remained male dominated; even though women often formed the majority of the individually affiliated members, these were far outstripped by the number of (largely male) trades unionists affiliated. Worley gives the example of Barnard Castle Labour Party in 1931; the membership of 4730 was formed of 3500 miners, 700 from the National Union of General and Municipal workers, 100 from the rail union, 30 from the Independent Labour Party, 150 from the Women's Section, and 250 from the individual members.[3] Women's sections and councils were subject to their local, male-dominated counterparts. The Women's Labour League and SJC were subject to no-one, however far they may have allowed themselves to be influenced; studying them allows us to see how women without the active constraint of male pressure acted, their priorities, their methods, and how they were influenced by feminist ideas.

For many decades, women were absent from Labour Party history. Traditional historians who recounted the story of Labour's elite missed women out by their choice of subject matter, as did others who concentrated on the analysis of a male social world. Historians of working people themselves formed a male-dominated clique and were interested in class to the exclusion of other categories. Some of the early 'big names' – Edward Thompson, Eric Hobsbawm, and John Saville – were none too friendly to the Labour Party itself. The Society for the Study of Labour History, which I joined in the 1980s, took about ten years to hold its proposed conference on gender; the 1997 conference at which the future of Labour history was discussed was a watershed that marked a far more open approach.[4] *History Workshop*, as conference and journal, aimed to redress the balance and feminist editors such as Sally Alexander and Barbara Taylor were important in ensuring discussion of gender and ethnicity. However, they also were apt to regard the Labour Party rather as a lost cause, in political and historical terms. This was the reason why Stephen Bird, Labour Party archivist, set up Labour Heritage, the Labour Party's own historical society. Together with Irene Wagner, Labour Party librarian, whose autobiographical account of politics in war-time Britain may be found in these pages, Stephen was very important in providing access to Labour

Party records. He remembers Henry Pelling coming to the library to research his groundbreaking book on the origins of the Labour Party,[5] and how this was important in founding the archives. I chaired some of the first meetings of Labour Heritage, which were attended by Lucy Middleton, wrapped in a fur coat; widow of Labour's original assistant secretary James, she was one of the first people to write about Labour Party women.[6]

Once given the will to tell the history of Labour Party women, one continues to encounter problems. There is good reason to be cautious about membership statistics. Early membership records did not differentiate by gender. Likewise, they do not distinguish ethnicity and social class of the membership is not recorded. For recent years there is work which provides some useful female membership figures.[7] Even here, it is women candidates and members of parliament that are most often analysed. Such statistics are useful for traditional history, which concentrates on people in positions of power, but are less suitable for examining experience at all levels. For women councillors it is more difficult to obtain numbers and for people active in ad hoc and special interest groups, such as the 1980s/1990s Women Against Pit Closures, it is almost impossible. In dealing with the League/SJC, however, one deals with identifiable women; they have left documents. In order to distinguish women's experience within the Labour Party in general, there is a need for more local studies such as Worley's, in which women emerge from obscurity. For instance, the study of women in the Labour Party in Wales shows a real sense of change through time in the way women participated, and the way in which regional socio-economic factors affected this.[8] However, authors Neil Evans and Dot Jones rather rush to a conclusion that 'From the standpoint of anyone with a commitment to equality of women its (Welsh Labour Party) record is appalling'.[9] Such a comment is doubtless justified by the statistics of women councillors and parliamentarians that they cite, but it is important to discover why such an invidious situation arose, and what factors were of influence.

Local studies can also get beyond the core people in constant membership to the more evanescent Party members; as I have written, a convenient metaphor to describe Labour Party membership is that of a church congregation, attending for occasional worship, taking part in particular activities; such a congregation resists quantification. The more usual 'rank and file' is misleading because it assumes that members serve a term, have coherence of purpose, are led and directed.[10] In addition, Labour Party women have often not distinguished between their political, industrial, and consumer-orientated activity. For instance, life-long labour activist Florence Davy wrote:

> When I was eighteen I joined the Labour Party...we were talking about setting up a League of Youth and I went along and came out secretary...that was in 1931 and I have belonged to the Labour Party ever since. I joined the London Cooperative Society in 1937: in the League of Youth they argued for this, it was all part of the "three winged approach". I joined my trade union when I was sixteen...the Union of Post Office Workers. Within two years I was its representative...I was also an organiser for UPW. The unity of the Labour Party, the trade union movement and the Cooperative Movement is essential for success.

Similarly, Joan Davis, who went on to become Labour Party Group Leader of Epping Forest District Council, remembered:

> We used to go to the Labour Party women's section with my Mum, although I remember more about the Cooperative Guild, they used to be big meetings, fifty to sixty was a small meeting.[11]

In the 1950s, Joan was minute secretary of Kensington Cooperative Party, belonged to the Cooperative Trading District Committee and the League of Youth and was on the general committee and executive of North Kensington Labour Party. Labour's 'complex system of representation and delegation', its affiliated socialist societies and trades unions, has been described as federal;[12] regarding women's participation, the structure might rather be described as labyrinthine. For Labour Party women federalism was institutionalized in the SJC.

While women's Labour history remained obscure, women's history in general was progressing, seeking to find a place in the academic schedule, a function of the feminist movement rather than the development of Labour historiography, using different methodologies such as oral history and life history.[13] A qualitative methodology is more satisfactory in uncovering women in Labour's federated congregation. A life history approach has much to offer and I was fortunate in belonging to Labour Heritage, and its Women's Research Committee, set up in answer to the over-confident assertion of an Iron and Steed Trades delegate to one of the early conferences, that trades union men founded the Labour Party. The Women's Research Committee convened a loose network of historians in constituency parties. There were few problems of memory,

Labour Party: Labour women labyrinth

Labour Women's Organizations	Labour Party
	Labour Party 1900– Affiliated socialist Societies and trades unions
Women's Labour League 1906	Affiliated 1908
Standing Joint Committee of Industrial Working Women 1916 (WLL, WTUL, NFWW, WCG)	Advises Labour Party
Women's Councils 1918	Individual membership 1918 Labour Party affiliates to SJC 1919
SJC secretary becomes Labour Party Chief Women's Officer 1920	
SJC Working Women's Organizations	
Women's Councils expand	
National Labour Women's Advisory Council 1951	Advises Labour Party
National Joint Committee of Working Women's Organizations 1952	

dealing with women who remained politically active and alert, who often knew each other and shared familiarity with past events. More problematic was listening without allowing preconceived ideas; for instance, as Sarah Perrigo (historian, feminist and Labour Party activist) found, it was initially hard to hear that many women were satisfied with their local party career, had no idea of being 'passed over' for office and valued their contribution to its social life.[14] Some women, notably Irene Wagner, who had been engaged in secret war work, had confidences that had to be respected.[15] A bonus was that many women had been involved with other political parties, the Communist Party or the Independent Labour Party, and thus had an informed and comparative approach to understanding their Labour Party career.

I edited the bulletin we produced, but the interviewees often wrote up their own accounts: we jointly made decisions on how many bulletins to print; production and distribution was a joint effort. Labour Heritage also preserved its members' histories by recording them for national sound archives.[16] Some groups, such as Derby South constituency women discovered their history by displaying and discussing extant Women's Council minutes along with leaflets, banners, photographs, and other memorabilia. Such events have their own history; in

1934 the Pageant of Labour at London's Crystal Palace included scenes from the Matchgirls' strike and the Rochdale Pioneers[17]. It was as a direct result of my participation at a Labour Heritage conference that I was able to borrow Hilda Smith's papers and write this book. It was the loan of Hilda Smith's papers that prompted me to take a fresh look at this subject. Hilda Smith was a member of the National Joint Committee of Working Women's Organizations in the 1970s and 1980s, at a time of great feminist activity, technological and economic change. Her committee had to deal with the new economic approach of Margaret Thatcher's governments, a political situation which meant the rethinking of its traditional method of lobbying Labour Governments and its alliances with other women's organizations.

Now Labour history is again rather in the doldrums. This may be on the one hand because, as Stephen Bird found, based on his experience of queries to the archives, there is less interest in Labour Party history when Labour is in government. My 2008 enquiries to Labour Party headquarters fell on stony ground; the long-serving and historically informed officers of the past are no longer to be found; there is no Chief Women's Officer; due to a shortage of office space, conference reports are no longer stored. At the Labour Party archives and Study Centre, the very helpful archivists Pearl Robinson and Darren Treadwell were hampered by the fact that since Peter Mandelsohn's 1987 reforms, the conference reports no longer contain the National Executive Committee report for the previous year and are not indexed by subject. On the other hand, recent studies are focused on 'New Labour', following the 'Third Way' to social inclusion. As Stephen Fielding and Duncan Tanner have written, 'Studies of contemporary Labour politics have focussed on explaining Tony Blair's rise to prominence, and especially on the existence of a "revisionist" rather than "radical" strand within the Party'.[18] Such writing tends to ignore differences of gender, of ethnicity, of region and of class; women appear in the index as part of the electorate. It is the leaders who are visible, rather than the membership, so that leading women politicians take the stage briefly. In a way we have turned full circle, back to the account of the elite group and the statistics of voting figures. Further discussion of New Labour and how it relates to contemporary expressions of feminism, and how both may affect Labour Party women, may be found in the conclusion.

Meanwhile the history given here of the Women's Labour League and its successors reveals something of Labour's female congregation; it shows how feminism was reflected by these separate groups; it shows how women organized their activities and their priorities. Some of the biographies and autobiographies draw on Labour Heritage work; I was also concerned that there be female agency, that women should speak for themselves. I have used my own archives and memory so that the later part of the book is partly ethnographical in methodology; I was a trades unionist, a feminist, and a Labour Party activist before ever I was an historian. This book draws on my existing body of work on women and the Labour Party and on internationalism. Everything, however, has been rewritten because my own ideas have changed.

Part I
Representation: The Women's Labour League

The representation of working people in parliament was one of the main political issues at the beginning of the twentieth century. The right to vote for working men had been gained, although, largely due to the combination of a mobile labour force and deficient electoral registration, it was often not exercised. Legislation to ameliorate workers' conditions, in the workplace, at home, and before the inevitable onslaughts of sickness and age, although widely debated, remained to be achieved. Workers' perceived political allies, reforming Liberals and some Conservatives, the latter often representing textile areas, seemed ineffective. Socialist politics therefore attracted new adherents, members of a variety of clubs and political parties, while trades unions developed a more modern and radical approach. From this mixture of trade union and political activity emerged the Labour Representation Committee (LRC), formed in 1900, with a goal at once moderate and revolutionary: the election of working men to parliament in order that they might enact legislation in their own interests – in other words, the parliamentary road to socialism. The LRC, an agency consisting of affiliated organizations, was renamed the Labour Party in 1906. In the LRC/Labour Party men predominated, an inevitable function of its role as agent for the trades unions and socialist societies in which men formed by far the greater part of the members. There was no individual membership of the Labour Party until its constitution was redrawn in 1918. As parliament and the parliamentary suffrage were entirely male, this gender limitation was, at first sight, excusable. However, on the one hand, LRC policy was to win full adult suffrage for working people; on the other, the limits on female suffrage were gradually being lifted; generally, wherever a new authority was created, women could vote. Women were therefore being elected to parish and district councils and Poor Law Boards.

At the same time, new ideas current in the arts and the sciences, and the development of relatively new disciplines such as sociology, psychoanalysis and sexology challenged the received wisdoms of Victorian times. Women were active in socialist and trade union circles, and there was a large and vociferous movement for women's suffrage: first wave feminism reached its zenith in the movement for women's enfranchisement. The case for women's suffrage was closely argued on several heads. There was the simple case that propertied women paid taxes and thus should not be denied representation. In addition, when women had the right to vote for local bodies there was no logic in denying them the parliamentary franchise. More fundamentally, drawing on a century of feminist argument that women should be independent and have equal rights to education and work, the case was made that women should not be denied citizenship on the grounds that they were subservient within the family. It was also strongly argued that women should not be put in the same category as those denied voting rights because of felony, poverty or insanity. Campaigners looked back to a past 'golden age', preceding industrialization, claiming that women had enjoyed a greater degree of equality in the mediaeval manors and towns where they could win licence to brew, weave and spin. Yet the arguments seldom stopped at merely claiming the right to vote; it was the ability to seek social reform through the ballot box that was being claimed. Such arguments turned on a gender ideology that cast women in the role of guardians of welfare rights, often citing women's performance of domestic duties, motherhood and control of the budget for household goods. There was thus a dilemma inherent in the suffrage campaign, in that it sought equality with men on the one hand while claiming a special role for women on the other.

In Britain the campaign for women's suffrage was divided into several groups, professing various arguments.[1] The National Union of Women's Suffrage Societies (NUWSS), about 50,000 strong, was the biggest, while the smaller Women's Social and Political Union (WSPU) with about 5000 members, run by Emmeline Pankhurst and her daughter Christabel, received the most publicity. The WSPU was formed in 1904 as a direct result of the exclusion of women from a branch meeting of the Independent Labour Party (ILP). Not all feminists supported the cause of women's suffrage, as British suffrage remained based on property holding. When women claimed equal voting rights with men, they were demanding inclusion into a voting system that excluded working people; some campaigners thus joined people's suffrage groups, perceiving women's suffrage as perpetuating, rather than diminishing, disadvantage. Illustrating the diversity of the suffrage groups, one of Emmeline Pankhursts's other daughters, Sylvia, led a people's suffrage group, the East London Federation, while another, Adela, emigrated to Australia and was active in the suffrage movement in her adopted country. Tactics varied as much as arguments.

The NUWSS supported any male politician who propounded their cause, while ideologically more in tune with the Liberal Party; the WSPU, however, denounced the Liberal Party for failing to achieve votes for women. NUWSS suffragists followed tactics of winning influence through debate and drawing attention to their case through non-payment of property taxes. The WSPU minority, termed 'suffragettes' by the contemporary press, used more violent means, ranging from cutting up golf courses to arson, and risking prison through demonstrations and then fasting when arrested. The fame of Emmeline and Christabel Pankhurst was such as to be synonymous with violent militancy. Government responses were equally violent, including force-feeding in prisons. These more aggressive tactics, needing generalship and thus giving power to the leaders of the groups, were seen by some as masculine and hierarchic, contrary to the spirit of the movement as a whole. However, the division between groups and tactics should not be overstressed; many women were active in more than one group or moved between groups and joint demonstrations were frequently held. The very diversity and vigour of the debate richly contributed to feminist ideology.

Women's representation in its ranks and women's suffrage were thus bound to be issues for the LRC/Labour Party, just as the existence of the Labour Party was a factor to be addressed by women's organizations and women suffragists. It was Labour movement women who squared this circle, by creating their own organization, the Women's Labour League. The following sections discuss the foundation of the League, its relationship with the suffrage movement and the Labour Party, and its consolidation. The short biographies, which close this first part, illustrate the experiences of individual women dealing with these issues.

1. Foundation of the Women's Labour League

This first section of Part I examines the foundation of the Women's Labour League, its relationship with the Labour Party and with suffrage organizations, and its direction under its first leaders.

It was Mary Fenton MacPherson of the Railway Women's Guild, a sister organization for the families of men in the rail unions, who first promoted the idea of a women's Labour organization attached to the Labour Representation Committee. On the model of the Guild, she envisaged a nation-wide group, run by women for women. She had to overcome the LRC's indifference; her initial approaches resulted merely in a resolution to the LRC's 1905 conference that, where the LRC was standing a parliamentary candidate, a local women's organization should be formed. While signifying that to achieve the Labour Party's primary goal of the representation of working people, women's help would be welcome; this fell far short of the autonomous women's organization Mary Fenton MacPherson wished to create. Accordingly, she continued to work independently from the LRC to interest women in her original idea. She was eventually rewarded by the foundation of the League at a meeting on 9 March 1906, held in the home of Margaret MacDonald, wife of LRC secretary Ramsay. An executive committee was elected whose duty was to encourage local branches. Margaret MacDonald became the League's first president. Mary Middleton, wife of Ramsay's assistant James, shortly took over from Mary Fenton MacPherson as secretary. A public meeting held a month later to inaugurate the Central London branch drew press attention and also served as an occasion for individual Labour Party men, including the party leader Keir Hardie, to give support. The League's original objects were stated as: 'To form an organisation of women to work for independent labour representation in connection with the Labour Party', but these were successfully amended at its first conference (Leicester, 1906) by suffragist Isabella Ford to include: 'and to obtain direct representation of women in parliament and on local bodies'.[2]

Local branches were quickly formed. While the number of members in each branch varied a great deal and the record of their subscriptions was haphazard, it would seem to indicate a total of 250 League members by 1907 (£2.1s.8d at 2d per member) and a total of 770 by 1908 (£6.17s.10d). The League success was part of the efflorescence of socialism in towns and villages throughout Britain; it was a time of frequent by-elections and three general elections (1906, January and December 1910) when the attention of both the Labour and the women's movements was directed to political activity. At its height, around 5000 women were in membership of the League, which networked with other women's organizations, in particular the Women's Cooperative Guild, the National Federation of Women Workers and socialist women's groupings. Although strong in London, the League was by no means confined to the capital, and provincial branches were far from the leadership's sphere of influence. The League was very weak in the Home Counties, but gained substantial support in the North East industrial regions and in the Lancashire and Cheshire area of the North West. South Wales was also well represented. Some cities, such as Birmingham and Manchester, had several branches. The total number of known branches, drawn from conference reports, League correspondence and the executive committee minutes was 201, but these fluctuated and perhaps half were active at any one time. An address book compiled in 1910 records 86 branches and the *League Leaflet* of 1911 reports 100. Of the branches recorded in 1910, nine are known to have been formed in 1906 and 1907, ten in 1908 and 11 in 1909, indicating a small, but resilient, core of continuity. The 1911 affiliation of the Railway Women's Guild, which then had 88 branches, therefore doubled the area of League influence.

The beginnings of a League branch were very much a local affair, an evolution from the local Labour community. The LRC or ILP would hold a meeting, sometimes asking a national League woman, perhaps Katharine Bruce Glasier or Margaret MacDonald, to speak. The Birmingham branch, for instance, was formed following a meeting of 25 women; an executive committee of seven was chosen and Margaret Fiorci was elected secretary. She wrote to 27 women in socialist societies such as the Labour Church, the Socialist Centre and the *Clarion* Cycling Club, delivering the letters by hand to save postage.[3] Birmingham Trades Council was asked for the names of women trade unionists and, having to report there were none, was very receptive to the idea of a League branch. At the formal opening of the Jarrow branch in 1907 Lisbeth Simm, who lived in Newcastle with her husband M.T. Simm, ILP North Eastern Region organizer, gave an address on 'the Labour Movement', which was followed by a character sketch from *Nicholas Nickleby* performed by some of the younger members. The secretary took names and it was decided to meet on alternative Tuesdays: 'some of the women present said they knew little about Labour politics', reported the *Northern Democrat* that October, 'but their husbands had voted for Curran (the successful Labour candidate) so they had come to learn further'.

It was hard work organizing where women were isolated and had traditionally been excluded from politics, for instance, in rural colliery districts. Lisbeth Simm wrote to Mary Middleton (her emphasis): '*Where branches seem to be most needed*, as say, the mining villages where women are almost an unknown quantity, there it is most difficult'.[4] Lisbeth's husband edited the *Northern Democrat* in which she wrote a regular women's column. She therefore had ready-made channels of publicity and advertisement. For instance in August 1908 she asked for names of women who felt 'disposed to join' a League branch in Newcastle, promising that work would be arranged to meet members' needs and that there would be both educational and social meetings. Men, who had learnt to appreciate women's work at election times, were asked to forward names. 'The subscription is very small, the mutual help of organized women is very, very great.' Having set up such a branch, Lisbeth wrote 'voluminous correspondence' if it lacked business. She suggested a consecutive pattern of work for branches to follow and urged the central leadership to follow up new branches quickly. One of her recruiting methods, which she used in Jarrow and recommended in *Labour Leader* (13 September 1911), was that each member, 'by persistent persuasion, visitation, leaflets and personal talks', would recruit one other member in the year. Nursing mothers, she suggested, could be reached by means of a cup of tea and talk about the care of babies. Lisbeth also advertised the League by speaking at open-air meetings. This could be extremely hard work. She rejoiced when the 'open-air season' of the 'wintry summer' of 1909 was over (*Northern Democrat*, October 1909). In September 1908 she had spoken at 25 open-air meetings and had felt unwell and unhappy.

Initially, the League's relationship with suffrage groups was not strong, although many members, particularly in the North East, were also members of the NUWSS. Labour women's organizations were generally supportive of, but not obsessed by, the campaign for women's suffrage. Partly, they were swayed by the people's suffrage argument; the Socialist International Women's Council, which met for the first time in 1907 decided in favour of people's, as opposed to women's suffrage. In the case of the Women's Labour League many members were already committed to suffrage organizations and joined the League to fulfil other goals; there was no need to duplicate the efforts of the NUWSS or WSPU. Moreover, the League was successfully ensuring the election of women to local bodies. Women were eligible to stand for parish and district councils from 1894 and some of the League's first recruits had already won election to these councils. From 1907 women could be elected to county and borough councils and several League members won their seats. The League did not work for Labour Party candidates who opposed women's enfranchisement.

The League did join the NUWSS on several demonstrations, although it was less comfortable working with the WSPU. There were several reasons for the League to distance itself from the WSPU. First, in its early days when it addressed a range of grievances expressed by women in the Labour movement, the WSPU was a direct competitor. Second, the WSPU's autocratic style of leadership was antithetical to the League's more relaxed style. Third, increasingly aggressive militant tactics, dramatic in intent, were costly to produce; WSPU fund-raising was a cause of concern. Lisbeth Simm, for instance, was appalled at the amount of money the WSPU collected in distressed areas; she went to one of Mrs Pankhurst's meetings and 'wished I'd my shilling back'.[5] The entrance fees were 6d, 1s and 2s: 'most ILP-ers had complimentary tickets, but a great crowd had to pay'; the hall was full and a collection was taken which raised a further £30, perhaps two years' wages for local working women. Lisbeth felt the WSPU organizers had little idea of the poverty of the region or the hardship their fund-raising would produce and lamented: 'we have to be content if a dozen join and never mind about raising funds'. She disliked the style of the meeting: 'How very theatrical they are.' An example of the way the WSPU aroused increasing antagonism in a Labour movement that was, initially, reasonably supportive, was the Cockermouth by-election of 1906. The Labour candidate was Robert Smillie of the ILP, secretary of the Miners' Union and supported by them. The ILP had been divided about limited women's enfranchisement; Christabel Pankhurst and Theresa Billington Greig went to Cockermouth during the election and conducted a campaign of votes for women; the ILP perceived this as hostile to Robert Smillie, who was resoundingly defeated. Mrs Pankhurst and Christabel resigned their membership of the ILP the following year. Nevertheless, the WSPU was attractive to some League members and this did cause controversy within the League. The President and general committee of the Preston branch resigned from the League on the issue, although there had already been a dispute over campaigning for secular education.[6] All of the Nelson branch left the League because insufficient attention was paid to women's enfranchisement and Charlotte Despard, a campaigning suffragette, resigned the League executive on the issue.

League relationships with the Labour Party were, if anything, more problematic. Its objects required the League both to form its own organization and to work with the Labour Party. The latter proved a difficult task and disappointment was expressed at the lack of Labour Party support. Affiliation was the first business discussed at the 1907 conference, resolved upon and duly sent to the Labour Party together with resolutions urging initiatives to be taken on inspection in dangerous trades and free school meals. A Labour Party fraternal delegate had been invited to the conference: John Hodge, British Steel Smelters, Iron and Tinplate Workers' secretary, was chosen to go, although he had been the only member of Labour's executive to vote against the gesture. Hodge demonstrated his reluctance: he did not wish to add to, or duplicate the present number of exchanges, he did not know where the conference was to be held, it was one of his few open Saturdays, could not someone else go? Finally he assented, explaining, 'I was not sure if it was the other crowd or not.'[7] However, won over by the conference, John Hodge said he could vouch for every Labour Member of Parliament being heart and soul with the League; he did point out that the Labour Party constitution would have to be amended to allow the affiliation of the League.

The League requests for affiliation explained that it was a combination of women drawn from exactly the same sections as the Labour Party drew its strength and that the League 'gives a channel for the expression of the special knowledge and experience of women of the party'.[8] The Labour Party executive, however 'declined to comment on letters from societies not already affiliated',[9] which in effect preserved male predominance. The Labour Party was thus described as 'lopsided' at the 1907 League conference. Similarly, in April 1908 *Woman Worker* expressed the fear that the Labour Party 'might grow too exclusively on the side of the male members and thus be one sided and incomplete'.

The executive's intransigence did not necessarily reflect Labour Party rank and file opinion. Labour Party men were often helpful to the League when it began to organize. Hebburn ILP, for example, put back its meeting by half an hour so that the League could meet in its hall from 6.30 p.m. to 8.00 p.m. In towns such as Jarrow and Preston the opportunity existed for more practical assistance; in Jarrow the local LRC lent its rooms free of charge to the League and in Preston the Weavers' Union made a room available. Gateshead men acknowledged they 'had not been able to win their wives over' and hoped the League would be more acceptable. The League sent delegates to local party meetings, arranged joint events, shared platforms at public meetings and proved its worth at local elections. Reinforcing the local labour community, League branches benefited from organizational strengths that community had already established – access to the local press, to accommodation and to the homes of local Labour personalities. In some areas, however, women were already active in the LRC and possibly resented League attempts to separate them out, feeling their participation would be diminished; the Leeds Branch reported: 'We have at Leeds a number of women attached to LRC branches which operates against us some-what.' In contrast, some local Labour parties appear to have formed women's groups that were not affiliated to the League.

The Labour Party executive finally agreed to recommend the necessary constitutional changes to the 1908 Labour Party conference. The League staged a coup; its conference was held at the same time, January, and in the same place as the Labour Party (Hull). Rooms were requested and granted, although Ramsay MacDonald found it necessary to write to each executive committee member for their opinion; Pete Curran replied angrily that of course the request should be met and there was no need to ask. League events were not advertised on the Labour Party agenda, but proved a huge success. On the Saturday evening before the conferences started the women held a social; John Hodge sang. Katherine Bruce Glasier, presiding, said:

> They were hoping as a League that their relationship with the Labour Party would, with that conference, have passed beyond the dubiously delightful stage in courtship known as a friendly understanding...into a definite engagement, soon to develop into a life-long union for mutual service.

Keir Hardie spoke in favour. William Robinson of the Beamers' and Drawers' Union was the Labour Party fraternal delegate and commented that the sooner the women were in the Labour Party, the greater their effect would be.[10] However, with everything set for affiliation, the Central London branch successfully moved a resolution that must have put it in jeopardy; the League resolved to accept in membership societies of women not eligible for membership of the Labour Party. This was a clear indication that women's interests remained a major concern of the delegates.

The outcome was a compromise. The Labour Party conference report commended the League election work. The much amended and heavily scored draft report shows that the exact nature of the recommendations for League recognition was the subject of intense debate. The League was to contribute to the general, but not the political fund and consequently not to vote on the latter. The League could not take part in the election of the Labour Party national executive committee 'and we could not very well give it a representative of its own.' The League was thus excluded from any real power within 'the Men's Party'. However, League women were to be allowed to send representatives to the Labour Party conference. 'Should a national organisation of women accepting the basis of this constitution and the policy of the Labour Party be formed', continued the proposal, ignoring the fact that it was at least two years out of date, 'it shall be eligible for affiliation as though it were a trades council.' The League accepted the terms. On 21 March 1908 Ramsay MacDonald was able to write to Mary Middleton: 'I placed your letter...before the executive and it was the unanimous decision to accept the affiliation of the Women's Labour League.' Equality and integration had not been won; as the League wrote in the trade union journal *Woman Worker* (no. 8, April 1908), 'we are only free lances making our way and trying to justify our existence'. The League could now enjoy Labour Party recognition, while enjoying the benefits and experiencing the pitfalls of separatism.

During the period of its freelance role under Margaret MacDonald and Mary Middleton, League organization was characterized by an amateur style that succeeded because of its vigour, an enabling, rather than a controlling leadership, which allowed plenty of scope for autonomous branch life. In return, branch strength had given the League credibility in establishing itself nationally and encouraged the freelance spirit to prevail. Dorothy Lenn of the Central London branch (also Margaret MacDonald's secretary for the Women's Industrial Council) wrote in *Labour Leader* (vol. 23, August 1908) of the diversity of women who joined, from civil servant to social worker, industrial worker to schoolteacher, married and single women. Professional women were attracted (such as Ethel Bentham, a medical doctor and Sister Kerrison of the Seaman's Hospital, Greenwich) and women trade unionists were well represented (Mary MacPherson, Margaret Bondfield, Mable Hope of the Post Office Clerks and Mary MacArthur of the National Federation of Working Women). As was reported in *Woman Worker* (January 1908):

> We feel the women's side of the movement will be incomplete unless we have all classes represented: each makes their own contribution, the seamy side of experience was helped by the educated one to put the case clearly and plan the detail of remedies, whilst book learning and enthusiasm are very empty qualities without the experience of the realities of life.

Not only did the League redress the gender imbalance, it provided a friendlier alternative to the Labour Party. Branches made a conscious effort to ensure their meetings were congenial to women. Some welcomed children at meetings; St. Pancras, for instance, reported a meeting 'with four babies and three children to make it homelike'. Many branches alternated evening and afternoon meetings. At the 1908 conference Margaret Bondfield suggested women should arrange a rotating crèche. Women perhaps had different expectations from their meetings than did men; at a Newcastle Labour movement gathering held to welcome Keir Hardie from a foreign tour in June 1908, which was immediately followed by a concert, Lisbeth Simm detected 'much disappointment... comrades from outlying districts had not an opportunity of speaking with their friends... (I wonder if the men arranged it?)'.[11]

In theory, League policy-making was conducted by the annual conference, to which each branch sent a delegate for every 25, or part of 25, members. No men were allowed to the early conferences so that women would learn to manage for themselves. After 1908 the conference was always held to fit in with that of the Labour Party, the League day and a half beginning a week of Labour activity in the chosen venue. The local branch hunted out cheap lodgings and provided a social gathering. A decision would be taken at that conference on which resolutions should be forwarded to the Labour Party conference and a delegate to that body was elected. The outgoing executive committee gave its report and elections were made to the new committee from nominations submitted beforehand. Florence Harrison Bell reported in the *Northern Democrat* (March 1911) on the last conference held (at Leicester) under the MacDonald/Middleton leadership. On arrival, with six other delegates, she was taken home by Councillor Mrs Riley, 'who fed us and saw us made tidy.... The treatment meted out to the prodigal son pales in heartiness to the fellowshipping which took place at the evening's reception.' The conference began the next morning, 31 branches being represented by 41 delegates 'who sat themselves down anyhow'. There was no platform, the chair's table being on the floor amongst the delegates. London delegates preponderated. Fraternal delegates from the Women's Cooperative Guild and the Labour Party were welcomed. In the morning there were debates on armaments, the Osborne Judgement (which made the trade unions' sponsorship of the Labour Party illegal), divorce laws, the franchise, a Labour ministry, women on juries and retirement age. 'The photographers were a terrible bore.' The afternoon was 'devoted to home and the child' and a discussion on workers' co-operatives 'which brought out general instances of a kind of tentative co-operation going on in many places'. Florence Harrison Bell's summary was: 'We were very earnest and at times angry in our hearts and very serious, but dull never unless by a chance a delegate got out of harmony with the conference.'

Every new executive committee met immediately after the conference, and thereafter every two months, at the MacDonalds' home in Lincoln's Inn Fields. The executive committee was drawn largely, but not exclusively, from the London Branches. During the MacDonald/ Middleton period the most frequently elected executive committee members were these two and Mary MacArthur (six times each), Sister Kerrison, Minnie Nodin (five times each), Margaret Bondfield, Katharine Bruce Glasier, Mary MacPherson and Lisbeth Simm (four times each). Leadership was fairly diversified, 27 women in all being elected to the executive committee during this period. The chair should have rotated but after 1910 was nearly always held by Ethel Bentham. There were *ad hoc* executive sub-committees (for instance on sweated work and medical inspection of school children) and standing committees (general purpose and literature-publicity). The literature committee undertook most of the written propaganda by producing leaflets on subjects ranging from pithead baths, women and the Labour movement, medical inspection of school children, to advice on the work of a Poor Law Guardian. All the socialist press was used, for instance, *Clarion* and *Labour Leader.* *Woman Worker* kept a page for League notes until 1909, when its editor Mary MacArthur fell into dispute with Margaret MacDonald at the Women's Industrial Council over minimum wages (see below). The non-socialist press, in particular local newspapers, gave reasonable coverage to the League, the contemporary (and invaluable) habit being to report meetings almost verbatim. Some editors were late in noticing the League's existence; the *Westminster Gazette,* for instance, reported on 22 October 1908 that 'a female Labour Party' was 'the latest idea'.

The League maintained separately an organizing fund and a general fund. The former was financed by donations and spent on election work; the latter was financed by a hotch-potch of delegates' fees, concerts, bazaars, sales and the affiliation fees. Each branch had to forward to the general fund 2d per member per year, which was usually raised by a local subscription of 1s per year. The general fund was spent on publication, printing and postage, office equipment and the conference arrangements. Margaret MacDonald contributed generously. In January 1909 individual Labour Party Members of Parliament and candidates were asked for financial help, and then LRCs in constituencies where Labour Party candidates were standing were asked to contribute; only two were able to help. The League eventually received a direct grant from the Labour Party in 1910.

Active in encouraging branches in the North East, Lisbeth Simm made a sustained attempt to introduce regional organization to give League branches a coherent pattern. Organizing trips took Lisbeth around the colliery districts where she had been born, to the Durham Miners' Gala, ILP conferences and into Scotland. In early 1911 Lisbeth spent a week in the Glasgow district, where she tried to get joint meetings of interested women from the town and surrounding areas. She wrote in *Labour Leader* (17 March 1911) that this should be the pattern for League recruitment for all big cities. Later that month she was in Edinburgh and then travelled to Leith. Lisbeth felt bitter that, unlike the WSPU, she could not offer the tea and entertainments so conducive to winning members. Indeed, she had to use her housekeeping money as League petty cash and was reluctant to claim her expenses. She wrote to Mary Middleton in June 1908 that she had meetings in Durham and would have to stay over: she had little cash in hand and had been using the housekeeping money; £1 or so would do, but £2 would be better if it could be spared. The problem was that Lisbeth had no friends in Durham and would have to lodge. Also, she had to pay someone to do her housekeeping while she was away. Eventually a scheme was worked out whereby Lisbeth was paid a fixed sum for each meeting and travelling expenses; if she had to stay overnight, the fee would be increased and Lisbeth would undertake some visiting.[12] Knowing these details illuminates Lisbeth's courage in facing the daunting task of going into a city where she was unknown, travelling by train, seeking out a lodging in a strange house, in order to publicize the Labour movement amongst working people. It is noteworthy that where Lisbeth's network did exist, it consisted largely of ILP members. To hold her cluster of branches together, Lisbeth initiated district meetings in the North East. She gave Margaret MacDonald three months' notice of such a meeting, open to the public and tempted Margaret to speak: 'The WLL is much discussed up here now. Once we show we are able to do things our cause is won'. 'The branches must be linked', Lisbeth wrote, 'and we think this is the best way.' She hoped she had not offended but 'the executive committee give me such a free hand that if I have exceeded the limits of my duties I don't think I am to blame'.

Events following the 1909 League conference, however, indicated that there was some difference of opinion about how the League should be organized, and that Lisbeth Simm and Margaret Macdonald did not always see eye-to-eye. They also reveal a ruthless streak to Margaret MacDonald. The conference was held in Portsmouth; Lisbeth did not attend because the fare was prohibitive and she therefore missed the meeting of the new executive committee.[13] The committee decided that, because of Lisbeth's travelling difficulties, Margaret Bondfield and Mrs Bellamy should organize branches, and that the League would approach Labour Party MPs and candidates for funds in order that a permanent organizer might be appointed at £150 per year. Lisbeth's work 'in her own north-east corner' was indeed commended, but there was no debate about paying her or offering her a full-time job. Instead, Dorothy Lenn was described as 'in all ways suitable'. The General Purposes Committee engaged Dorothy at £2 a week. Lisbeth attended the next executive committee (30 April 1909) at which Mary MacArthur queried whether the General Purposes Committee had exceeded its authority. Margaret MacDonald followed the classic mode of gaining consensus, taking the offending issue in two parts, the first being the more generally acceptable. She moved and Katharine Bruce Glasier seconded 'That we confirm the appointment of a permanent organiser. That the salary be two pounds when at work for the League', plus travelling and reasonable expenses. Minnie Nodin, the treasurer, and Mary Macpherson voted in favour; these might be termed the old guard. Mary MacArthur and Lisbeth voted against. It was then proposed that Dorothy Lenn be the organizer. Only Margaret MacDonald, Katharine Bruce Glasier and Minnie Nodin were in favour. The others abstained; Margaret MacDonald had therefore won approval for Dorothy Lenn's appointment by three votes against five abstentions. There are records of a spring tour by Dorothy in Wales and the North West and of a subsequent autumn tour in Wales. She found it difficult to get branches to be involved in winter organizing and intended to spend this time at the London Labour Party election rooms. The Women's Industrial Council paid a portion of Dorothy's wages. When this support ceased League funds were low. Dorothy's services were 'discontinued', but not until she had made a substantial contribution to League work in the January 1910 General Election. The East Birmingham branch which she had formed in the process of canvassing was said to be 'quite getting the honours' in the election.

Two more part-time organizers were appointed, Bertha Ayles for the South West and Annot Robinson in Manchester. Bertha Ayles (nee Batt) had moved to Bristol in 1910 with her husband Walter, who worked there as an ILP organizer. By 1911 Walter Ayles had published plans for a socialist local council in Bristol, with municipal housing, better control of planning and sanitary regulations and plenteous provision of education. Mrs Ayles was able to start conferences in the South West by the summer of 1910, building on Dorothy Lenn's work of the previous year. By January 1911 delegates were attending from Cardiff, Barry, Newport and Bristol. Swansea branch sent a report and Nantyfflon branch sent their greetings. This conference lasted all day and was followed by a more intimate 'round the stove' meeting of the activists (*Labour Leader*, January 1911); in the evening the women held a public meeting. Mrs Ayles spoke on the subject of municipal lodging houses for women, her theme that where women worked in industrial areas there was need for cheap accommodation that would provide both companionship and common cooking and washing facilities.

Meanwhile, Mrs Ayles was returning to her home surroundings of Lancashire to organize. The Lancashire and Cheshire area was a League stronghold. At its start in 1906 two branches were formed, Preston (secretary, Mrs Rigby, succeeded by Kitty Ralphs and Mrs Duckett) and Wallasey (secretary, Bertha Lancaster, succeeded by Mrs Stallybrass and Mrs Wade). Wallasey remained continuously active, returning Katharine Bruce Glasier to the League executive committee. Katharine had worked amongst Lancashire ILP women, encouraging them to join the League. In 1907 Nelson (Mrs Acton) and Bootle branches were formed; Preston branch split, its officers leaving to join the WSPU, but the branch continued. In 1909, the year of Dorothy Lenn's organizing tour, Blackpool (Mrs Suttland), Warrington (Miss Robinson) and St Helens (Mrs Bell) gained branches. Four of these eight branches were active in 1910; St Helens branch split in two, with Mrs Burt secretary of the seceding faction and, reflecting the general strength of the League in this year of two elections, three branches in Wigan were added and branches in Blackburn (Mrs Hulme), Burnley (Miss Burley), Hyde (Mrs Bradley) and Lancaster (Mrs Fort and Macclesfield (Mrs Pimblott).

A major city in the Lancashire and Cheshire area, Manchester had five branches, which Annot Robinson was asked to organize. Annot was committed to socialism and to women's suffrage and was active in the WSPU. She came from Dundee, where she had worked for the ILP. She was a graduate of St Andrews University (Lady Literate in Arts, an external degree). On arrival in Manchester, then Annot Wilkie, she was admitted to Central Manchester ILP branch, from which Mrs Pankhurst and Christabel had just resigned (June 1907).[14] She is next mentioned in the ILP branch minutes as the bride of Sam Robinson, the propaganda secretary (December 1907). In February 1908 there was a demonstration organized by the WSPU in London; Annot attended and was arrested. Manchester Central ILP sent both Annot and Christabel, also imprisoned, messages of support and sympathy. This gesture of solidarity possibly healed the breach between the ILP and WSPU locally; certainly on her release from prison, Annot became a regular attendee at ILP meetings. Sam and Annot quickly had two babies; Annot sent Margaret MacDonald a photograph of her first baby and Margaret responded with the invitation to organize for the League. Annot, who had given hospitality to Dorothy Lenn, was concerned about the latter's position. Margaret replied: 'we shall do more wisely if we have some part-time district organizers... as we have been doing with Mrs Simm'. A certain ruthlessness in Margaret's character was again revealed: 'Miss Lenn will be able to get work quite easily I think'; 'Don't feel you are ousting Miss Lenn. We needed her until the Election as we wanted to be able to send someone to every place which had a candidate and we did.' Annot was offered the same terms as Lisbeth Simm: payment for meetings and travelling expenses. As this usually amounted to £2 each month, Margaret suggested that Annot should carry out an appropriate amount of work. Her second baby was born in 1911 when Annot was 37 years old and was given a 'socialist christening': 'Baptismal rites and the usual formula were entirely dispensed with'; Keir Hardie came to the ceremony to sponsor the child and pinned the badges of the ILP and Women's Labour League to its clothes.

While branches and regions had local interests, there were several national campaigns organized by the League. The biggest single League campaign was its prolonged attempt to enforce the adoption by local authorities of the permissory Education (Provision of Meals) Act of 1906. The waging of this campaign demonstrates the importance of representation at local and national level in achieving reform. The Act resulted from parliamentary discussion of the report of the Inter-Departmental Committee on Physical Deterioration, set up in 1904 after the South African wars because of the concern at the ineffectiveness of the undernourished and unfit British infantrymen. Included in its recommendations was the feeding of schoolchildren and the recovery of costs from parents wherever possible. In 1905 Poor Law Boards of Guardians were empowered to give relief to children without insisting their fathers entered the workhouse, provided steps were taken to recover the cost. Few boards availed themselves of the opportunity. The Education (Provision of Meals) Act was the next step, giving local authorities discretionary powers to feed schoolchildren, who were unable to benefit from education because of hunger, either by co-operating with voluntary agencies or by spending the product of up to a halfpenny rate. The Parliamentary Labour Party accepted the limited Act. The League, however, did not find the discretionary measure acceptable: its impact on local education authorities was negligible and children continued to go hungry. The League therefore campaigned for the Act to become mandatory, so that locally there could be no evasion and as a corollary, to make state funds available to underwrite local expenditure.

Liskeard branch first (1907) raised the issue of school meals within the League.[15] Birmingham branch reported that the City Council had adopted the Education (Provision of Meals) Act. Hull branch urged its adoption on the local education committee and lobbied its Members of Parliament. Portsmouth branch urged the Act's adoption, then Leeds. The London County Council, despite having a special committee on physical deterioration, refused to adopt the school meals Act. St Pancras League branch, two of its members being school managers, collected evidence for the Council committee and suggested a petition asking the Council to reconsider and make a rate to carry out the Act.[16] Branch members on the care committee of a local group of London schools were able to persuade the authorities to begin school dinners in their area. Central London branch began collecting evidence on which districts of London contained needy children, how many there were and of what age and where the parents worked. A resolution was then sent to the London County Council asking for the adoption of the Act; it was refused: Central London branch collected 1000 signatures and petitioned the Council to receive a delegation; they were denied. However, a central Council care committee was set up, on which Dr Salter (League member Ada Salter's husband) served; at a League meeting he spoke of the 60,000 London children who needed ophthalmic treatment, the 10,000 needing orthodontic treatment, the thousands suffering from tuberculosis. Eventually in 1908, the London County Council agreed to raise £10,000 from the rates to feed school children.[17]

Leicester branch perhaps displayed the most remarkable feat of organizing. The education committee had adjourned its debate on the Act, so the League branch organized a huge demonstration in the market place. J.R. Clynes (one of Labour's most prominent Members of Parliament and once a textile worker) and Margaret MacDonald spoke; a petition was sent to the Council, where 'our Labour men worked harder than ever because they felt the force behind them'.[18] However, the Council decided to leave feeding schoolchildren to charity. Leicester branch then organized a repeat meeting in the market place, at which local women spoke and collected signatures to a further petition. They were opposed locally, by the Charity Organization Society, on the grounds that parental responsibility would be diminished. After repeated lobbying, a conference was held, attended by representatives of the Charity

Organization Society and the National Society for the Prevention of Cruelty to Children, and a voluntary scheme was proposed. Leicester Town Council decided to cooperate and formed the Children's Aid Association that provided school meals.

Lisbeth Simm chaired a meeting in Gateshead 'for the purpose of calling attention to the condition of many Gateshead's schoolchildren' (*Northern Democrat*, March 1908). Gateshead Council's trust in voluntary charities' ability to feed children was misplaced: 'about sixty of the worst cases have been supplied with breakfasts; the others...do without'. Margaret MacMillan, an ILP member whose chief concern was the welfare of schoolchildren, said that among the children of the better class artisan 8 per cent were at the age of 12 and deformed – that is, had crooked backs or rickets; 28 per cent suffered from adenoids, a throat and nose disease which would never cure of itself; 25 per cent were anaemic – blood in a poor and unhealthy condition. Margaret MacMillan had carefully investigated the quantity of real food required by a school child. 'To provide this, 2s per week was required for food for each child, so that a man and his wife with a family of five would need to spend 17s to 18s a week on food alone. With the average wage of about a pound a week, for many working men such a proceeding was impossible!' Margaret MacMillan's arguments had been accepted in her own town of Bradford, which was the only town in which the Guardians had provided out relief under the 1905 provision for any length of time. At Gateshead, a resolution was taken, with only one dissentient, urging Gateshead Council to adopt the Act and a petition was organized.

Humanitarian but half-heartedly funded, experimental, introduced in an *ad hoc* way rather than as part of a structured programme of reform, it was not surprising that, Bradford apart, the provision of school meals was clumsy and chaotic. The original wording of the Act had been taken to mean meals could not be provided outside school terms, because no educational benefit accrued. The original stimulant had been to ensure physical fitness; however, health was rarely used as a criterion for deciding provision. Poverty was the factor most frequently used and was variously defined. Selection was usually made by teachers; where it was left to parents to refer their children it was found that very few meals were provided. The stigma of pauperism and the punitive Poor Law were feared, and there was antipathy to contact with any form of state bureaucracy. League branches were amongst those organizations that had to make sense of piecemeal reform on the ground. They needed a universal measure that did not stigmatize the parents or the child, and that was simple and involved no complicated system of referral to an alien authority. They therefore initiated collective League action, asking the executive committee to co-ordinate their campaigns. It was an issue that the leadership had studied in depth; Margaret MacDonald had collected evidence from women's groups in France, Belgium, Switzerland and Austria.[19] Surprisingly, it took a while for the executive management to decide on action: it seemed content to leave the branches to cope; the pressure for a national petition, however, became irresistible. The latter came into use by 1909 and read:

> We the undersigned women of…petition our local authority to put into force the Act for the providing of meals for necessitous schoolchildren and consider that the expenses should be defrayed entirely out of public funds without any appeal to charity.

League campaigns continued, using this petition, but new legislation did not result.

Poor Law election work had been urged upon branches at the League's first conference. League women stood as candidates wherever elections were open to them, at district and parish councils and at the Poor Law Boards of Guardians. The Guardians were local bodies funded mainly through the rates, although there was some attempt at area pooling of resources and some central government provision. In many urban areas private bodies were also active in schemes for poor relief and the Charity Organization Society had, in some cases, managed these. This had pioneered casework with its clients, the obverse side of the face of progress being that the COS still believed poverty to be the result of individual failure. A Royal Commission had been set up in 1905 to study the Poor Law. The Poor Law Amendment Act of 1834 was still in force; its philosophy was that the recipient of poor relief should be in a worse condition than anyone who could provide for herself or himself, and that any relief given outside the workhouse ('out relief') should therefore be kept to a minimum: the 'less eligibility' and 'workhouse' tests. The social surveys of the late nineteenth and early twentieth centuries had illustrated, and the progressive spirit believed, that poverty was due to environment and social conditions rather than individual indolence and degeneracy. Rowntree's survey of York, in particular illustrated the poverty cycle; a child born in poverty would achieve relative comfort when first at work without dependants, would be impoverished by low wages coupled with growing responsibilities and thus be unable to save for an old age of miserable dependency. Measures were growing up outside the

Poor Law system to deal with specific causes of poverty, notably the old age pension introduced in 1908.

Nevertheless, the Royal Commission on the Poor Law did not report until 1909. Majority and minority reports were then produced, their common ground being the recommendations to abolish Boards of Guardians and improve co-ordination of public and private resources, with greater attempts to categorize poor people and provide more specific relief. The argument between the minority, who wanted the complete abolition of the Poor Law system, and the majority, who would have retained some such comprehensive approach, detracted from the impact of the Report and no measures to amend the Poor Law were introduced. The President of the Poor Law Division of the Local Government Board remained wedded to the principles of 1834 and many local boards reflected his philosophy. Receiving relief was still a real stigma, labelling the recipient 'pauper' and as such, disenfranchised. This, of course, meant that nobody receiving relief could vote in the Guardians' elections.

The total number of League members elected to Boards of Guardians is unknown. Sister Kerrison had been serving in West Ham since 1897. Mrs Cawthorne, secretary of the Hull branch, was the first to stand as a League candidate in 1906. Hull Trades Council chose her as candidate, donated £5 to her expenses and promised active support. Mrs Cawthorne intended to canvass every household and asked Margaret MacDonald to speak on her behalf: her agent wrote that it would not be possible to pay Margaret's expenses as 'we are only workmen's wives and our incomes are taxed severely for our movement'.[20] Despite strong opposition, Mrs Cawthorne was elected at her first attempt. Lisbeth Simm was elected to the Gosforth Board in 1908; she perceived her election as a 'woman's fight', believing that women could contribute to understanding the poverty which the Guardians had to address. Mrs Gibbin of Benwell branch came top of the poll at her first attempt in 1911 and wrote in *Labour Leader* (3 March 1911) that women should stand as candidates because the Guardians dealt so largely with women and children, the sick and the aged. There had been flooding in Benwell pit and many men had lost work; some had lost their lives. Mrs Gibbin campaigned for out relief to widows, as going into their workhouse added to their misery and prolonged their poverty.

Calling on women to act politically according to traditional gender roles was integral to the Middleton/MacDonald philosophy of gender, and this belief in the value of women's experience was explicitly stated in the *League Leaflet* on Guardians' work (no. 6): 'All sorts of questions arise which a woman knows more about, or can tackle better than a man.' An example was given: 'there are the children, thousands... have no other parents than the state,... others... have to be protected against their own parents. These children want *Mothering* (original emphasis)'. In the opinion of League members, the skills demanded of a Guardian were particularly applicable to women who managed a household budget. Women who were used to distributing inadequate resources in a caring way, for the good of the whole family, could bring these skills to bear in community work: 'The work of the Poor Law Guardians is like housekeeping for a very big and very difficult family', stated the leaflet; 'we want women's help to run this publicly managed household, just as much as to arrange for their own homes'. Seeing the public economy as an extension of that of the household was another typical strand of Middleton/MacDonald philosophy.

The conscious emphasis on women's contribution and skills may have distinguished League women from socialists already serving on the boards. Alternately, it may have acted as a base for gender solidarity and provided a means of approach to the benevolence of women Liberal and Conservative Guardians. However many boards had been male preserves and a particular importance of the League was to provide the organizational and imaginative support that gave women the courage to stand in such areas.[21] Lisbeth, for instance, felt her campaign aroused a new interest in public affairs amongst the working women of the district. As a woman candidate, she also experienced antagonism: 'I was solemnly charged to "stay at home and take care of my husband". Again and again I was told to "realise what a dreadful thing it was for one women to go and sit there amongst so many men"', reported Lisbeth in the *Northern Democrat* (May 1908). She thanked not only the women who had worked in the campaign, but also those whom prejudice had prevented from contributing. Once elected, Lisbeth indeed found that attending the meetings was rather 'a dreadful thing':

> Ours is a 'truly rural' Board. A drowsy atmosphere pervades the room, and except for the monotony of the chairman's voice, and an occasional 'Agreed' from a few members we might as well be in Church... When all is said and done, the Poor Law is a hopeless machine.

Lisbeth felt the need for a supportive voice at the meetings: 'Our next work must be to continue in preparation and education, for one woman among a crowd of over sixty men sorely needs a companion.'

In 1909 Glasgow League women lobbied Lord Provost to demand practical training for unemployed women in domestic work and hygiene and elementary sick nursing. They asked for provision of a Distress Committee workroom. Their case was remitted to a special committee of the Corporation (the Unemployed Workmen's Committee). The Distress Committee ran a labour colony where unemployed men could work on the land and were given basic accommodation and a small wage. It is interesting that in 1909 Mrs Joseph Fells served on the League executive: Joseph Fells had financed a labour colony for London unemployed men. Near Glasgow there were 800 acres on the heights of the moor, land previously not used for farming, where up to 700 men had found employment, thereby avoiding the workhouse. League members visited the colony and thought that women also should be employed, in market-gardening, vegetable-growing and poultry-keeping, and lobbied the Distress Committee to that effect in 1911. At their meeting with the committee, League women drew attention to the estimated 17,000 prostitutes in Glasgow and suggested that the dire need for work could be met by providing needlework and work on the colony. The men of the committee withdrew to consider and on their return announced that the Unemployed Workmen's Committee would resume meeting and obtain information and statistics 'from the ladies'.

The way some women resolved the need for an income while caring for children was to take in sweated work (long hours of work for little reward) that could be carried out either at home or in small local workshops where they could take the children.[22] Such establishments were not subject to regulation by any authority; local councils had power to deal with homework, but it was, of course, extremely difficult to monitor. Very few sweated workers belonged to a trade union. Sweated workers were seasonally employed, especially in the hat, glove and dressmaking trades, and were laid off for long periods; they were therefore forced to suffer long hours in times of employment. The 1905 Unemployed Workmen Act did cover such seasonally employed women, making provision for local authorities to set up workrooms (such as those the Glasgow League branch campaigned for) so that the women would not be dependent on Poor Law relief. The only such workroom recorded was that set up by the Central London Distress Committee. Generally, there was a lack of knowledge about female labour, despite the efforts of campaigners. The Women's Industrial Council, set up in 1894, had vast experience of studying sweated labour. The Council consisted of two hundred or so women, who collected data and lobbied politicians with the results. Margaret MacDonald was the Council's legal secretary and as such gave evidence to the Royal Commission on the Poor Laws regarding women's work and wages.[23] The Council participated in the sweated industry exhibition run by the *Daily News* in 1906. This exhibition had an enormous impact on public opinion and led to the founding of the Anti-Sweating League. A Select Committee of the House of Commons was set up (1907) to inquire into sweated work. Ramsay MacDonald presented a Homeworkers' Bill to the House of Commons, seeking to introduce regulations that would improve conditions.

It was the *Clarion* woman's column editor, Julia Varley, who offered the League what she called a 'golden opportunity to make propaganda over sweating' in February 1907. The *Clarion* was to hold a handicraft exhibition in London, the hall was free, so should the League decide to staff a stall with six workers at £1 per week for six weeks, the cost would be trifling. The executive committee decided to accept the offer; branches collected examples of cloth made up very cheaply by women for local tailors. This involved enquiry into the sweated trades and contact with women homeworkers to the benefit of the branch; holding the exhibition contributed to raising interest at Westminster while Ramsay MacDonald's Bill was on the timetable. A League member from Lowestoft took back items from the exhibition and arranged her own showing at the local adult school.[24] One dress was shown at the exhibition for which the machinist was paid 1s 1d and the finisher 2s 0d; the retailer paid the tailor 12s 6d and priced the dress at 16s 6d. The tailor was named Mr Cohen; he had appeared before the House of Commons Home Industry Committee. He offered to pay the League £100 if their figures, and his involvement, could be proved within 15 days. He stated that his design had been stolen and asked the League to pay £25 to a charity of his choosing should they default.[25] The correspondence between the League and Mr Cohen lasted longer than the 14 days; the League obtained legal advice and offered to produce evidence before arbitrators, asking for the Board of Trade to be represented. Mr Cohen demanded to see the identifying marks on the costume, perhaps in an endeavour to trace and penalize the worker who had given the information. Neither side moved from their position, but the press coverage helped the publicity on sweated work to reach a wide audience. The League gave evidence before the Select Committee about Mr Cohen.

A letter sent to the League from a woman then in the Royal Infirmary illustrated the desperation of women sweated workers and the difficulty of finding a remedy. The woman wrote that she had reared her children alone with the aid of her sewing machine: 'such a Bill (as Ramsay

MacDonald sought to introduce) would have crushed me'.[26] Many women workers resented any interference with their right to work. Women's trade unions had traditionally preferred to rely on free collective bargaining to improve pay and conditions, but wanted workshops licensed to make sure they were safe and clean. The Women's Industrial Council, on the other hand, had a history of supporting legislation to improve conditions for women workers. It now fell into dispute about the wisdom of legislation on introducing trades boards to regulate pay and conditions in specific trades.[27] Margaret MacDonald supported the trade union position, preferring negotiated rates. Mary MacArthur was in favour of trades boards and spoke at the 1907 League conference to that effect. Angry correspondence between the two ensued. On 20 November 1907 at the Central London League branch meeting, Mary MacArthur spoke for and Margaret MacDonald against trades boards; the following year the branch agreed to cooperate with the Women's Industrial Council in an investigation of married women's work. At the League executive on 11 February 1908 Margaret spoke against sending a representative to the Anti-Sweating League demonstration because of the difference of opinion within the League, but Mary Macpherson was, nevertheless, chosen and attended as League representative. Bad feeling caused Mary MacArthur to resign from the League executive, but controversy within the League continued. Finally, the 1909 Trades Board Act introduced a minimum wage for around 200,000 women in tailoring, paper-box making, lace and chain making trades.

In 1908 Margaret Bondfield, Sister Kerrison, Edith Macrosty, Mary Macpherson, Minnie Nodin and all League executive committee members were also Women's Industrial Council members, in addition to Margaret MacDonald. Dorothy Lenn was employed to help in the investigation of married women's work; she worked in Leicester, where Margaret MacDonald raised funds for the investigation, donating some of her own money. Margaret Bondfield carried out an investigation in Yorkshire. In 1910 there was an argument over the handling of a book on sweating, later edited by Clementina Black, and over proposed changes in the structure of the Women's Industrial Council (which would have given more power to its leadership). Margaret MacDonald and the League women all resigned from the Council.

Despite occasional controversy and sometimes high-handed leadership action, the freelance role was played out in full spate of enthusiasm until 1911, Mary Middleton remaining as secretary and working in close partnership with Margaret MacDonald. A systematic and coherent structure had been achieved for the League. There were three provincial organizers, four districts holding regular conferences and the executive presence in London. A system of 'live and let live' had been established at national level with women's trade unions and socialist party women's sections. Affiliation to the Labour Party was achieved, and a special place for women provided. The annual conference, in concert with the Labour Party, illustrated that 'the Men's Party' had accepted the League. Nationally, the League had done little on suffrage although individual League members were active in the struggle for women's enfranchisement, a notable example being Annot Robinson. League members had been elected to Poor Law Boards. In all, a type of constitutional socialist feminism could be acted out and thought out in a context alien to neither the turn-of-the century women's movement, nor the quest for working people's democracy. Combining the thrust of both movements into a new philosophy was an attractive challenge, which won the League substantial support. Then, both Mary Middleton and Margaret MacDonald died in 1911. Mary Middleton had fought bravely against cancer since 1909. Margaret MacDonald's death was thought to be due to poisoning, inexplicable to the medical practice of her time. The greatest epitaph to these women was the survival of the League that they had managed in its freelance role.

2. Consolidation of the Women's Labour League

This second section examines the fortunes of the League from 1911 when, following the death of its two original leaders, the League evolved from the decentralized body of the 'freelance' years into a more highly organized campaigning group. This transition was not easy for the League; nevertheless, it increased in vigour. Membership rose 500 per cent from the 100 women at the first conference in 1906 to the 5000 credited in Labour Party *Annual Reports* of 1913 and 1914. As its national profile grew stronger, so did the League's independent character as a woman's organization, despite its Labour Party affiliation.

Under Margaret MacDonald and Mary Middleton, and given its original modelling on the Railway Women's Guild, the League had been open to the charge later levelled against it by suffragist Theresa Billington Grieg, of consisting 'chiefly of the wives and daughters of labour fathers'.[28] There would always be an element of truth in such a charge, as the Labour movement was, to some extent, a self-contained world that facilitated relationships between its members. However, on the one hand, the evidence does not support the case that the 'wives and daughters' lacked their own political conviction; on the other, there were from the start many single League women who led independent lives (for example Sister Kerrison, Mary MacArthur and Ethel Bentham). The League's new leaders, Margaret Bondfield and then Marion Phillips, were single, professional women to whom Greig's charge in no way applied. Margaret Bondfield was a trade unionist from a working class background and Marion Phillips a highly educated economist.[29] Marion Phillips had been involved in the suffrage movement and the League's involvement in this struggle increased under her leadership, while the League's greater involvement in trades union activities reflected Margaret Bondfield's interests. Other new areas of discussion included birth control and peace. The League's long-standing campaigns continued, for instance the school meals campaign, but were waged in a more centralized manner.

On Mary Middleton's death in April 1911, the League executive committee decided to create a new role of organizing secretary, a paid officer (£2 per week, with six weeks paid holiday) who would support Margaret MacDonald by helping with secretarial work and also assist the Labour Party at by-elections. Margaret Bondfield slid into the role. According to her biographer, Margaret Bondfield was:

> the moving spirit of the little group of women in London – Mary
> MacArthur, Margaret MacDonald, Gertrude Tuckwell, Julia Dawson

and the rest – who were the life and soul of the Labour movement in all its relations with their own sex... to whom the equal place of full recognition to women by Labour is largely due.[30]

At this time, aged 38 years, Margaret was good-looking with a speaking voice renowned for its clarity and melody. According to Sylvia Pankhurst, Margaret used her looks and voice to good effect: '...attired in pink, dark and dark-eyed, with a deep throaty voice many found beautiful. She was very charming and vivacious and eager to score all the points that her youth and prettiness would win for her'.[31] Margaret's career had been spectacular; she had worked as a shop assistant, joined the Social Democratic Federation and became assistant secretary of the Shop Assistants' Union. She had worked as a propagandist for the Labour Party and for the ILP, which she joined having become disillusioned with the rather stern Social Democratic Federation. Margaret worked with Clementina Black on the report on married women's work for the Women's Industrial Council and with the Women's Cooperative Guild on maternity and child welfare. She thus had experience across the range of socialist societies and with women as workers, politicians and consumers. Nevertheless, there were some points of discord; Margaret was a great admirer of Mary MacArthur, and supported the minimum wage, which had been the cause of MacArthur's dispute with Margaret MacDonald. Margaret Bondfield believed women's separate organizations to be a preliminary step to integration into the full, mixed body, rather than the League approach to women's organizations as separate-but-equal partner.

When Margaret MacDonald became ill, Margaret Bondfield took over some of her duties; on Margaret MacDonald's death in November 1911, Margaret Bondfield also fell sick. The general secretaryship was offered, temporarily, to Marion Phillips, who was at the time organizing secretary of the Women's Trade Union League. She was a very different type of leader than Margaret MacDonald; a trained and experienced administrator, Marion Phillips had graduated from Melbourne University and won a research scholarship to the London School of Economics, where she qualified DSC in Economics. She worked as an investigator for the Royal Commission on the Poor Laws until 1910. Marion had founded North Kensington Women's Labour League and was also elected to the executive committee that year. Civil servant A.J. Braithwaite, who had conducted negotiations with women's organizations over the new National Insurance scheme (see below for details of the scheme), considered that she had 'the best brains of the whole lot'.[32] Marion was paid

£1 per week for part-time duties, 10.30 a.m. to 1.00 p.m. every day in the office, plus expenses of 7s per day for work outside London.

There ensued a difficult period of rivalry between two households. Margaret Bondfield, her friend Maud Ward and Ethel Clarke shared one dwelling and Marion Phillips, Mary Longman (also an investigator for the Poor Law Commission) and Ethel Bentham another. All were League members. Margaret Bondfield wrote:

> I have decided not to hold office in the League. I shall be a member of the executive committee only. For the first time I have met with people with whom I *cannot* work…At present my attitude divides the Executive Committee and is frightfully bad for the League. I do not choose to be the nominal head without any real power.[33]

On the one hand, Katherine Bruce Glasier wrote to Ramsay MacDonald:

> I wish I had Margaret Bondfield's confidence or quite understood her: but her friendship with Maud Ward which your dear wife dreaded got right between us. These violent attachments don't seem to help, or to be good servants of the commonwealth. They have in them all the disproportionate heats and chills and passionate impulsive actions against outsiders who touch one of the beloved one's supposed interests or dignities that belong to lovers.[34]

On the other, she opined:

> …the personality of Dr. Phillips is a real difficulty. If only your dear wife had lived to train her, hold her, *compel* her to less egotism she might have grown great as well as clever to a degree, and capable…she is as hard and cold as glass. Brilliant as diamonds are and *none* of us can love her except Dr. Ethel Bentham.[35]

It is hard to know what to make of all this. Margaret Bondfield was ill and had the responsibility of a sick mother, yet given her wide political and trades union experience she cannot have been easily intimidated. As stated, she was not one hundred per cent in accord with the original League objectives, and between her and Marion Phillips there were different attitudes to women's suffrage, as is shown below. There are unsubstantiated hints in Katherine Bruce Glasier's letters of lesbian relationships in the two households. Whether or not the relationships were sexual, they were obviously self-sufficient, separatist and childless, and may have antagonized heterosexual League women. Katherine, however, as was shown by various disputes over the ILP's journal *Labour Leader*, for which she wrote, tended towards purple prose and was quick to spot a plot.

In the event, Margaret Bondfield resigned as organizing secretary in January 1912. The executive continued to pay half her wages until June; she had made her flat available to store League literature, and Ethel Clarke worked on the literature sales and accounts. Her resignation was finally accepted in September 1912 and she left the executive committee in 1914. Marion Phillips's position was ratified and made permanent at the 1913 League conference. The League again asked Margaret Bondfield to accept the post of organizing secretary but she decided not to commit herself full-time to League work. Marion Phillips was then paid £100 per year as general secretary, a position she held for the rest of the League's existence, apart from a few months in 1915 when Mary Longman stood in for her. Katherine Bruce Glasier was almost reconciled: '... she (Marion Phllips) identifies the Women's Labour League with herself and toils for it untiringly...we have accepted Dr Phillips amazing energy and powerful lead as the only thing to do in very difficult circumstances'.[36]

During these changes, the League continued to use space in the MacDonald house, eventually agreeing to pay £25 per year for two rooms and a storeroom. Ethel Bentham guaranteed the rent. Ethel Clarke (until 1913), Miss Schloesser and Agnes Brown provided secretarial assistance. District committees and conferences on the Lisbeth Simm model were encouraged. A call for district representation on the executive committee was, however, bypassed. Innovations, which gave more power to the leadership at conference, were that the morning session was devoted to a paper presented for discussion and that branch reports were relegated to last from first place. Marion Phillips gave the paper in 1913, a skilled and detailed account of 'How to raise money for public services without increasing the burdens of poverty'. Taxation on consumption, property and capital, and local taxation were considered and recommendations made that taxes should be levied on luxury consumption and a graduated tax set on income from property and profits. Resolutions for the Labour Party conference were now despatched directly by the executive committee without discussion at the League conference. Newcomers to the executive committee included Mary Longman, Scottish socialist Clarice McNab,[37] and Louise Donaldson, whose Christian Socialist husband Frederick later became Canon of Westminster. Representation on the executive committee from outside London was reduced and it was decided that standing com-mittees would be comprised of Londoners. Marion Philips undertook few of the speaking tours for the League at which Margaret MacDonald had excelled. The *League Leaflet* became more professional and was sold through newsagents, evolving by April 1913 into a full-size magazine, *Labour Woman*.

From 1911, the League was granted £50 from the Labour Party gen-eral fund and £50 from its special fund. The more metropolitan and more centralized shape of the League meant that contacts between the League and the Party leadership were facilitated and these contacts were strengthened by the League's insistent lobbying of Labour MPs on issues such as national insurance and suffrage. In 1913, the Liberal Govern-ment enacted legislation to pay MPs so that parliament should not be restricted to members with private means. This went some way to redress the effects of the Osborne Judgement, which had outlawed trades union contributions to political parties. Released from the need to sup-port its MPs, the Labour Party could afford to be more generous with affiliates, and the League grant was doubled. However, there was a sting in the tail; the increased cost of publications and office expenditure soon used up the grant, and a special meeting of League and Party officers was called to discuss finance. Arthur Henderson, Party secretary, wrote to Marion Phillips: 'There was a feeling that branch organisation of the League, so far as it has come to the notice of members of our committee, was not as efficient or as strongly developed as it could be'.[38] Marion Phillips agreed to forego her salary, the hours and pay of the office clerk were cut and the pages of *Labour Woman* reduced.

Meanwhile, the strained relations between leading figures in the League were exacerbated by the dispute over women's suffrage, which had come to a head in 1909. Margaret Bondfield was then delegated to the Labour Party conference and had to put forward the League motion on suffrage. She was president of the People's Suffrage Association and had tried unsuccessfully to get the League to affiliate to this body; the League conference had voted against this in 1908 and 1909. The League motion with which Margaret Bondfield was entrusted demanded that women's enfranchisement be a central part of any suffrage reform mea-sure introduced and that failing this, Labour MPs should oppose the reform in its entirety. Without authority, she amended the motion to exclude the part about total opposition, and faced severe criticism from some League executive members. Despite this, the executive merely recorded that the conference report had been received and Margaret Bondield's action endorsed. At the January 1911 League conference, an amendment in favour of women's enfranchisement to a resolution in favour of full enfranchisement of men and women was defeated by 32 votes to four.

Nevertheless, League involvement in the women's suffrage campaign grew under Marion Phillips's leadership. Although now in favour of people's suffrage, Marion Phillips had a background of work for the NUWSS. Branches were asked to pass resolutions in favour of the Local Authority (Qualification of Women) Bill, a positive step that had not been taken previously. The League became one of the organizing societies of a conference of the Women's Suffrage Joint Committee and the Adult Suffrage Society called specifically to discuss the vote and working women. Following this, the League decided to support the Joint Committee in urging the immediate introduction of a Reform Bill; branches were again asked to pass resolutions in favour and the Prime Minister was asked to receive a deputation. The catalyst that may have stimulated the League to greater activity, as it stimulated so many women to militancy, was the introduction of a Franchise Bill into the House of Commons, which did not include women, by the Liberal Prime Minister (Asquith) in 1911. The ILP campaigned against this action and the Labour Party conference finally took the decision that no franchise reform was acceptable unless women were included. With the Labour Party now committed to support, a restraint on League activity was removed.

NUWSS and many Liberal Party women, appalled at the Prime Minister's action, were drawn towards cooperation with Labour. H.N. Brailsford, a radical Liberal academic and journalist, approached the Labour Party on behalf of the NUWSS and, with great patience, cajoled both groups into an alliance. The leadership of each organization was reluctant, the NUWSS articulating a desire to remain non-party-political. There is no record of League involvement in the discussions; Catherine Marshall, of the NUWSS, dealt directly with the Labour Party men. Eventually, an Election Fighting Fund was set up to combat constituencies where the Member of Parliament was not committed to women's suffrage, and to fight these on behalf of the Labour Party. In the constituencies chosen for combat, NUWSS women and Labour Party men appear to have worked well together and to have been reasonably successful. There were 32 by-elections from June 1912 until August 1914, five of them in mining constituencies; as mining was labour-intensive, it was particularly important to win support from the mineworkers, who because of their numbers could dominate politics within their constituency. The NUWSS and Labour Party alliance fought eight seats, including mining constituencies; although the Labour candidate was not returned in any of these eight constituencies, the Liberal vote was reduced in each.

By October 1912, the League was sufficiently active on women's enfranchisement to allow the Women's Freedom League (formed by secessionists from the WSPU in 1907) to inscribe the League name on a scroll recording societies that supported women's suffrage, with the wording, 'Unity in Adversity' as its logo. The League executive committee joined the Women's Freedom League at its international fair and took part in the Women's Freedom League national conference in December 1912. A special suffrage edition of the *League Leaflet* was issued late in 1912 (no. 23); a statement of the Labour Party position on suffrage and that the League was working for its achievement. This was signed by Marion Phillips and started in a stateswoman-like way, regretting that the WSPU had seen fit to campaign against Philip Snowden (ILP and Labour Party) in his constituency. It was reported that the Labour Party was trying to persuade the House of Commons to adopt an amendment to the Reform Bill then before it, to include women's enfranchisement. The WSPU position was that the amendment was inadequate and therefore the whole Bill should be rejected; the *League Leaflet* reiterated that such a course would be a betrayal of Labour women in constituencies that had returned Labour Members of Parliament. Philip Snowden wrote that the feeling of the House of Commons was moving in favour of women; what was needed was constituency pressure and the support of the Irish Members of Parliament. (The latter were seeking Home Rule and supported the Liberal Government in so far as it seemed inclined to grant their claims.) What course the Labour Party should take if the Bill were to reach its third reading in parliament and still not refer to women was hotly debated, Marion Phillip's advice being to wait and see:

> Let us, who represent the working women in politics, be forward in the fight, pressing our supporters in the House of Commons onward to the victory which justice demands. And let us do this from within our own ranks, under our own banner of freedom and hope, not scattered through our societies, but solidly organized as Labour women demanding economic and political equality for working women and working men.

In order that, in the event of women not being included in the Reform Bill, the Labour Party would be equipped with the right response, the

League executive committee decided on the safeguard of a further resolution to the Labour Party conference. They also decided to take part
in a national suffrage conference. These actions were supported by the
1913 League conference, the year Florence Harrison Bell, an ardent suffragist, was elected to the executive committee. The executive began to
take its own direct action on women's suffrage, deciding on 31 March
1913 to send resolutions to the Prime Minister, Lloyd George (Chancellor of the Exchequer), the People's Suffrage Federation and the Labour
Party, demanding the immediate introduction of a government measure to enfranchise women. Having been offered the chance to discuss
this action with a League delegation, the Parliamentary Labour Party
offended by replying that MPs would meet League women together
with delegates from the NUWSS and the Women's Co-operative Guild.
From tentative support, the League had moved to claiming the right for
its own voice to be distinctly heard on the issue of women's suffrage:
it claimed, 'as an organisation of the Party', the right to a private
deputation and discussion.

Some executive committee members, such as Katharine Bruce Glasier,
felt that concentrating on suffrage reduced the ordinary membership
of the League to a 'stage army'. Involvement in the suffrage campaign
was conducted by the London leadership and set in Westminster, an
issue of high politics. However, the coercive measures against the militant suffragettes furthered their cause and there is no record of branch
rebellion against the leadership. A resolution calling on the House of
Commons to redress the grievances of women and protesting coercion
was sent to the Prime Minister, the Labour Party and the press. Marion
Phillips, on behalf of the League, urged Labour MPs to abstain or vote
against a Reform Bill unless it enfranchised women. As the Bill currently
under discussion was primarily intended to abolish plural voting – the
right to vote in more than one constituency where ownership of property or residence qualified the elector – which discriminated against men
of the working classes, asking the Labour Party to forgo the legislation
illustrated how committed the League had become to the suffrage cause.

As reprisals against suffrage campaigners grew, so did the League support for their cause. Delegates were sent to the conference held to protest
against the Cat and Mouse Act (which enabled women prisoners on
hunger strike to be released until they had recovered sufficiently to
complete their sentence). The poster produced to publicize the hor-
rors of the Cat and Mouse Act was exhibited and the League called
for a Labour Amendment to the Address following the King's Speech.
Marion Phillips wrote an obituary for Emily Wilding Davison who was

killed when she threw herself under the King's horse at the Derby.[39] Applauding her courage, Marion Phillips wrote that Emily Wilding Davison 'stood rather apart from the organized disorder of the militant movement'. As this indicated, there was no *rapprochement* between the League and the WSPU. A sizeable number of WSPU members retained their League membership; the executive decided they must choose between the two bodies. The outbreak of war prevented further progress; however, the League had travelled a considerable distance along the way to supporting women's, as opposed to people's, suffrage.

The growing confidence of the League was also demonstrated in the way it pursued its less contentious campaigns on social policy. Now making use of its national petition for free school meals, the League applied pressure at Westminster, producing pamphlets and calling on Labour Members of Parliament to introduce amending legislation. Branches urging their own local Members of Parliament to act, reinforced this campaign. During 1911–12, of 322 authorities, 131 made some provision for feeding schoolchildren.[40] Margaret MacMillan later wrote that the Bradford experiment had been influential in proving to local authorities that community feeding minimized labour and the cost of each portion of food; socialism made sense:

> Bradford grasped the nettle... Its splendid Central School kitchen with its scientific equipment, its worked out menus, its fine transport, its expert direction and trained staff helped lift the whole question into a new atmosphere.[41]

Bradford schoolchildren, after eight years of experimentation and investigation, were being provided with a variety of 17 different dinners at a cost of 3s 4d to 1s 1½d per meal. The district auditor regularly made a surcharge because the meals were provided in school holidays as well as term time, and the product of a halfpenny rate was exceeded. Lisbeth Simm reported her joy at witnessing this operation (*Northern Democrat*, March 1912): 'It was just dinner time and the smell of savoury meat and potato pies greeted us at the door.' Three teachers and six of the older girls served the dinners. Every child either bought, or was given, a dinner ticket 'so that they were all on the same footing at the feeding centre'. There was full use of new technology; a central kitchen prepared the dinners, which were sent out on vans: 'I... admired the wonderful appliances for lightening labour... "Here we wash all the plates with hot water, slide them down that board into the cold water and then put them in this rack, and turn on a hot air tap to dry them."'

Pressure was not relaxed; at the 1914 Labour Party conference, D. McCarthy criticized Labour MPs for not pursuing the issue with enough 'holy zeal'; Marion Phillips again moved a League resolution demanding compulsory provision of school meals and also asked that catering be carried out by local authority employees, not left to contract labour. In that year it seemed success was in sight, when the government announced that the exchequer would grant half the cost of school meal provision and that proposals to legalize feeding schoolchildren during the holidays would be included in next session's Education Bill. War destroyed this immediate chance of progress.

Birth control, a new subject of discussion for the League, was considered in the pages of *Labour Woman*. Florence Harrison Bell wrote in August 1913 that family limitation would help working people, who would otherwise be thrown into poverty by coping with large numbers of children. Emily C. Fortey replied the next month that birth control was an evil, although she would not condemn working people, faced with poverty, for following a custom already set among the upper classes. A lively correspondence ensued, the majority of which was in agreement with Florence Harrison Bell. Jennie Baker wrote that ways and means should be explained for working women to follow. She later became the first president of the National Council for the Unmarried Mother and her Child.

A new field of activity for the League was also campaigning on the proposed National Insurance Bill. This was one of the Liberal Government's flagship reforms aimed at providing sickness and unemployment cover for workers but it dealt chiefly with men and provisions for women were inadequate. Assisted by Margaret Bondfield, who gave a description for *Labour Leader* (21 July 1911), Birmingham branch conducted a house-to-house canvass:

> At 11 a.m. a few members who had risen early and finished off their housework and I started to canvass. The shyness soon wore off, and each took a separate section of the streets. Oh! the lonely lives of these women, hidden away at the back of a network of small mean streets.

The measures in the final Act were the result of prolonged negotiations with interested parties – the medical profession, Friendly Societies who ran sick pay schemes, insurance companies – and within parliament. The budget proposed by the Chancellor Lloyd George to enable the Act had provoked the House of Lords into rebellion, causing the Liberal Government to hold the two 1910 general elections. The Parliament

Act of 1911, which restricted the power of the Lords, resolved the constitutional crisis. The Act was in two parts; the first made sick pay and medical treatment available to workers who contributed weekly to a fund into which their employers and the state also paid a share. The second allowed for 15 weeks' unemployment pay in specific industries. The very few women engaged in steady trades were eligible for unemployment benefit; this was achieved as a result of insistent lobbying by women's trades unions and political organizations, including the League. As the sick pay contributions were weekly, the casual female workforce and unregulated sweated workers were similarly excluded and the benefits of sick pay and medical treatment were in practice confined to the adult, able-bodied male. Health cover for widows and orphans had been lost in the negotiations and no dependants were covered. Within the Labour movement as a whole the Act was controversial, some welcoming the provisions, some preferring wage rises that would allow workers to make their own provisions. Labour MPs voted against each other in divisions during the passage of the Act. The League, however, was consistent in its view that women should be included; they joined demonstrations and lobbied MPs to that effect. When the National Insurance scheme came into effect, League branches were instructed to seek representation on local bodies operating the scheme. The Industrial Women's Insurance Advisory Board was created in 1912 with representatives from the League, the Women's Cooperative Guild and the National Federation of Women Workers; board meetings were held in the League offices.

The 1911 Act also provided for a maternity allowance to the wife of an insured man. There was some dispute as to whether the allowance should be paid to the man or direct to the mother. Those Labour MPs in favour of the provision were not agreed as to the payee, while most trades unions, arguing for a 'family wage' for their members, were opposed to the idea of allowances. The dilemma for the League was that payment of the allowance to the mother presupposed that she alone would be responsible for raising the child and, as League campaigners well knew, most working women did precisely that. Margaret Bondfield was amongst those who were opposed to the idea of women being paid an allowance to stay outside the workforce. It was the Cooperative Women's Guild, who dealt with women as consumers, who successfully campaigned in 1913 to make the payment the legal property of the mother.

League support for industrial women continued under its new leadership. Many League branches worked locally in support of women's trade unions, for instance, amongst the dressmakers and staymakers of

Portsmouth on short time and low wages, the card room workers at Preston, the laundry girls at Liskeard who were intimidated from joining the National Federation of Women Workers. The tailoresses at Birmingham gave in their names to the Tailor, Machinist and Pressers Union at a League meeting addressed by Mrs Pankhurst.[42] Birmingham, Keighley and District Trades Council had a mere 1500 trade unionists from 45,000 'in this benighted town' and was optimistic that the League would help redress the balance. In Wigan *Labour Leader* reported (27 April 1911) that the League was organizing the pit-brow girls to become members of the Miner's Federation. During the great wave of industrial unrest of 1911 the Hull seamen and dockers went on strike (*Labour Leader*, 31 July 1911); League women set up a relief committee. Mrs Hill, Hull League president, was caretaker of the local ILP hall that was used to organize relief. They separated themselves into ward committees and made house-to-house visits. In London, League women took care of strikers' children during the dock strike.

The industrial agitation of 1911 was also vigorous in South Wales. Women and young girls employed in cigar-making, bottling and laundry work came out on strike and Mrs Scholefield, president of Cardiff Women's Labour League, assisted by Margaret Bondfield, met them to give advice: 'We went into the highways and the parks, holding odd meetings in odd places', reported Margaret Bondfield in *Labour Leader* (4 August 1911). The laundry workers got together and organized a committee; Margaret Bondfield drafted a Laundry Workers' Charter with them. The employers set up their own association and met representatives of the laundry workers; the Charter was agreed and the employers 'came to terms'. The Workers' Union were so pleased at this success that they signed up Mrs Scholefield temporarily. She held meetings at Barry Docks on women and children and the effects of the strike.[43] The 1912 executive resolution to the League conference congratulated women who had stood 'shoulder to shoulder' with men in the disputes. At the 1914 conference, delegates were reminded that 'the wives of strikers had participated in the rough and tumble of the movement outside their home. In some cases they taken their turn when picketting was to be done'. Fifteen League branches had strike funds by 1914. Twenty branches were helping unions operate the new Trades Boards that regulated wages and conditions in various industries.

The League did have contact with the National Union of Women Workers. This was rather misnamed, being an organization of philanthropic and religious women rather than of industrial trade unionists. However, it was affiliated to the Labour Party, unlike many of the smaller women's trade unions. Margaret MacDonald had been a member of the NUWW executive council since 1896. Lisbeth Simm was a guest at the NUWW 1911 conference and read a paper on education and women of the working classes. The Scottish Council for Women's Trades kept in touch with the League, Margaret Irwin writing frequently about sweated workshops and the conditions of women's employment. The National Federation of Women Workers was in close touch with the League while Mary MacArthur sat on its executive, but did not affiliate. Neither did Margaret Bondfield's former union of shop assistants.

League women had to be careful not to tread on the toes of women's trades unions. In Hull, for instance, despite their work to relieve distress, the League branch was 'flatly told we were not wanted to help organize women workers'. Lisbeth Simm, when working in Glasgow amongst the 'intelligent and not easily humbugged' dressmakers and weavers, was careful to ensure that the League executive committee did not send Mary MacArthur to speak. As secretary of the National Federation of Women Workers, she obviously had an interest: 'we really have no right to bring in a trade union organizer to the women, they are competent to choose organizers for themselves and would certainly resent us sending one to them'.[44] Some actions did stretch friendly relations, such as the sheets of signatures collected by branches in support of a full dinner hour for Co-operative women jam workers, which were sent by the executive to Margaret Llewellyn Davies with a letter deploring the jam worker's low pay.

While the League profile at home was raised under Marion Phillip's leadership, its interest in international affairs was broadened. Although the 1907 Labour and Socialist International Women's Congress had instructed delegates, including a sizeable British contingent, to organize more coherently among women, little progress had been made. League women had, indeed, made many individual trips to women's groups abroad; Margaret MacDonald, Margaret Bondfield and Annot Robinson were among those visiting America, while trips to Europe were frequent. British women attended the 1910 International but, regrettably, displayed domestic differences. The debate on suffrage took up most of the two days and the British delegation came under fierce adverse criticism for supporting limited women's suffrage. Four League motions on the subject failed to be discussed. Moreover, Ethel Bentham, Marion Phillips and Mrs Despard had been chosen to speak on behalf of the British delegation, but Dora Montefiore of the Social Democratic Federation was called to speak in their place. Ten League delegates walked out in protest. However, the International had called for a women's council to be formed in each affiliated country and the Women's International Council of Socialist and Labour Organizations (British Section) was duly formed. The League affiliated, Margaret Bondfield becoming chair and Margaret McDonald secretary. Unfortunately, no records survive of this body. However, the pages of *Labour Woman* indicate increased attention to international news. Jennie Baker took over the relevant column from Mary Macpherson in April 1914 and headed it 'Our Sisters Abroad'. The activities of European and American socialists were reported and space was given to the women's council of the Socialist International. Greetings were sent to German revolutionary socialist and theorist Rosa Luxembourg, on her arrest in April 1914. Mary Longman took over the secretaryship of the Women's Council in 1913 and her speech at a peace demonstration in Germany was reported in July 1914.

One of the executive committee resolutions sent to the League 1912 conference condemned secret diplomacy, and the government, for acting as if war were inevitable. At the 1913 conference Katherine Bruce Glasier moved the first resolution, which protested militarism and an expansion of war in the Balkans. Lisbeth Simm wrote an article entitled 'War against War' for *Labour Woman* in July 1913, arguing that '... the Labour Party had always stood for international friendship and peace'. She found army training and discipline degrading, turning men into alien beings. She remembered seeing a military camp as a child: 'it seemed to us as if these soldiers were not men, but something that was drilled while sober, and drunk and helpless when off duty'. Lisbeth wrote that the price of production of life for mothers was too heavy for it to be wasted and that war demoralized a nation. The League's leaflet *Facts and Figures* for November 1913 recorded that Britain spent £18,729,000 per annum on education, £27,860,000 on the army and £44,085,000 on the Navy; spending on the armed forces amounted to 12s 4d per head of the population. The 1914 conference argued against arms expenditure, against conscription and in favour of the joint action of workers internationally against war.

This increased interest in international affairs foreshadowed changes in the League priorities that are dealt with in Part II. Already, under its new leaders, the League had developed and consolidated. Its organization and agenda were much more ambitious than those originally envisaged by Mary MacPherson. The 'freelance' period of relatively loose central organization, which had enabled branch autonomy and individual initiative, had been replaced by a more centralized and directed approach. Both Margaret Bondfield and Marion Phillips were able to bring to the fore their own concerns, and Marion Phillips's character in particular is revealed as energetic and driven – 'brilliant as diamonds'. By 1914 the League had consolidated its position as a funded Labour Party affiliate, was active and effective in the industrial and political spheres, saw its school meals campaign nearing fruition, its members elected to Boards of Guardians and local councils, and its profile in the suffrage campaign strengthened. Externally, the suffrage movement had an effect upon the League, but how far the greater involvement in this campaign was a result of Marion Phillips's interest and how far the effect of the broader campaign is difficult to tell. However, by 1914 the League had made great strides in achieving representation for women, not only at local level but in lobbying government, for instance on national insurance. This raised profile was to stand the League in good stead as it met the challenge of wartime organization.

3. Enid Stacy, Marion Barry and Clarice McNab Shaw

The experiences of these three different women illustrate some of the campaigns discussed in this first part. All three were involved in both trades union and political activity and publicly advocated Labour movement involvement in speeches and writing. However, their different backgrounds are a reminder of the wide variety of women attracted to socialist and Labour organizations. Enid Stacy was an educated woman from an English middle-class background, Marion Barry was a tailoress of Irish origin and Clarice McNab Shaw came from a Scottish farming family. Enid Stacy had some experience of alternative lifestyles and eventually married a clergyman. Marion Barry and Clarice McNab Shaw married men who were active in the Labour movement. All three followed the parliamentary road to socialism. Enid Stacy was active at the turn of the nineteenth and twentieth centuries and the widespread range of her activities is typical of this period, when socialist societies were flourishing in Britain. Marion Barry's activity started in the same period and continued until 1910. She joined the Women's Labour League in 1907. Like Clarice McNab Shaw, Marion Barry was primarily an organizer, a function made necessary by the very success of the groups formed in the earlier period. Clarice McNab Shaw joined the Women's Labour League in 1910 and continued in Labour politics until 1945.

Enid Stacy

Enid Stacy (1868–1903),[45] trades unionist, politician and educationalist, was the eldest of four children of Henry Stacy, painter, and his wife Rose Deeley. Enid was born and spent her first 25 years in Bristol, leaving in 1893 to join the Starnthwaite Home Colony at Kendal. Thereafter Enid lived in the North of England, first in Newcastle and then Littleborough. She married Percy Widdrington, clergyman, and they had one son. She was awarded a BA degree by London University and taught at Bristol.

The Stacy family was at the heart of Bristol's lively left political and social life; Enid's younger sister, Edna, became a ballet dancer and Rose Deeley was a pianist. Enid participated in the singing that closed political gatherings and was later commissioned (1896) to prepare a songbook for the Independent Labour Party (ILP). Her politics were the cause of Enid's leaving Bristol. Enid was a member of the Gas Workers' Union and was elected to the Fabian society in 1891. She was already building a reputation as a speaker. She was Honorary Secretary of the Society for the

Promotion of Trades Unionism Amongst Women in Bristol and helped organize a strike of women confectionery workers in 1892. Teaching posts were thereafter closed to Enid. She journeyed North with Ben Tillett, Bristol-based leader of the Dockers' Union and Pete Curran, General Secretary of the Gas Workers' Union (later Labour Member of Parliament for Jarrow[46]) to attend the ILP inaugural meeting held on 12 January 1893. She then took up residence in the Stornthwaite Home Colony in the Lake District. This had been founded by a local clergy-man as a self-sufficient alternative to the workhouse, but was perceived by its residents as an experiment in communal living. Not without disagreements between its residents, the colony scandalized the neigh-bourhood because of the mix of male and female lodgers. They were forcibly evicted and Enid used her subsequent appearance at the magis-trates' court to enhance her reputation as a speaker. In 1893 she spoke at about 50 meetings; thereafter she addressed around 300 each year until the birth of her son, when she limited her engagements to six months of the year. In Mersyside, where unemployment was severe, the police broke up Enid's meetings. In 1895, Enid was appointed by the Fabian Society to its travelling Hutchinson Trust lectureship.

The ILP had women's sections and guilds, but no national body to pro-vide these with a focus. In 1894, Enid had suggested the formation of a women's association, but this suggestion was never acted upon. She was elected to the ILP National Administration committee from 1896–99. Supporting the majority position that the Socialist International be limited to those committed to parliamentary socialism (as opposed to anarcho-revolutionary means), Enid was given the task of examining British delegates' credentials for its 1896 meeting. She topped the vote for the International's Commission on Education. The International's meeting was adjourned to enable delegates to attend a demonstration at a magistrates' court where Mrs Pankhurst was appearing (at this time Mrs Pankhurst was an ILP member, before her rise to national status as a suffragette leader). Enid was chosen as a major speaker at the demon-stration and was booked to speak during the forthcoming Trades Union Congress conference week.

Enid's experience at Stornthwaite and her political involvement made her an ideal contributor to Edward Carpenter's 1897 volume on alternate social and political lifestyles.[47] Carpenter himself followed a semi-communal, socialist, self-sufficient lifestyle and was influenced by new work on sexology, homosexuality and sexuality in women. Her essay on women's rights for Edward Carpenter's collection expounded Enid's belief that the equality on which socialism was based was impossible without political and social rights for women. In Stacy's view, women should be able to vote as an expression of their citizenship. As wives, they should have perfect equality with their husbands; they were free to choose motherhood and would then share guardianship of children with their father. Women should be educated and free to choose appropriate work, limited only by their capacity. Work regulations should apply equally to men and women.

Enid continued her publicity work by taking charge of the Clarion Van in 1898 and 1899. The Van had started as a soup kitchen and was named after and funded by Robert Blatchford's *Clarion* visionary newspaper. At the outbreak of the South African wars in 1899, Enid made pacifist speeches. She undertook two speaking tours of the United States. In 1903, Enid's work for socialism and feminism ended when she died, due to an embolism, at the age of 35. Enid's family legacy was notably inherited by her nieces Angela and Joan Tuckett. Angela was a prominent Communist Party member, historian and folk musician,[48] and Joan founded the left-wing Bristol Unity theatre.

Marion Barry

Marion Barry[49] was a trades unionist and member of the Women's Labour League. Her origins are obscure. She was of Irish descent and lived in London and Jarrow. Marion married Pete (Peter Francis) Curran, leader of the Gas Workers' Union, who was elected Member of Parliament for Jarrow in 1907. They had two daughters and two sons.

From 1895, Marion represented the East London Tailoresses, which later affiliated to the Women's Trade Union League (WTUL). She became assistant secretary to that body in 1896 and began a punishing schedule of meetings. The first meeting Marion addressed for the WTUL was at a vinegar and pickle factory in Gloucester, where she formed a union of 200 young women. In May 1896 Marion spoke at a meeting of launderesses, held under the auspices of the Gas Workers' Union. That year she attended the Trades Union Congress as observer for the WTUL. Nominated by the London Trades Council, Marion was elected to the Technical Education Board of the London County Council in 1897. After a relatively quiet period following her marriage, Marion, now styling herself 'Mrs Pete Curran', was appointed WTUL organizer in 1906; one of the WTUL's main concerns was the exemption of largely female, largely home-based industries such as the shirt and collar trades from industrial regulation and the subsequent exploitation of the workforce. Marion helped organize the 1906 *Daily News* Sweated Industries Exhibition, which gave rise to the formation of the Anti-Sweating League. In 1906 and 1907 Marion's organizing trips included Halstead, Londonderry, Edmonton, Tottenham, Silverton, Woolwich, Derby, Norwich, Oxford, Abingdon and Taunton.

In the summer of 1907 this activity was increased by Pete Curran's candidacy in Jarrow, with meetings and handbills to prepare, chalking the pavements and leafleting factory gates to publicize the meetings, at one of which Margaret MacDonald of the Women's Labour League was the main speaker.[50] Marion assisted in the foundation of and served as secretary to the Jarrow branch of the Women's Labour League, calling the Labour Party 'the men's party'. The Jarrow branch held fortnightly meetings on subjects such as infant mortality, women's suffrage, school meals and married women workers. It was the campaign for school meals that became one of Marion's chief concerns. She lobbied Jarrow council, sitting with other Women's Labour League members in the gallery to witness the progress of the proposal that the Education (Provision of Meals) Act be adopted so that schoolchildren could be fed from public funds. The council meeting was adjourned for the mayoral banquet and reconvened, Women's Labour League and ILP members filling every visitors' seat. The motion to adopt the Act was ruled out of order and referred to the Education committee. This committee had no Labour representative and referred the matter to the School Attendance sub-committee whose members declared themselves unaware of any child suffering through lack of food and therefore declined to take action. Defeated here, Marion resumed her campaign against sweated work by forming part of the WTUL and Women's Labour League organizing committee for the Women's Labour Day, held at Earl's Court in 1909. This 'Great Labour Fete and Carnival' had as its theme the exploitation of women in the workforce. Pete Curran, who served on the general council for the Women's Labour Day, posed parliamentary questions on sweated work and was a supporter of women's suffrage. Marion was elected to the Women's Labour League executive committee in 1908 and 1909.

The executive committee stood in silent respect to commemorate the death of Pete Curran shortly after his defeat at Jarrow in 1910. The *Women's Trade Union Review* recorded:

For many years we owed much to the generous advocacy, unstintingly given of Mr. Pete Curran ... our loss is complete ... Mrs. Curran who, an occasional organiser, comes constantly in touch with the League and its officers, knows how deeply her husband's work in claiming for women a place in the trade union movement was appreciated by it and them, and how sincerely he has been and will be mourned in all quarters where the power and worth of combination amongst women workers is recognised.[51]

Marion's trade union work was thereafter confined to giving occasional support to new staff. She was active on Hackney Labour exchange, but her later life is as obscure as her origins.

Clarice McNab Shaw

Clarice McNab Shaw[52] was a politician and a member of the Women's Labour League, becoming a leading figure in Scottish Labour politics. She was born in Leith, probably in 1882, and died at Troon, 27 October 1946. Her father was Bailie McNab. Clarice McNab taught music in Leith when a young woman. She became National Secretary of the Socialist Sunday Schools. Following its recruiting tour of Scotland, Clarice McNab joined the Women's Labour League, helping to form a Leith branch in 1910 (secretary Mrs Cruickshank). Clarice McNab was Leith delegate to the League conference in 1911, served on its executive committee and headed its Scottish district from 1917 to 1918. This position gave her a seat on the executive committee of the Scottish Advisory Committee (later Council) of the Labour Party. Clarice married Ben Shaw, secretary of the Scottish Labour Party.

Women could be elected to County and Borough Councils in Scotland from 1907 and Clarice McNab was elected to Leith Town Council in 1913. In 1918 when the Labour Party was re-organized and the Women's Labour League disbanded, she remained active in women's organizations within the Labour Party nationally and in Scotland. She became secretary to the Joint Committee of Labour, Co-operative and Trades Union women formed in Scotland in 1934. She retained her seat on the Scottish Council national executive, to which she was elected chair from 1939 to 1940 thus presiding at the 1940 Silver Jubilee conference, where a special presentation marked her unbroken yearly re-elections to the Council. Clarice served on Troon Town Council and Ayr County Council from 1932 to 1936, where she headed the Public Health Committee for a time. After standing unsuccessfully in the 1929 and 1931 elections, Clarice was selected as their parliamentary candidate by the Kilmarnock constituency in 1944 and won the seat in the 1945 general election, gaining 23,837 votes to her Conservative opponent's 16,300.

Clarice McNab Shaw was prevented by illness from taking her seat, which she resigned. She died shortly afterwards at 36 Titchfield Road, Troon. She was survived by her step-daughter Marjorie, a journalist who worked in Moscow during the war and its aftermath.

Part II
War: The Standing Joint Committee

The single greatest cause of change in the organization and activities of the Labour Party and women's groups was war. The experience, during the First World War, of organizing a Party consisting of affiliated organizations, which were not always of the same mind, was an important factor in the adoption of a new Labour Party constitution. This provided for individual Party membership and made the constituency the heart of Party organization but entailed the disbanding of the Women's Labour League. Labour women's contribution to the war effort was a factor in the creation of the Standing Joint Committee of Working Women's Organizations (SJC) that, to an extent, replaced the League. In the Second World War, the constituency base, which had served the Party well, was disrupted by bombing, evacuation and conscription into the services or industry. Greater workplace organization favoured the Communist Party. During both wars, women's participation in the labour force greatly increased. In the Second World War older and married women formed a greater part of the female workforce and women worked for the first time alongside men in heavy industries. As a result, women's union membership started to grow; industrial women's representation in the Labour movement was thus strengthened.

The inter-war decades were marked by grave problems at home and abroad, which tested and divided Labour politicians. The Labour Party won two brief periods of government, in 1924 and 1929–1931, but was felled by the financial crisis of 1931. The National Government formed thereafter by Ramsay MacDonald, and which he headed until 1935, consisted predominately of Conservative MPs. MacDonald and those Labour leaders who followed him into the National Government were expelled from the Labour Party, which thereafter formed a small parliamentary opposition. For their part, the trades unions were defeated in the 1926 general strike and deeply wounded by the restrictive Trades Unions and Trades Disputes Act of 1927. Not only the political imperatives of unemployment and poverty at home, but also the rise of fascism and the development of sizeable Communist movements in Europe, demanded responses both from the Labour movement and from the disparate feminist movement. Labour women sought to represent primarily the interests of working women and were not always in accord with feminists who had alternative priorities. This was a period of unparalleled international Labour and socialist organization. In this situation, the record of the participation of SJC members in international organizations was impressive.[1]

In both wars, women's changing experience provided a grounding for the development of feminism. To an extent, the impact of the First World War undermined traditional notions of femininity, as women were needed as munitions workers and won the right to nurse the troops. In addition, the collapse of the European empires gave some space for fresh ideas to flourish. However, war also reinforced notions of masculinity and emphasized the need to breed future soldiers, prioritizing women's value as reproducers of the nation's warriors. The reinforcement of patriarchal attitudes caused by the war was illustrated by the addition of the notorious Clause 40D to the Defence of the Realm Act, which made it an offence for women to infect troops with venereal disease and allowed their compulsory treatment. A positive effect of dislocation in the First World War was to make change in electoral registration procedures essential; the resultant franchise reform, including limited women's suffrage, helped resolve the question of representation, which had dominated the early years of the twentieth century.

The post-suffrage years were once seen as a hiatus in the development of feminist theory and activity, the height of suffrage activity being over while second wave feminism had yet to flourish.[2] More recently, the diversity of feminism in the inter-war period has been valued for its vigour in facing the problems of gender stereotyping and disadvantage, which continued once some women had won the right to vote. Some women continued to concentrate on arguing for full enfranchisement; the NUWSS was reformed as NUSEC (The National Union of Societies for Equal Citizenship). Other women turned to challenging different heads of disadvantage, such as married women's right to work and equal pay. Yet others argued for women's rights to leisure and for family endowment, to enable mothers to fund their work at home. The arguments turned, as before, on whether women's stereotype as wives and mothers was accepted or challenged. Those who demanded women's rights on equal terms as men without proclaiming women's special status were sometimes seen as promoting 'me too' feminism. Feminist thinking on sexuality continued to challenge societal norms, inspired partly by the prevalence of venereal disease amongst the First World War troops and partly by the renewed interest in married women's sexuality which was the counterpart of the need to ensure the supply of future soldiery. Marie Stopes set up a pioneering contraceptive clinic in London and was one of the first to publish the marriage manuals popular in the period. A botanist, she used flower images to explain sexuality. In contrast, the Swedish feminist Ellen Key promoted the idea of single mother-hood, enabling women to raise children free from prevailing notions of masculinity and femininity. Radclyffe Hall's novel *The Well of Lone-liness* (1928) brought her personal experience of lesbianism to a wide audience.

The diverse collection of inter-war women's groups included the Open Door Council and Six Point Group, who aimed to increase career opportunities for women; groups representing various trades; and those campaigning on issues such as contraception and abortion. NUSEC itself split into the National Council for Equal Citizenship and the National Union of Townswomen's Guilds. Many women were members of more than one group and groups often worked well together, so that in effect they formed a women's network.

Internationally, women's suffrage and socialist groups remained sepa-rate; the difference should not, however, be overestimated, some women remaining active in both groupings. Large Communist movements in Germany, mid and central Europe promoted an end to separate female and male spheres of life and women's familial subordination. In con-trast, fascists promoted the idea of '*kinder, kirche, kuche*'; that women's role was to look after children, go to church and cook. The women's peace movement, which began in the First World War, continued through the work of the Women's International League for Peace and Freedom. During and immediately after the Second World War it was the campaign for equal pay that was at the forefront of the feminist agenda.

4. The First World War

The outbreak of the First World War meant that the activities of the Women's Labour League were redirected and its organization and contacts with the Labour Party and other socialist and women's groups were affected. This section examines the effect of the First World War on the Women's Labour League, the demise of the League and the foundation of the Standing Joint Committee.

The triumph of the militarism condemned by the League at home and through its international connections, shattered the known landmarks of the political ground throughout Europe. 'In one short week the whole fabric of civilisation has been shaken', wrote Marion Phillips for the September 1914 issue of *Labour Woman*. She hoped the suffering would end in greater humanity and the furtherance of the interests of the working classes. Next month *Labour Woman* carried a League manifesto that declared 'the interests of the League lay in peace'…'every soldier slain left a woman desolate'. Secret diplomacy was at fault and apathy and self-interest; the Labour and Socialist movement in Europe should '…stay aloof from the rancour' and seek '…a United States of Europe, a free Belgium, free Finland, free Poland, free womanhood and free working classes'. Enforced enlistment was opposed, whether it was the result of conscription or domestic poverty, and the use of women to persuade men to volunteer was condemned.

Some League members were pacifist. For instance, Mrs Ayles, in poor health and with a young child, supported her husband Walter, who was one of the founder members of the pacifist No Conscription Fellowship. As a conscientious objector he was repeatedly arrested, finally being released from a sentence of prison with hard labour in 1919. However, the League executive accepted the inevitability of war in its 1914 report, delivered at the 1916 conference: 'The League has accepted the position that there is no ground on which we can adopt a policy of opposition to the war'. Ada Salter had proposed a resolution that called on soldiers to lay down their arms, but this had been watered down until it became a restatement of the manifesto position. The League affiliated to the Union of Democratic Control, founded partly by Ramsay MacDonald, which argued for democratic control of foreign policy, sought a negotiated peace and opposed conscription. The League motion to the 1916 Labour Party conference opposed conscription and called for industrial action should it be introduced. In the face of opposition from Arthur Henderson, who took a seat in the War Cabinet, thus becoming Britain's first Labour Minister, the first part of the League motion was agreed by 1,718,000 votes to 360,000, a splendid victory for the League. The second part was narrowly defeated, by 649,000 votes to 614,000.

Ada Salter's 1914 speech showed an increased class-consciousness:

> They noted all over the world signs of the change that was coming, and women of the working classes have taken the foremost place in it. A tremendous transformation was going to take place on this earth; and the injustices of the ages, the misery of the oppressed classes, and the sorrow of the poor, and the tyranny of the wealthy were going to be swept away for ever. Nothing could stop the movement. When the trades union movement fully realised that all the workers, men and women, youth and maidens, were members one of another, then they would hear more than the rumble of revolution in the distance; the revolution would be here.[3]

This type of chiliasm was unusual for the League, but was to be found in the rhetoric of socialist parties throughout Europe, despite their participation in the war. Workplace agitation increased and there were strikes against price rises. Ada Salter's contribution was to position the League amongst those more radical, feminist socialists, who insisted that gender equality precede the revolution. Prime examples were Rosa Luxemourg and Clara Zetkin, arrested for their activity in Germany, and Alexandra Kollontai, who was expelled from Sweden. These incidents were reported in *Labour Woman* (January and November 1915). The League sent delegates (Mary Longman, Marion Phillips, Ada Salter and Margaret Bondfield) to the 1915 Labour and Socialist Women's International convened by Clara Zetkin and held at Bern. There, women from Germany ('at greatest danger'), France, Belgium, Russia, Poland, Italy, Holland and Switzerland declared: 'War against War'

> War against War! We demand a peace that will recognise the rights of peoples and nations, both large and small, to independence and self government, will enforce no limits and unsupportable conditions against any country, and will require expiation of the wrong done to Belgium, thus clearing the way for the peaceful and friendly cooperation of the nations.[4]

The Russian revolution of 1917 furthered these sentiments of internationalism and class-consciousness. The Russian dictatorship had long been protested by the Labour movement; for instance, in *Labour Woman* (April 1915) Mary Longman had denounced the Allies' agreement to unite their financial resources as tantamount to supporting the destruction of Finland, the arrest of socialists in the Duma and the persecution of Jewish people. The revolution was thus welcomed and the League received an invitation from the Petrograd Council of Workers' and Soldiers' Delegates to be part of a Labour delegation to Russia. Mary Longman was chosen but, along with the other Labour delegates, was refused a passport. League women attended a June 1917 conference to 'hail the Russian revolution', supporting resolutions which called for peace but not the resolution calling for the immediate creation of Workers' and Soldiers' Councils in Britain. Throughout its existence, the League retained the secretaryship of the Socialist Women's Council of the International, now renamed the Women's National Council.

At home, branches were urged to take on local distress work, making sure women received pensions and agitating on behalf of those who were ineligible (for instance, dependants of merchant seamen). Norwich branch had an early success in raising the problem of women not being able to pay the delivery charge of unstamped soldiers' letters; the Postmaster General agreed that such mail be delivered free of charge.[5] League women were instructed by Marion Phillips to ensure they were elected to local citizens' committees. They were to demand free meals for school and pre-school children, free milk and meals for nursing mothers and their children and adequate housing for dislocated workers. Grieving women needed support and Belgian refugees had to be cared for. There was prejudice against aliens to counter and work to be done in preventing the smashing of aliens' property. The League campaigned for changes in the Bastardy laws. There were no Forces' allowances for children born out of wedlock; in some cases soldiers were unaware of their babies' existence. The mothers' only recourse was the Poor Law; abortion was of course illegal and women found guilty of infanticide were hung. The League demanded that children born to parents who married after the birth should be declared legitimate and that the prospective mother should be able to get an affiliation order before the birth of the baby. Related to this, was a fear articulated by some League women, that men who had served in the forces would learn to think of male sexuality as an impulse to be accommodated without regard to consequences. The League accordingly affiliated to the Association of Moral and Social Hygiene, which campaigned against licensed brothels in France; League branches arranged lectures on venereal disease. There was correspondence on the use of contraception or celibacy as a protest against the government wasting young male lives in war.

While this new work increased running costs, the traditional means of fund-raising through entertainment was clearly inappropriate. The Central London branch *Annual Report* for the year ended 31 March 1915 illustrated the effects of war:

> The depression and misery all over the world were necessarily reflected...and made it hard to carry out its work. When the war broke out, members felt that it was impossible to keep to the usual lines of work, and especially to hold the same social gatherings as have been held in past years.

Central London branch had welcomed deportees from South Africa and held educational meetings such as 'Small Nations and the War', 'The Terms of Peace' and 'The Work of the French Women's Socialist Group'. Delegates had attended meetings on war work, pay and prices; branch members had worked on the allowances paid to soldiers' and sailors' wives and the supervision of these women by the police. (A circular had been issued requiring wives to register at local police stations and giving the police the right to visit their homes, enquire into their behaviour and admonish them when it was deemed to be necessary.) Campaigns had ranged from the building of state cottages for disabled soldiers to protesting the employment of schoolchildren in agriculture. Members and supporters were sewing children's clothes and maternity outfits at home.

Housing became a major League campaign. The construction of houses to eliminate unnecessary labour in climbing stairs, heating water and carrying coal had long been a League concern. A housing committee was set up of Jennie Baker, Marion Phillips, Ada Salter and Averil Sanderson Furniss of the decorating family, who was expert in the subject.[6] Each branch was to elect a correspondent and report to the housing committee. Fifty thousand copies were sold of a leaflet which enquired: 'what are the chief defects of your home?'; 'where do you think the larder should be?'; 'where do you want cupboards?'; 'what floor is the scullery?'. Many of the questions were debated at women's meetings, some of them arranged by the Co-operative Women's Guild, before replies were sent to the committee. Averil Sanderson Furniss wrote that while middle class women were consulted by architects, working women were ignored by jerry builders who put price first; she demanded that the women who experienced the problem should have first say in its remedy. Some branches had already begun work on housing; Glasgow branch set up a Women's

Housing Association in 1915 and Annot Robinson was a member of a similar group in Manchester. The League supported an experimental model public kitchen in London. The Ministry of Food and local authorities ran national kitchens with restaurants attached to help overcome war shortages and disruption. However, Averil Sanderson Furniss commented that these, and public wash houses, should be run by professionals rather than merely making machinery available to be used by each woman in turn; also, women wanted their own home to be self-sufficient. Marion Philips sat on the Women's Advisory Committee of the Ministry of Reconstruction and the replies to the League leaflet contributed to that committee's two reports. Averil Sanderson Furniss served on the Ministry of Health Housing Department advisory council after the war and pressed for women to sit on local authority housing committees.

The League conference was postponed in 1915. A clerk was engaged for the League offices at 10s per week; Marion Phillips resigned as secretary, although she retained the editorship of *Labour Woman*, and Mary Longman took over. In 1916, the memory of the League was nearly lost to future historians. Ramsay MacDonald intended to move from his house, which had also been home to the League office since its inception; the League hurriedly moved to the Labour Party offices at 1, Victoria Street. Ramsay MacDonald burnt most of Margaret MacDonald's papers; Marion Phillips was instructed to destroy correspondence before 1912 and unimportant letters written thereafter. Fortunately the minute books survived the flames, plus a collection of papers saved by Mary Middleton, in the keeping of James Middleton and finally rescued by his third wife Lucy Cox.

Also in 1916 the League was left a legacy, with which it was intended to pay a full-time organizer; Mary Longman resigned and Lisbeth Simm was offered but refused the job. Miss Coates was appointed, after exhaustive interviews, for a sixth-month trial period, Marion Phillips meanwhile acting as honorary secretary. The executive committee was increased and was to be elected at conference, together with an unpaid general secretary and treasurer; all other officers were to be appointed by the executive committee. Miss Coates was dismissed when her six months' trial expired and, after another lengthy interview process, Miss Stevens appointed. Conferences were held in 1916 and 1917, but the entertainment provided was restricted in 1916 and non-existent the following year. District conferences were encouraged and Lisbeth Simm and Miss Scholefield were appointed as salaried district organizers. Other regions were run by unpaid organizers, including Clarice McNab in

Scotland. At every executive committee, however, the list of branches that had collapsed was ominously long. Thirty branches overall closed during the war years while 16 opened.

The reduced expenses in the League office met with Labour Party approval; a supplementary grant of £150 was made. It was left to the relatively inexperienced Mary Longman to conduct negotiations with James Middleton on the future of the League. Mary set out her stall:

> The executive would like to be regarded not merely as one among a number of societies affiliated to the local Labour Parties, but as something much more closely connected, as part of the Labour Party itself – meanwhile the League asks that the Labour Party Executive Committee if they will help, firstly by pressing on the local Labour Parties the view that the League is an organic part of the Labour Party – its women's section – and as such has a special claim on it for support and help.[7]

The difficulties still facing the League were made clear when Mr Higginbotham, Labour Party organizer, spoke to the Wolverhampton Labour Party. The League delegate at the meeting heard that:

> ...he did not know how many members the League had in Wolverhampton, but he ventured to say we were not growing and he advocated the starting of a Women's Labour Association for social functions, say to meet the prospective candidate and his wife, and to have a cup of tea provided and light refreshments, etc., he thought we might get recruits for the League when their ideas were more advanced.[8]

A League committee (Mary Longman, Ada Salter, Marion Phillips and Minnnie Nodin) drafted proposals, which Mary Longman put to James Middleton. These were largely concerned with publicising the League at local level, providing assistance with rooms for branch meetings and calling women's meetings with League speakers when new Labour Party branches were formed or Labour Party organizers visited a district. In addition, it was suggested that League branch representatives should meet with the Labour Party executive and organizers at the annual Labour Party conference. The Labour Party organizing sub-committee discussed these proposals in 1916.

A joint sub-committee with the Labour Party was formed, consisting of four League women (Jennie Baker, Marion Phillips, Ada Salter, and

Minnie Nodin) and four Labour men. It was intended to involve trades union secretaries and to address the question of appointing women organizers in each of the League districts, agents common to League and Party and financial help to the League. The cost of appointing organizers in League districts was estimated at £1000 per year, to be financed half by the legacy and half by the Labour Party. Furthermore, it was agreed that the League be an integral part of the Party, while preserving independence of expression for women.

Meanwhile, leading Labour figures including Arthur Henderson were engaged in drafting a post-war constitution for the Labour Party, which would allow individual membership of local branches affiliated, as would be trades unions, to local constituency parties. Some such reorganization would be necessary following the disruption of the war and would provide a firmer local base for the Labour Party, with the constituency now the heart of activities. This individual membership, open to women and men, went far to overcome the problems which had hindered women's membership of the 'men's party'. The philosophy of the Party was restated:

> To secure for the workers by hand or by brain the full fruits of their industry and the most equitable distribution thereof that may be possible upon the basis of the common ownership of the means of production and exchange and the best obtainable system of popular administration and control of each industry and service.

Labour Woman (November 1917) called the new constitution 'a transformation', 'almost a revolution in itself'. Arthur Henderson attended the League executive committee meeting on 12 October 1917 to explain the proposals for women's organization. These were that women's sections in local constituency parties be created and four National Executive committee seats be reserved for women. The League minutes record: '...in the discussion it was felt very strongly that special provision should be made for women to have opportunities of discussing special women's questions or problems from the women's standpoint'. Marion Phillips then successfully proposed that 'any further discussion be postponed until after the Labour Party was more settled'. Nevertheless, discussion did continue, the sticking point for the League being the holding of an annual conference of women's sections and the creation of a Woman's Advisory Committee at national level. It had been agreed that *Labour Woman* continue in publication. The League held a conference in January 1918 to discuss these proposals; a detailed record does not survive, merely the executive reports, in its minutes and *Labour Woman*. From these it appears that the proposals were accepted with just two branches dissenting. Branches did insist that some sort of national women's forum continue. The League also protested the proposed reduced subscription fees for women (6d as opposed to 1s for men). Otherwise, the proposals were largely nodded through.

The last League executive committee raised the clerk's salary to 15s per week; the Labour Party accepted responsibility for all expenditure after 1 January 1918. Some branches, districts and executive committee members continued to argue for an annual conference, but the question was shelved. League affiliations to other bodies were discontinued, the Railway Women's Guild being urged to join the Labour Party. On 14 June 1918 the League money, office furnishings and fittings and literature were handed over to the Labour Party. However, the position of women in the newly reorganized Labour Party cannot be fully understood without considering the result of League participation in joint enterprises undertaken during the war.

A major change that the League addressed in the war years was women's employment in trades usually restricted to men. Initially, women faced unemployment; many domestic servants lost their jobs. By 1915, however, women were being reemployed in industry and were joining trades unions in large numbers. Mary MacArthur became secretary of the Central Council for Women's Employment, formed in August 1914 to help deploy women workers and safeguard their interests. This body raised some suspicion in the Labour movement, which created its own organization, the War Emergency: Workers National Committee. From this body, four League women were delegated to Mary MacArthur's committee, Marion Phillips, Margaret Bondfield, Mrs Gasson and Susan Lawrence. Their first job was to prevent volunteers putting seamstresses and tailoresses out of work and insisting that government contracts were put out to skilled women. The committee's demands included equal pay for equal work, a living wage and work after the war. League women felt that there were four interests to consider: the employer; the male worker; his dependants; and the woman worker. In May 1916, the League held a conference on 'Industrialized women after the war, to which 125 trades unions and societies sent delegates. Marion Phillips wrote in *Labour Woman* the following month that neither the trades unions nor the women's organizations could be entrusted to respect the interests of both the male and female workers.

To help address the concerns of industrial women, the Standing Joint Industrial Women's Committee was founded in February 1916.

The League, the Co-operative Women's Guild, the Railway Women's Guild, the Women's Trade Union League and the National Federation of Working Women were represented. Mary MacArthur was elected chair, Margaret Llewellyn Davies of the Co-operative Women's Guild vice-chair and Mary Longman secretary. Miss Coates took over from Mary Longman, followed by Marion Phillips. The parliamentary committee of the Trades Union Congress (TUC) was invited to delegate Margaret Bondfield to the new organization. Eligible for membership were representatives of industrial women's organizations that were national in character, consisted of women only and had at least 1000 members. Each member organization instructed its branches to work together locally, especially on pensions' committees. With the three wings of the Labour movement conjoined – industrial, consumer and political – Marion Phillips, as secretary to the SJC now had a firm base as spokeswoman for most of the pre-war Labour movement single sex groups. As the League continued to ask for a Labour Party national women's advisory committee, Marion Phillips now suggested that the SJC fulfil this role and that it consist of eight League delegates and four from each of the other groups. The Labour Party unanimously agreed this in April 1918.

The issue of women's representation within the Labour movement was thus resolved. At the close of the war, the question of women' parliamentary franchise was addressed. The arguments in favour had been made by 1914 and would have been a major issue at the abandoned 1915 General Election. The war split the suffrage movement; the WSPU dissolved itself in favour of supporting recruitment to the forces while the NUWSS formed military and pacifist wings. The pacifist wing evolved into the Women's International League for Peace and Freedom. Franchise reform however, could not be entirely shelved during the war; absence from home on war service magnified the faults of an electoral registration system based on property ownership. The SJC declared in 1916 that the principle: 'every man in the fighting forces should have the vote' was insufficient and demanded, in place of the electoral registration measures proposed by the government: 'a Franchise Bill to give full suffrage rights to all men and women'.[9] A Speaker's committee was set up to address the problems of registration. Labour MPs who supported women's enfranchisement, including Arthur Henderson, had joined the wartime coalition government. One of the Labour MPs assigned to the Speaker's committee was Mr Wardle, who had helped inspire Mary Fenton Macpherson's original proposals for a Woman's Labour League. Both the League and the Labour Party appear to have considered women's enfranchisement a foregone conclusion. The League set up a sub committee on 'the organization of women as voters' while the Speaker's committee was still deliberating. In the event, it was a last minute amendment to the committee's recommendations that secured the enfranchisement of woman aged 30 years and over. The recommendations were accepted and included in the 1918 Reform Act.

In the process of integration into the Labour Party, we may ask how far League women were mistresses of their own fate, and how far they were affected by external sources. The Labour Party had its own agenda, negotiated by James Middleton and Arthur Henderson, but the less experienced Mary Longman was nevertheless successful in achieving her goals of integration plus a national women's advisory body and conference. Marion Phillips was, of course, instrumental in this success and won the position of leading woman in the Labour Party and of the separate women's body for working women. The result of the foundation of the SJC and of the graceful demise of the League before the new constitution in fact meant that thereafter women had two bites of the cherry: on the one hand, they enjoyed direct access to the Labour Party through individual membership, with women's councils at constituency level; on the other, they could affiliate to the SJC which represented the female membership of the trades unions, the Co-operative movement and the Labour Party. They could look back on the success of the Women's Labour League, while all women aged 30 and over could benefit from the success of the suffrage campaign. By far the greatest changes in principles and practices were those brought about by the First World War. The League's involvement here is an insight into what war meant for women at home, and the League's stance against militarism and pro-internationalism left a legacy which, little known, has been undervalued.

5. The inter war years: the Standing Joint Committee

The further history of the SJC is recounted in this section, explaining its connections with the Labour Party and discussing its organization and activities. The relationship of the SJC to other women's organizations is considered, in the continued campaign for full adult woman suffrage and over the vexed question of protective legislation for women workers. The SJC identity as an organization for working women is illustrated.

Because of its close links with the Labour Party, the SJC held a distinct place in the inter-war women's network. The Labour Party affiliated to the SJC in 1919;[10] SJC meetings were held at Labour Party headquarters; the Labour Party Chief Women's Officer (Marion Phillips) was SJC secretary. From 1922 the SJC advised the Labour Party on matters of interest to women and arranged the National Conference of Labour Women. However, the SJC was independent, corresponding directly with external organizations such as the League of Nations, the Labour and Socialist International, government departments and with its own affiliates. In 1929 the SJC claimed to represent 'over a million women in the Labour Party, Trades Union and Co-operative Movements'. The Women's Co-operative Guild remained strong. Within the Labour Party, the Women's Councils proved popular, despite not being able to decide policy and having no direct representation on Labour's ruling executive. Women joined local Labour Parties in larger numbers than did men and by 1923 the membership of Women's Sections was around 120,000; between 1927 and 1939 women's membership was from 250 to 300,000, half the party membership.[11]

Marion Phillips addressed the new situation brought about by women's enfranchisement and also supported the continuance of separate women's organizations:

> ...it is felt that women are so newly come into political life that their development will be hindered and forced along the ordinary lines of political thought amongst men, thus losing the value of women's rich experience, if the whole of the work is conducted in organisations including both sexes.

Expanding her theme, she gave her opinion that:

> ...there are certain matters in which the experience of women is far wider and closer than that of men can ever be... home life, the

nurture of the young, the care of the sick and weakly, the planning
of the dwelling itself, are especially women's questions...because it
is only by women turning their own experience into the common
knowledge of all that the right solutions can be found'.[12]

She published several pamphlets of advice and encouragement for the
Women's Councils, writing that 'the object of the Women's Councils
is to bring more women into the Party by making a special appeal to
them, to educate women in public affairs, and to express the point of
view of Labour women'. Business meetings were suggested, mixed with
education meetings, propaganda, tea parties, expeditions and outings,
very much the previous Women's Labour League programme.[13]

The SJC emphasized the importance of its newly enfranchised
affiliated members identifying with the Labour Party. In so doing, it
identified consciously and openly with working women, acknowledging a class prejudice that some feminists deplored. The SJC explained
its reasons: the seemingly neutral Women's Party, descendant of the
militant suffragettes, supported the Conservatives while truly neutral
Women's Citizens Associations must either become talking shops or
negotiate with political allies; only Labour could be trusted to further
the interests of industrial, working women. While it was important to
get women into parliament 'it is still more important that these women
should have the aims of the working class movement at heart and prop-
erly represent the women they will serve'.[14] It is noteworthy that Lisbeth
Simm, who had been so active prior to and during the First World War,
no longer appears in the records. Her husband, M.T. Simm stood as a
Liberal/Labour candidate in the 1918 election. All those who accepted
Liberal backing – the so-called 'coupon' – were denounced by the Labour
Party. This serves to remind us that the Labour Party was then trying to
make its impact on the political scene, fighting to establish its identity
and promote its cause. Marion Phillips and her co-workers were as intent
on this cause as the Labour Party leaders.

Nevertheless, until 1928 when women were enfranchised from the
age of 21, the SJC continued to give qualified support to the suffrage
campaign. Labour women were fairly successful in lobbying Labour MPs
in this respect; Labour's 1919 Bill for Women's Emancipation demanded
equal franchise and that women should be allowed to sit in the House
of Lords; this measure was defeated by the introduction of the government's less advanced Sex Discrimination Act. The SJC supported Ellen
Wilkinson when she spoke at a NUSEC demonstration and SJC members joined a demonstration at the House of Commons; Marion Phillips
lobbied Labour's national executive for a franchise Bill. However, after

1928 the SJC ceased activity on equal suffrage. At the same time, gender solidarity was demonstrated when women MPs of all parties who were not SJC members were invited to attend meetings as observers.[15]

Of Labour's prominent women, Marion Phillips and Margaret Bondfield were both elected to parliament. Susan Lawrence, of the old guard, continued in activity both on the London County Council and in parliament, and younger women such as Ellen Wilkinson came to prominence.[16] When Margaret Bondfield became Chair of the TUC in 1923 the SJC recorded:

> this is not only a great personal honour and mark of recognition... but an honour which raises the whole position of women in the Labour Movement and gives recognition to women's place in the Labour World.[17]

Margaret Bondfield, of course, went on to become Britain's first woman Cabinet Minister. However, accused by some of treachery, she suffered the fate common to the Labour politicians who mismanaged the 1931 crisis. Her fine career was overshadowed when, faced with huge unemployment insurance costs, she promoted the Anomalies Bill, which would have excluded some married women from receiving payments. In contrast Marion Phillips, an economist, was secretary to the Special Committee, which the Labour Government formed to examine the issues of currency and exchange. The Committee's advice was rejected and Marian Phillips continued to oppose government policy. She died in 1932 and was replaced by Mary Sutherland as Chief Woman's Organizer of the Labour Party and secretary to the SJC.

Under both Marion Phillips and Mary Sutherland, the SJC continued with the same style of investigation that the Women's Labour League had used during the war when enquiring into housing. An exhaustive questionnaire with plenty of space for comment would be sent out, followed by debate at committee and the production of a draft discussion memorandum. The SJC later explained:

> We desire...to emphasise the importance of 'collective' views expressed by groups of women after detailed discussion at meetings. It is through discussion...that new ideas emerge and progress is made.[18]

The SJC investigated issues such as maternity hospitals and housing design, and the results were used to inform government. School meals remained an issue for Labour women and formed the subject of Susan Lawrence's 1924 maiden speech to the House of Commons.

The National Government which took office in 1931, influenced by its perception of economic crisis, sought cuts in education costs, which were protested by the SJC. The SJC formed an 'Economics in Education' Sub-Committee in 1932 and held several demonstrations against government cuts, including one in Mile End Baths, London in October 1932. All affiliated organizations were asked to send two or more delegates to join a deputation to the Board of Education, which was examining school fees. The SJC in particular protested circular 1421, which limited the number of free places in secondary schools and applied a means test. SJC affiliates managed to get support from some local authorities, for instance Lancashire and Glasgow, which passed resolutions objecting to the provisions of the circular and asking their local members of Parliament to raise the issue. In 1933, questions were put in the House of Commons and demonstrations continued. The SJC's interest was recognized when the Board of Education Consultative Committee requested that the SJC give evidence. The SJC memorandum in reply maintained: 'the views we put forward... are not from the standpoint of the educational expert, but of organized working women, and especially of working class mothers who have a very real interest in education'. The SJC claimed to speak for over a million women encountered at conferences and in its affiliated organizations. The SJC asked that the school leaving age be immediately raised to 15 years and to 16 years in three year's time, this to be accompanied by a maintenance allowance. Every child's right to education at 16 was asserted. In the SJC's view, there should be a varying curriculum for different needs, although these modifications should be managed under a single system and bound by the same regulations. The SJC concluded: 'Until school education is free, class distinction in education, the most indefensible of all class distinctions, will persist...'.[19]

The working conditions of women in domestic service were an area of SJC interest. Despite middle and upper–class concern at 'the servant problem' many women continued in service and the weakened trades unions found it difficult to contact this group of workers, never easy to organize. The SJC investigated the problem in its usual detailed style. A questionnaire was sent to women's sections, employers and employees, plus the Cooperative Women's Guild, and drew 971 responses, representing 43,168 women. Following discussion, a Domestic Workers' Charter was produced which, when the Labour government promised a Domestic Service Commission in 1931, formed the basis for a deputation to the Ministry of Labour. The SJC asked that domestic workers be covered by unemployment insurance. Margaret Bondfield, then Minister of Labour, tried to tackle the isolation of domestic workers, writing to Michael Brooks MP that before setting out for a position prospective servants should have the name and address of the relevant employment exchange and addresses of women's welfare associations in the area. As Marion Phillips pointed out, domestic workers formed a quarter to a third of female voters in constituencies such as Kensington and Westminster. It proved difficult, however, to interest the TUC, whose women's advisory committee despaired of effective union activity in this field.[20] With the fall of the Labour government, no further progress was made.

Concerned as it was with industrial women, the SJC favoured protective legislation. Julia Varley, a leading women's organizer for the Workers' Union, who had been active for two decades in the struggle to win decent working conditions for women, was one of the chief campaigners for health and safety and statutory limitation of working hours. She had participated in action to institute trade boards, at which employers and workers' representatives agreed regulations for those industries where working conditions did not facilitate local regulations. Her 1927 report for the International Federation of Working Women on homework in Britain illustrates and explains Labour women's desire for continued protection.[21] Varley reported that the British TUC had demanded government action to regulate small workshops, especially in the clothing industry, where homeworking predominated. Food and metal trades were the other major employers of homeworkers. Homeworkers were nearly always women. She wrote that: 'Under whatever form of production, capitalist or socialist, it is an absolute necessity that work is carried out in healthy conditions'. In Britain, in some cases, factory legislation applied to homework, in that the rate for the job and the job description had to be specified to the worker. The Home Secretary had the right to demand, from all employers, registers of homeworkers and local authorities had the right to inspection. Some local authorities were more diligent than others: 'opportunities to bypass regulations are countless'. If the home environment, or the work, was dangerous to the health of the worker or the eventual consumer of the goods, the work could be prohibited. Varley was of the opinion that some trades, such as the fur trade, or sorting feathers, should never be done without adequate regulation. She pointed out that employers used homeworkers not merely to save money on rent, light, heating and insurance, but to avoid factory legislation. For instance, work with celluloid, which was highly flammable, was heavily regulated in factories, but not at all in the home. She gave an example of the difficulties of enforcing regulation; if a workshop with a hundred workers closed, and contracted out its work, the local authority had a hundred homes to visit. As many homeworkers distributed tasks amongst neighbours, the problem was multiplied.

As Varley wrote, homeworking was an issue of gender. Echoing contemporary male trades unionists, she expressed the need for a male worker to earn enough to support his family. Varley did, however, recognize that women had to supplement family income, even if the 'head of the family' was in full-time employment. She implicitly acknowledged the existence of a primary-masculine, and secondary-feminine labour market. At this time, there was a tertiary market in addition, as children were in employment. Varley understood that some women chose homework, not only because of their family responsibilities, but because they could direct their own labour, gaining 'a certain sense of freedom'. However, this applied to older women; young women 'prefer to work in the factory and be rid of all work when they come home'; as women's circumstances improved, older women were disadvantaged by patriarchal practices from which the younger generation was, to an extent, emancipated. Varley wrote of the double burden of domestic and wage labour for older women: 'Such circumstances are regrettable and must be acknowledged by any society which lays claim to progress'.

Homeworking allowed casualization of the labour force: 'having a certain supply of workers available when business is good without having to expand their company'. Casualization enabled employers to benefit from skilled women workers who had left factory work, perhaps because of marriage. Varley explained that 'all levels of work are represented at home' including highly qualified work. Advanced technology, however, was seldom required, so that on-the-job training was possible. Homeworkers, of course, had to provide their own rent, heat and light; many had to provide their own materials but where the trade was regulated, could claim a refund on expenditure on material.

Varley's opinion, despite the lack of reliable data, was that homework was decreasing. This decrease excluded the fine tailoring section of the clothing industry and that of consumer durables, which may have been due to a government-inspired home building programme in Britain. She wrote that British trades unions wanted the complete abolition of homeworking. Low wages and poor conditions 'pose a threat to the living standards of other workers'. Varley described the difficulties of union organizers who had many homes to visit, where the worker was in isolation, and had to be convinced 'that their interests were the same as those of numerous other workers who they do not know and have never seen'. These workers did not perceive homework as part of an industry. Poor employers, who could otherwise be closed down by unionization, remained in the industry and were also a threat to other workers. Varley, therefore, clearly saw homeworking as an evil, and the twin remedies as union organization and regulation.

Feminist organizations such as NUSEC and the Open Door Council were strongly opposed, arguing that protection restricted women's working opportunities and pay; both sides to the argument had international support. One of the reasons why few countries adopted the Hague and Montevideo conventions of the League of Nations, which would have given women equal citizenship rights, was concern that it would annul legislation to protect women workers. When, in 1929, feminist organizations lobbied the Labour Home Secretary, Clynes, about repealing factory legislation, he asked Gertrude Tuckwell of the TUC to organize a 'counter -blast'. The SJC already had this in hand and asked all affiliates to send a representative to the deputation. The TUC refused an invitation to participate, but Clynes avowed: 'as far as he was concerned, he would not be a party to removing the protection which women enjoyed at present'.[22] In this case, refusal to take action accorded with the SJC's programme.

In the press debate which accompanied the dispute over protective legislation, Labour women illustrated their knowledge of the female industrial labour force; that it was under twenty-five and impermanent. The youth of the labour force was partly a function of the operation of the marriage bar. Labour women's conferences repeatedly protested this bar and the SJC campaigned strongly for married women's right to work, finding the bar divisive of women workers, while mothers of young children were given menial work as if this were a charitable action. Eleanor Barton, SJC chair in 1934, attacked the bar on three counts: one, unequal treatment of married women, of whom unpaid labour in the home was expected while its value was ignored: 'why then expect every women to be good at housework'; two, no account was taken of widows and deserted wives; three, why should married women 'stay at the level of his achievements?' Susan Lawrence conducted an exhaustive enquiry into London County Council school cleaners and was successful in winning their freedom from the bar, although SJC deputations failed to extend this exemption.[23]

On issues of sexuality and birth control, the official records of Labour women's involvement are largely silent. Jennie Baker, of the Women's Labour League, took the presidency of the National Council for Unmarried Women, formed in 1918. In the campaign by the Labour Party women's membership on birth control, the SJC appears to have been largely inactive. In 1923, there was a sub-committee on birth control (Florence Harrison Bell, Ethel Bentham, Mrs Hobbs, Mrs Hood, Mrs Rachan and Mrs Lowe) but their resolution in favour of extended provision to the National Conference of Labour Women was defeated without a vote.[24] The dismissal of a health visitor, from a maternity and child welfare clinic, for giving birth control information renewed debate but John Wheatley, Labour Minister of Health in 1924, refused to take further action. Subsequent resolutions in favour that were taken by Labour Women's Conferences were side-tracked at Labour Party conferences until 1926, when, despite support from the miners' unions, the resolution was soundly defeated. In common with most other Labour women MPs. Ellen Wilkinson, acknowledging that class issues were paramount, did not campaign on birth control. A notable exception was Dorothy Jewson, MP for Norwich 1923–1924, ex Women's Labour League. Reluctance to act possibly had to do with fear of losing the Roman Catholic vote; Wheatley himself was a Roman Catholic.

There is some contemporary and explanatory evidence of the Labour Party leadership's reluctance to take a stand. Rose Witcop and her companion Guy Aldred, anarchists opposed to Labour Party gradualism on this and, indeed, all issues, were involved in publicising the work of American birth control reformer Margaret Sanger. Guy Aldred published Sanger's pamphlet 'Family Limitation' under his own name. Approaches were made to Margaret Bondfield, Susan Lawrence and suffragist Mrs Pethwick Lawrence to write a preface and several Labour Party women's sections expressed interest. Witcop wrote to Sanger that: 'the Labour Party does not want to be obliged to state its attitude towards birth control but...the rank and file is almost entirely with us'.[25] The outcome illustrates how entrenched contemporary opinion was on birth control and was not happy for Guy Aldred, who was prosecuted and fined for obscenity. Facing the Labour Party up to dealing with women's sexuality was a challenge to the patriarchal attitudes displayed in its rhetoric in favour of family life. Labour does have another, and still hidden history; that of the single women who found fulfilment in the Labour world. Some single women lived together in life-long friendships; some of these relationships may have been lesbian.

In the inter-war period, the SJC did manage to sustain both its connection with the Labour Party and its organizational independence. It is clear that the parliamentary lobby was used to great effect by the SJC. When Labour governments were elected, the SJC could lobby for its policies, for instance on domestic service and protective legislation. When the National Government was in power, it was more difficult to get a hearing, for instance on education cuts. Weakened trades union organization made it difficult to make progress on gaining better conditions for women workers. Continuing campaigns started by the Women's Labour League, for instance on school meals, and foreshadowing later campaigns of its successor (the National Joint Committee of Working Women's Organizations) such as education and the marriage bar, the SJC undertook a thorough investigation of the conditions of a working woman's life. The SJC maintained a distinct position within the women's network by clearly prioritizing working women, their conditions of work and their right to continue in work after marriage. Both Marion Phillips's insistence that affiliates vote Labour and the SJC's sustained campaigning on protective legislation drew accusations of 'class prejudice', a prejudice that the SJC proudly acknowledged. With personal knowledge of the conditions of work and home life of working women, gained in some cases through trade union activity, in others research or constituency work, SJC members could sustain and argue their case at governmental level. Prioritizing class issues, the SJC was largely timid and silent on the issue of sexuality. In terms of numbers, the SJC was a success; the record of women forming half the Labour Party membership at the outbreak of war in 1939 was an impressive one, owing much to the organizational skills of Marion Phillips and then of Mary Sutherland as Chief Woman's Officer of the Labour Party, and to the wide reach and constant activity of the SJC, which boasted of communicating with 'over a million women'.

6. Bronwen Tall Brittian, Florence Davy and Mary Sutherland

The two autobiographical notes and the short biography below illustrate some of the events described in this part. Bronwen Tall Brittian
lived in Wales during the general strike and miners' strike of 1926
and she describes its effect on her community. It was this strike that
brought Bronwen into political activity. For Florence Davy, it was the
poverty of inter-war London that provided her political education. Florence also describes her war work and her attempts to influence the
local council, on which she served, to provide deep underground shelters. Mary Sutherland, Labour Party Chief Women's Officer and secretary
to the SJC came from the same sort of poor background as Bronwen
and Florence. However, having won a bursary, Mary received a university education. It was through trade union activity and journalism
that she rose to prominence. All women were life-long Labour movement activists, Florence Davy believing firmly that the Labour Party,
trades union and Co-operative movement should work together, a belief
of course shared and put into practice by Mary Sutherland. The three
accounts show how location affects women's experience. Mary Sutherland dealt with women across Britain as SJC secretary and, as is evident
from discussion of the SJC in this part, was aware of the importance
of receiving opinions from women in different situations. She also represented Britain at women's international socialist meetings. Florence's
and Bronwen's autobiographies arise from talks they gave for Labour
Heritage, in which organization they continued their work for the
Labour Party.

Bronwen Tall Brittian: autobiographical note, 'And I saw that day a hungry baby' (Wales 1926)

The 1926 strike in Wales went on and on,[26] so did the sunshine. I was
aware that our newly built ambulance hall was now being used for
general community purposes – our limited St John's Ambulance unit
was small fry in face of the needs of the community. I can remember
there were dances three nights a week, and there was none of this business of 'unwaged' horror but 3 pence admission was charged to one
and all (is there some lesson there for human rights or human dignity?). My guilt about humanity stems from then, because I had a job,
you see.

   In September the sun continued to shine and I suddenly noticed
something else – the women – let me repeat, the women – suddenly

emerged as the social organizers; afternoon cricket functions, all ages included, picnics, fairgrounds brought in, small but exciting events organized within the limitations of no or very little money. And the good weather continued. Then I noticed something else – everyone was wearing gym shoes.

In December the good weather ended and the miners gave in. They never forgot the betrayal of Jimmie Thomas and the NUR. I immigrated to London in 1929. In 1938 I went to Wales for my annual summer visit home. By now the unemployed total was somewhere about 3 million.

I observed an extraordinary social structure in South Wales. Large families were the norm, but five out of six were unemployed or married to unemployed spouses. I visited cousins in the next valley: my host, one of five brothers was the only one of the family in employment. The other guest that day was the young sister of my hostess who had been married for five years and whose husband (about 26 years old) had never had a job. The hostess's sister and youngest child spent one day a week as honoured guests, but really to be adequately fed for at least one day a week. My hosts fed one or other of the relatives seven days a week. This is when I fell in love with the Welsh because of the gentle courtesy of this sharing of hospitality. Did you know, by the way that on those days the dole adequately fed you for only three and a half days a week. *And I saw that day a hungry baby.*

There were one or two parts of South Wales that fared a little better during this period because somehow in the previous 20 years the miners of my native valley had organized life in such a way that they had established what were known as Workmen's Institutes which had very well equipped libraries, reading rooms and provision for billiards and snooker. So at least the male part of the population was catered for – not that women were inhibited from using the libraries – it just was not traditional. The other thing was that in this particular valley some of the miners had established a very successful prototype of the National Health Service. It was so successful, in fact, that I have never really understood the failure of the NHS. I can only conclude that it was because GPs were allowed to remain outside the system, thereby sowing the seeds of its own destruction.

But let me go on telling you about this successful local medical aid society; the valley was split into three main communities, each with its own heart, and our medical aid society established a large surgery in each of these centres. The doctors who came to service the society were of course all blackballed by the British Medical Association, so that by and large the doctors who came were largely one of two categories, they were either lazy blighters, who wanted a salary and had few responsibilities, but who nearly always had charming bed-side manners, or they wanted to treat their patients without being inhibited by capitation fees and the cost of drugs. This was one of the remarkable things about our Society – If a doctor said that a patient needed so and so, that patient got it. The refinements were that, Cardiff Royal Infirmary, which was our nearest teaching hospi-tal, suddenly acquired a regular income that they hadn't sought – they thought it was the easiest money they had ever acquired. But, you see, if you have an accident in the mine, you have more dead than injured, so that facility was never a burden to Cardiff Royal Infirmary.

We also had district nurses, and these were all employed like the doc-tors – I forgot to tell you, by the way, that because the doctors had been blackballed by the BMA they were all paid very high salaries as compen-sation. The next development was that the leading dental surgeon in Cardiff was hired for a very large fee to come and hold a surgery once a week in the valley. So everything we did you will notice was top qual-ity. Another need was pinpointed – anyone who had to travel to Cardiff for x-ray or consultation had his or her travelling expenses paid. If they were unable to travel on their own and had to be accompanied, these travelling expenses were also paid.

This was all done under very difficult circumstances. At that stage, coal had not been nationalized so all the collieries in the district were privately owned: in order to guarantee their income these miners had to persuade the colliery owners to make the deductions from pay of every miner to finance all this. I have to tell you that as far as my memory goes it was 3d in the pound from each man, of which 1d went to Cardiff Royal Infirmary and 2d to the Medical Aid Society to pay for all these services and all the drugs. In the way life goes on a colliery blacksmith emerged as a gifted administrator – he was not a Labour man, oddly enough, he was not a party political animal, but of course as party politics polarized he had to change from being an 'inde-pendent' councillor into being a Labour councillor. One colliery at the top end of the valley was not allowed to join our Medical Aid Society. David Davies, Llandinaw, owned the pit. His family was so wealthy they were legendary. At one stage his unmarried sister known to my grand-parents administered the colliery. The interesting development is that David Davies left no issue and after he died (then Lord Davies) in 1944, a 'Memorial Institute of International Studies' was formed in 1951 'to commemorate and continue the work of Lord Davies on the means of establishing a viable world order'.

The parallel development in South Wales at the time was related to the Co-operative movement. At that stage the Co-operative stores were very well established and serviced, I should think, at least 80 per cent of the population. They had big department stores, they had their own bakeries, and their own dairies and they were very well off indeed. So that when the 1926 strike started they were strong, they were economically viable and 80 per cent of the population depended on them.

By the end of that strike in December the majority of those families were in debt to the Co-operative society, and since a large percentage of miners never got their jobs back a lot of those debts remained unpaid. This was a very sad thing, it was a cleft stick because those who had been on strike were very poor at the end of the strike, some of them never got jobs again, as I told you, so the Co-op suffered, and it suffered grievously; I never heard any complaints about this – it was a fact of life and everyone had to adjust to it. But I don't think the Co-ops really recovered from that, because apart from the continued unemployment of quite a percentage of the local population, so many 'got on their bikes' and went looking for work in different parts of the country (did you know that about one-third of my valley landed in the new car industry at Cowley) and others emigrated.

You will have noticed how often I have mentioned how the sun continued to shine through those many months. Just imagine what life would have been like for those people if they had had bad weather. If it is cold and wet you don't survive very long in gym shoes: if it is cold and wet you need far more, and more expensive, food: so I began to get a little superstitious about this permanent sunshine; I eventually decided that God was on the side of the miners. The other interesting thought of course is that, if their hardships had been greatly increased would there have been civil disobedience. Some of you will have read the famous speech made by Ellen Wilkinson in the House of Commons after she led the march of the unemployed from Jarrow – in relating the conditions under which these people had to live she was interrupted by a Conservative member who accused her of exaggerating the facts, otherwise he said, 'if they were a bad as you say there would have been revolution'. To which Miss Wilkinson replied 'the half starved don't rebel'.

Mary Sutherland

Mary Sutherland,[27] CBE, JP, was born to a farming family at Burn-head, Banchory Ternan on 30 November 1895. Her mother was Jessie (née Henderson) and her father Alexander Sutherland, a crofter. Mary had two brothers, Alexander and James, who both served in the First World War.

Despite helping to care for her sick mother, who died in 1911, and deputizing for her at home, Mary won bursaries to Aberdeen Girl's High School and then the University of Aberdeen, graduating in 1917 and qualifying as a teacher at the Aberdeen Training College the following year. However, she soon moved into politics, becoming organizer to the Scottish Farm Servants' Union from 1920 until 1922, and editing the union's journal, *The Scottish Farm Servant*. From 1921 to 1922 Mary was vice-chair of the Stirling Trades and Labour Council. She was sub-editor of the Glasgow-based left-wing weekly *Forward* in 1923. In 1924 Mary became Labour Party Woman's Organizer for Scotland. When Marion Phillips died in 1932, Mary moved to London and took over as Labour Party Chief Woman's Officer, secretary to the Standing Joint Committee and editor of *Labour Woman* and held these posts until retirement in 1960. She carried on the SJC's tradition of prioritizing working women and dealing with women in industry, in politics and as consumers. Her time of greatest influence was, perhaps, during the Second World War, when she formed part of the Women's Consultative Committee to the Minister of Labour, Ernest Bevin.

In 1933 Mary became correspondent to the Women's Advisory Committee of the Labour and Socialist International (LSI) and acted as secretary to that body. This interest in socialist internationalism was life-long. She had been delegate to the International Federation of Landworkers meeting in Vienna in 1922. Mary was opposed to working with communists in popular or united fronts. In this she was perhaps partly influenced by the failure of the LSI women's campaign, which she had led, to free the Russian socialist Eva Broido, who had been tried and sentenced as a dissident in 1928. However, as a Labour Party official, Mary could be expected to hold the standard leadership position, which was that work with communists was divisive and enfeebled the Labour Party. In August 1939 Mary attended the international women's study week in Belgium, whose theme was 'Woman and War'. After the war, Mary became chair of the International Council of Social Democratic Women (successor to the LSI committee), and continued to attend meetings after her retirement from the Labour Party.

Mary Sutherland was awarded the CBE in 1949. Bessie Braddock, MP moved the tribute to her at the Labour Party conference in 1960. Suffering a stroke, Mary eventually left London to return to her Scottish roots. Following a second stroke, she died at Hairmynes hospital, East Kirkbride, on 19 October 1972. In memory of her work, Mary's name was added to the Marion Phillips International Fund, started by subscription in 1933, to enable socialist women from other countries to travel to Britain.

Florence Davy: from Zeppelins to jets[28]

My first memories are of being in a Zeppelin raid in London in 1917. I was a very small child of course, but it was quite a bad time. Bombs dropped nearby and I lost an aunt. Many men didn't come back from that war, and many who did had their health seriously impaired. I noticed a growing sense of poverty around me. There was terrible unemployment. The Board of Guardians ruled peoples' lives and would not give any money if there was anything in the house that was saleable. Some homes were so impoverished there was nothing left but sticks. I remember one particular family, a house I went into, of a school friend. There were six children and the mother and father but there was only one chair.

I noticed as a child the effect this had on the spirit of the people, which was very varied. Some people were so downtrodden that they were dispirited and couldn't speak up for themselves, while with others, there was spirit there and they were prepared to stand and fight.

I remember the General Strike of 1926, with the marches on London. We had terrible poverty. I lived in East London, which was not the wealthy section. My father was a postman and the wages were low, but my mother and father were both very industrious and made things we needed, so we got by. We weren't hungry; we weren't cold. Quite a lot of people had inadequate clothing in the winter and they used to reinforce their jacket or coat with paper. They made a lining to stop the wind coming through. Some had no bedclothes, just a mattress, one for the children and one for the parents. They were dirty and stained and they had only old coats (for bedclothes), there was just nothing left.

One day in 1926, I saw a man, he had on some old, striped, musty green trousers and was trying to look like a city boss. With a striped shirt, he had on an old black waistcoat and on top of his head a very, very old black high silk hat, with a placard front and back. He was obviously going off to a demonstration – it read 'I'm one of the bosses, this is what blacklegs have made me' I was astonished because I was a child, but I've never forgotten it.

I had a couple of uncles who'd come back from the war. They refused to buckle under and were trade unionists. If a man would work for 6d a week less than another man he would get the job. The other man would lose it and you had no security. You had nothing, but they refused to work below the rate that was laid down by the trade union movement. They really did suffer and we had as a family to help to support them.

There were suicides. There was a family we were friendly with and in summer we used to walk round and have a little chat. You couldn't offer a cup of tea. No one could do that. They didn't have enough resources, but they were friendly and comforting to each other. In this family, the man hung himself because he couldn't support his wife and children. He couldn't see any future. We also saw families that were put out on the streets. What they had got of a home, tables and chairs, were put in the road. The mother and the children would be sitting there. The look on their faces was like the end of the world; expressionless faces. There was the Board of Guardians and the workhouse; men and women were separated and they used to have to work and scrub.

Wages were absolutely minimal. Outworkers especially lived from hand to mouth. Delivery and collection was not laid on and the workers had to provide their own matching cottons. A tie worker earned 3 farthings per tie, and a shirt machinist earned 2 pence farthing for making a shirt excluding the collar. Since there was no old age pensions when people couldn't work any more they roamed the streets singing, playing a mouth organ etc., in their endeavours to keep out of the workhouse. I left school at the age of 14 years in 1927 and worked over 60 hours a week for 12/-.

They decided at school they would have a child speak for each of the political parties. My parents weren't political at all, although my father had helped Herbert Morrison in an election. In the face of what I saw and experienced, which seemed to me as a child so inhuman and unjust, I didn't like the way people were spoken to. (Wherever you went, whether it was the doctor or the hospital or to an interview, you were spoken to which such disrespect, because you were poor.) I said I would speak for the Labour Party. I don't remember anything I said, except that once I got up there I was telling the whole school about all this I'd seen and that it was all wrong and that there had got to be a change. So that was how I got my first affinity with the Labour Party and it made such an impression on my soul that it will live with me all my life and whatever happens I will never change what I believe in.

When I was 18 I joined the Labour Party. We were talking about setting up a League of Youth and I went along and came out secretary. That's what I usually did, because whatever I joined they were always looking for a worker. So I became a founder member of the North Hackney Labour Party, that was in 1931 and I have belonged to the Labour Party ever since. I joined the London Co-operative Society in 1937 because in the League of Youth they urged this, it was all part of the 'three winged approach'. I joined my trade union when I was 16 because I became a London telephonist and we had the Union of Post Office Workers. Within two years I was the union rep. I was elected to go onto the UPW London District committee and I also represented London telephonists on a National Tribunal. I was also an organizer for UPW and used to go round the telephone exchanges and when the girls came out for their tea break I talked non-stop and recruited quite well.

The blitz and war work (Florence had been elected to Hackney Council)

Hackney Council went in for a programme of surface shelters and strutted basements, in the main, for public use. As time progressed and after serious losses, it became clear that these were not adequate protection. The strutted basements caused a serious loss of life when the building above collapsed. Then there would be a risk of drowning and from gas when pipes fractured. I can remember one particular night on the corner of Coronation Avenue, Stoke Newington, we lost 400 people who were trapped below ground. We were experiencing the blitz ourselves too and trying to get to meetings – if you got to a meeting you couldn't get home, you had to stay there all night. For a time we had a fiasco, as an emergency committee of four councillors was set up to bear the responsibility and we were disbanded – but one of those four was a Tory. If you please! A quorum was one! At a special group meeting I said 'This is impossible, people are going to go into the Forces, people are going to be prevented from attending, but as many people who can get there should still make a quorum for a council meeting'. Unfortunately, I was the only one who disagreed with setting up this emergency committee, so I was rather labelled a bit of a rebel. The Tory was a local builder. But anyway we came back to having a full meeting and for a while I was on the civil defence and finance committee.

The AASTA (The Association of Architects, Surveyors and Technical Assistants) had a project for deep bomb-proof shelters, and although

I hadn't had support when I had tried to introduce this into the Council Chamber, it was later adopted.

When my husband went into the Forces in March 1941 I was in a collapsed state of health. I had been too near too many explosions and hadn't slept in my bed for months. Having relations in Harrogate I went there and commenced work with the Ministry of Aircraft Production. I was put onto contracts for the proofing of balloon fabric. (Japan had been the sole source of pure silk before the war so there was much to be done to find a substitute.) After a few months I was twice upgraded and finished up on the 'silk supply'. I was still in poor health and in a mean billet and at this stage – late in 1942 – my doctor recommended me to return to London in the care of my parents. I was transferred to Thames House to the Directorate of Machine Tools.

The bombing of London commenced with nightly raids with the use of 50 lb bombs. (The damage was similar to what I had seen after the Zeppelin raids in 1917.) But this was stepped up to saturation bombing both day and night. Our landmines captured in France were conveyed over us and dropped. We had daylight bombing and the bombs became larger, from 500 lbs to 1000 lbs. Incendiaries were being used and they lit up the target for the nightly raids. In the course of this I saw the Beckton Gas Works explode into the sky and witnessed many dogfights. On this particular occasion I counted 250 German bombers flying in full formation. Then could be seen a single fighter figure fighting out of the clouds and attacking the rear bomber. He got it! Then he tried again, but that was enough! Surprise was no longer on his side. I heard of one learner pilot in the air and suddenly faced with such a formation. Ground couldn't signal him down so he turned his plane and flew straight into the formation! What a brave man!

We also entered the phase of the 'flying bombs', but so long as you kept your eyes and your ears open you could drop for shelter (perhaps the granite kerb) as soon as you heard the engine cut out.

Before the war manufacturers had not ploughed back their profits into new machine tools, and Britain found itself at a terrible loss. Beaverbrook and Churchill left no stone unturned and America filled the gaps. I worked at the Directorate of Machine Tools until May 1943 when I had to retire to have my baby. Later, a newspaper heading told me what I'd worked on with the word 'whittle' across the headlines. I'd helped to set it up.

Then came the phase of the rockets. If you heard them you were safe, if not...?

The war completely changed our lives, and we had to settle down to the changed conditions.

The Labour government gave us so many good things including the Health Service. Previously the doctor had always to be paid for the medicine too. When people were too poor to pay, some doctors – one I remember as 'Noble by name, and noble by nature' still cared for their patients; but others would not treat anyone who owed them money. The chemist was the only hope then, but I heard of cases where people – and babies too – were allowed to go untreated – and died.

So what a blessing the Health Service was – let no one break it asunder.

We had always struggled for education for all and the opportunity regardless of wealth.

The workhouses were abolished and no one was allowed to starve. Later generations have taken our achievements for granted, but if they allow them to be abolished the fight will have to be made all over again.

Unity of the Labour Party, Trade Union movement and the Co-operative movement is essential to success, and tolerance and compassion over a wide field of opinion has to be achieved to gain success and maintain it.

7. International organization

This section of Part II examines women's international trades union and socialist organizations active between the wars, to which SJC members and British trades unionists and politicians were affiliated. The problems besetting the formation of separate women's committees are discussed, a reminder that the SJC's autonomous position at home was unusual within the international Labour community. However, the SJC was content to allow the Labour Party to nominate its members for service abroad, and respected Labour Party policy. The issues addressed internationally were those of suffrage, workplace pay and conditions, in general the issues of concern to the SJC at home. To these were added citizenship and the threat of fascism and war.

The International Congress of Working Women was one of the first bodies centred on working people to resume meetings after the First World War. British delegates, Marion Phillips, Susan Lawrence and Gertrude Tuckwell of the Women's Trade Union League proposed a resolution on behalf of the SJC, which demanded women's equality of treatment at work, irrespective of their family responsibilities. The Congress met in New York in 1920, now titled the International Federation of Working Women (IFWW). Mrs Raymond Robins (USA) was elected president and Mary MacArthur, vice-president.[29] IFWW next met at Geneva in 1921 with delegates from Belgium, Cuba, Czechoslovakia, France, Italy, Norway, Poland, South Africa, Switzerland, the United States and a group from China, in addition to the British delegation of nine women, the largest present. When Mary MacArthur died suddenly, the Labour Party and TUC appointed the British delegation, which included Marion Phillips. Mrs Raymond Robins retained her position; Marion Phillips was elected secretary and Mrs Harrison Bell (formerly of the Women's Labour League) treasurer; each country nominated a vice-president, Margaret Bondfield acting for Britain. The British delegation accepted the invitation of the congress to act as IFWW's Bureau. The main business was 'war against war', and action against unemployment. Work was started on an investigation into the labour conditions of women and children in the textile trade and a report made to the IFTU in 1923. Monthly supplements on women's work were to be published with IFTU press reports. Marion Phillips followed the Labour Party line that international bodies were advisory only, but also demanded rank and file involvement in international conferences, writing that: 'Delegates come to exchange and discuss information rather than pass a binding resolution, to find out about a subject and see it from each nation's point of view and discuss its treatment'.[30] At IFWW's 1924 Conference the British delegates promoted a Women's Section at the International Federation of Trades Unions, to replace IFWW. This happened the following year, Mary Quaile (Transport and General Worker's Union) being appointed British representative.

British trades union women made a trip to the Soviet Union in 1925 in order to discover; 'conditions affecting the work, health and general conditions of women and children in Russia.'[31] They were favourably impressed by workers' participation in factory management, that factories were 'light and spacious', with on-site medical and dental care and crèche provision. Whether the visitors appreciated that they saw model factories is difficult to judge; they were concerned to praise good practice but were not without criticism. It was noted that the 'new economic policy' had cut crèche numbers (1308 in 1924 from a height of 2509 in 1922) and cost some women jobs, because they were less well organized than men (forming about 25 per cent of trades unionists) and because their labour was costly, given the generosity of maternity leave. On the other hand: 'women at work on treadle machines and other occupations in which work during the menstrual period are unhealthy have two days off with pay during this period'. There were equal pay and sickness insurance covered dependants. Common dining rooms and children's corners lightened domestic drudgery and freed women to participate in political debate.

However, IFTU's Women's Section, now called the International Committee of Women's Trades Unionists, held only three conferences: Paris 1927, Brussels, 1933 and London 1936. The 1927 conference dealt with women's right to work. Professional women were described as vital to the economy, but handicapped by the opposition to working women, which kept wages low. The position of domestic workers, largely women, was considered: the conference resolved that domestic workers should have at least the average industrial wage. Other topics discussed were protection for women workers (as discussed in Section 5), an eight-hour day, regular workplace inspection, sickness insurance, the right to belong to a trades union, minimum wages, maternity leave and the prohibition of night work.[32] By 1933 international trades union women were remarking on the 'feminisation' of the contemporary labour force: in light engineering, electrical apparatus, textile, food and chemical trades, the number of male employees was falling and that of women rising. This trend was said to be encouraged by factory organization and the subdivision of labour; war had also shown that women could be effective, for instance in motor engineering work. In non-regulated trades, women were working 50–60 hours a week and suffering fatigue; night work was permitted because the International Labour Office directive prohibiting this had been amended. The right to work was again discussed, as a marriage bar had been placed on married women civil servants in Germany on 30 June 1933. In Austria and Italy also, fascist governments banned married women's work. In Yugoslavia, Belgium, France, Luxembourg and Britain, there was a similar tendency and attacks had been made on married women workers in the Netherlands and the United States.[33]

At the 1936 conference, women trades unions turned their attention to women's nationality rights; they planned to lobby the League of Nations to achieve equal nationality rights for women. A Women's Committee of the League of Nations, or a correspondence bureau was suggested. However, women trades unionists here faced a paradox of their own making; it was difficult on the one hand to request special protective legislation for women, on the grounds that women had special needs, and on the other hand, to argue for equal citizenship. Jeanne Chevenard (France) wrote that women demanded citizenship: 'although...it cannot be accepted by the Labour Movement, as it could allow for an interpretation which might exclude protection for women'.[34]

In contrast to IFTU, the LSI Labour and Socialist International recognized the need for a woman's section from the outset. Austrian women pushed for a women's conference and LSI secretary Adler may well have been in favour; certainly, he later worked amicably with LSI women organizers. LSI women did not operate from a basis of equality; but they did maintain their organization and activity throughout the inter-war period.

The International Congress of Labour and Socialist Women met at Hamburg in 1923. Delegates from Britain were Marion Phillips, Ethel Bentham, Beatrice Webb and Susan Lawrence. LSI accepted the women's proposal to convene regular women's congresses, although it did not implement the women's demand that the LSI executive committee should contain at least one woman. The LSI asked instead that a representative be sent to meetings to take part in discussions, 'although without voting rights'. Beyond these demands, the women's congress had resolved to work for women's enfranchisement; to consider an International Women's Day; to promote education and peace; to promote the welfare of mothers and children. Five presidents were elected: Marion Phillips, Adelheid Popp (Austria), Frau Bang (Denmark), Frau Juchacz (Germany) and Frau Tilanus (Netherlands).[35] Adelheid Popp was chosen to attend LSI executive committee meetings and, in fact, became known as the executive women's representative, so LSI women went a long way towards fulfilling their 1923 demands.

As agreed, the LSI called the first International Conference of Labour and Socialist Women together with its own Congress at Marseilles in August 1925. The SJC arranged the Labour Party delegation. IFWW experience was put to use by including Mrs Harrison Bell and Marion Phillips. The latter deputized for Adelheid Popp at LSI meetings. Agnes Dollan, who represented the Labour Party, Mary Carlin (Transport and General Workers' Union) and Mary Bell Richards (Boot and Shoe Operatives) were the trades unionists, Ethel Bentham and Rose Smith-Rose represented the Fabian Society. The Independent Labour Party sent Margaret Bondfield, Dorothy Jewson and Minnie Pallister.[36] At this conference it was proposed that a Socialist Women's Advisory Committee of LSI be formed. LSI Secretary Adler notified all affiliates of the council's existence and asked for names of representatives to be notified to him. Provisionally the committee included British, German, Austrian, Belgian, Slav and Balkan representatives. Eventually, Agnes Dollan, Dorothy Jewson and Marion Phillips represented Britain; Germany had three representatives, Belgium and Austria two, and the remaining countries one each. Susan Lawrence was elected to the presidium. Edith Kemiss was the first committee secretary, followed by Martha Transk (1928) and Alice Pels (1934). Support from Adler was important in allowing women to maintain an international profile. For instance, in August 1926 Adler asked affiliates for information on how many women were presented in national parliaments, how women had voted in the last general election, whether there was a Labour Movement women's press and what women's trades union organization existed.[37]

However, the Labour Party International sub-committee opposed the creation of a separate Women's Bureau and the proposal that the political wing in each country should elect its women's representatives 'in conjunction with women's organizations'.[38] British delegates accordingly voted against these proposals, which were dropped. Although SJC women were, in practice, consulted about representation, this was very different to empowering women to elect their own representatives directly. However, the SJC declared: 'the LSI speaks for them as full citizens and members of a political body which has…fully and without reserve accepted the economic, social and political partnership of men and women'.[39]

The resolutions for 1928 Congress set the pattern of the Women's Advisory Council agenda throughout the inter-war years. Topically, the

Polish proposal was to oppose the mobilization of women in war-time. Other resolutions addressed the position of women at work and in the home. There were proposals for a public medical service open to all, for state care of sick and physically disabled people and the prevention and cure of illness. The ILP resolution covered women in all aspects of life: 'for the sick', non contributory national insurance; 'for women in industry', a living wage and equality at work; public ownership of land, mines, transport, power, housing; 'for the mother and child', the abolition of unemployment and low wages, full maintenance for six weeks before and six weeks after birth, a 'scientific methods of family limitation'.[40] This resolution was interesting for they way in which it specified low wages and unemployment as problems for women bringing up a family and because it dealt with birth control. The Austrian resolution was also in favour of birth control: 'we consider the threat of penalties against artificial abortion to be objectionable'.

For the 1931 conference, the British resolution was on domestic work and again mixed concern for women at home and at work, including domestic service. Scientific organization of housework was demanded, deserving high pay.[41] At this conference progress was made on women's suffrage. It was one of the weaknesses of women's international organizations that women were politically disadvantaged. Even where women were enfranchised, for instance in Weimar Germany, their election to political office was subject to the patronage of male-dominated political parties. Weimar women found that party discipline was restrictive; and cross-party meetings of women were disliked, despite the fact that proportional representation in European social democracies often resulted in coalition governments.[42] In other social democracies, including France and Belgium, socialists participating in coalition governments feared to upset the balance of power by enfranchising women. Sara Huysmans of Belgium deplored the situation in *Labour Magazine*, noting that socialists feared that women would vote conservative and that Catholic parties were, therefore, generally in favour of women's enfranchisement.[43] It was a major success when the Women's Council persuaded Belgian delegates to the 1931 LSI conference to support women's enfranchisement; the French agreed to expedite their campaign for votes for women.

The Women's Advisory Council began, in 1931, an ambitious programme to investigate, compare and portray statistically conditions of life, including the cost of living, of women in European countries. The British were among the most conscientious in supplying statistics, but these were never wholly reliable and the project remained incomplete.

Other issues dealt with included women's nationality on marriage, the Women's Council being concerned that women should not become aliens in their country of birth.[44]

Attention paid to issues of gender diminished as the focus of international organizations became the struggle against fascism, with one curious exception. For reasons the files do not explain, the 1935 LSI Congress expressed the opinion that 'women seem to be too little concerned with questions of doctrine' and the LSI 'considered it urgently necessary' for the women leaders to 'see where they stood'. A long-postponed study week was therefore convened at the Belgian Labour College in 1936 on the theme 'Economic and Political Democracy and Women'.[45] This study week had originally been devised, by the Women's Council, as a ten-day conference for rank and file women, funded by women parliamentarians who would each donate a day's pay. Instead, the leaders of the women's parties attended a programme of lectures and seminars, outings and discussions. Maria Mahler, speaking on 'Trades Unions under Fascism' noted: 'we are looking here at the ground work for a fascist war'. Taking a leisurely approach and prioritizing discussion, with relatively low-level expectations, the women deemed their week 'a brilliant success'. LSI women continued to demand a rank and file conference. Mary Sutherland successfully proposed that an International Women's Week replace the conventional Women's Day, to spread the international spirit in face of 'the growth of fascism and menace of war'. The Women's International secretary was to provide information on each country and national parties were urged to attract visits from women comrades in other countries and to make group visits in return.[46]

The Spanish Civil War had a huge impact on women's international groups. The 1937 report of the Women's Committee reported women's activity and 'enthusiastic support to the efforts of workers' parties to help Spain' in all countries. To contribute to the international 'spirit', and meet Mary Sutherland's proposal, the secretary was collecting reports of a day in the life of a woman in each affiliated country; a qualitative, rather than quantitative attempt to provide this information. Making use of both this data and the statistics collected, two enquiries were being pursued, one on the needs of working class households and the second on the health of children and adolescents. However, it had proved impossible to contact the Women's Committee of IFTU (as we have seen, by then, almost non-existent) and the Women's Committee attached to the League of Nations had 'a phantom existence'. Information on women's employment and women's rights in each affiliate was therefore requested. The approach of war had re-politicized the birth control debate; the Danish representative of the International Women's committee (Naina Anderson) condemned the dictators' purpose and method in seeking population increase. She called for the reasons that people practised birth control to be attacked rather than contraception itself and demanded social legislation for this purpose.[47]

Thereafter, women's organization was increasingly difficult in the face of the fascist advance. Numbers dropped throughout 1938. Plans for a further study week to be held in the Netherlands were postponed until 1939 because the Dutch government had objected to criticism of its foreign policy, so that there were fears of police supervision. The event was then further delayed to 1940 and Britain was chosen as the venue. Meanwhile, the inquiry on the cost of living contin-ued but only Britain and Belgium were able to contribute information. The campaign to protect Spanish children and provide food intensi-fied. It was proposed that women operate a boycott of Japanese goods. Resolutions were taken against the Nazi annexation of Czechoslovakia and horror expressed at the disappearance of people in both Spain and Czechoslovakia. Solidarity was expressed with women exiles and pledges were made to help refugees. Norway joined the LSI and its Women's Council and Czechoslovakia left both. To complete the catalogue of disasters, Adelheid Popp died in 1939. However, women's unremitting attempts to understand daily life in other countries, unique in for-mal international organization, should be remembered; women had sought to become familiar with the countries where atrocities now took place.

This impressive record of international participation by the SJC was within the framework of mainstream Labour Party and trade union pol-icy. Indeed, the SJC were content to let the Labour Party and TUC choose its delegations and outline its policy positions. In addition, the SJC was confined to work with social democrat parties and eschewed collabora-tion with communists. At home, the SJC did not join with communist women, maintaining the Labour Party position of parliamentary social-ism. Some Labour women did manage to work in United or Popular Front Groups with Communist women, but even for prominent women such as Ellen Wilkinson, as the following section shows, such positions were problematic.

8. Ellen Wilkinson and Irene Wagner

The short biography of Ellen Wilkinson and Irene Wagner's biographical note follow the section on internationalism. That of Ellen Wilkinson is illustrative of political activity in the campaign against fascism. Irene Wagner was named for peace but, growing up as a member of a Jewish family under the Third Reich, was forced to flee her country, finding refuge in the wartime London Labour community. Both women started their political activity when young, Ellen at 16 years and Irene at 11 years old. Irene went on to become Labour Party librarian and was active in forming Labour Heritage, for whom her tale was first recounted. Both women differed from Labour officials such as Mary Sutherland in their readiness to make political connections beyond the Labour Party.

The early career of Ellen Wilkinson

Ellen Cicely Wilkinson (1891–1947) was one of four children.[48] She was born in Manchester and attended Manchester University, gaining an MA degree with honours in History. At university, she was briefly engaged to be married. A socialist and suffragist, she was elected to Manchester City council in 1923, as Labour Member of Parliament for Middlesborough East (1924–1931) and Labour MP for Jarrow (1935–1947).

Ellen's political career began early when, at 16, she joined the Independent Labour Party (ILP), remaining a member until 1932, when the ILP disaffiliated from the Labour Party. She was vice-chair of the University Socialist Society and later became a member of this body's national executive committee. In 1912 Ellen joined the Election Fighting Fund, an organization set up that year by the big women's suffrage organization, the 50,000 strong National Union of Women's Suffrage Societies, and the Labour Party, to help sympathetic Labour candidates to win parliamentary seats. The following year, Ellen joined the Women's Labour League and was secretary of its Tyldesley branch. She was appointed Manchester NUWSS organizer. In 1915, Ellen became National Women's Organizer of the Amalgamated Union of Cooperative Employees, which after a 1921 amalgamation became the National Union of Distributive and Allied Workers (NUDAW). She was a member of the Laundry, Corset, Dressmaking and Millinery Trades Boards and chair of the Workers' Side of the Laundry Trades board. Elected to MP for Middlesborough East in 1924, sponsored by NUDAW, Ellen was one of merely four women MPs. Ellen maintained friendly relations with other women MPs. She was at home in Parliament and a good orator. While she campaigned on major issues raised by the women's network, such as equal pay, and spoke for the Standing Joint Committee on women's suffrage, Ellen's parliamentary speeches reflected her socialism rather than her feminism. Working people, men and women, were her political passion throughout her short life.

Ellen lost her seat in 1931 when financial crisis caused the downfall of the 1929–1931 Labour Government. She did not support the policies of fiscal stringency, which contributed to this collapse. Rather, Ellen had signed the Mosley memorandum promoting Keynsian fiscal policy, the rejection of which led Mosley, then one of its rising stars, to abandon the Labour Party in favour of his own New Party, which evolved into the British Union of Fascists. Re-elected MP for Jarrow in 1935, Ellen continued to oppose the economic policies of the National government and supported her constituency's protest march to London in 1936. Jarrow was a north east shipbuilding town with over 70 per cent unemployment. A group of 200 men marched to London. They wanted to show Parliament, and people in the south, how difficult life was in their region but that they were responsible, orderly citizens. They demanded that a steel works be built in Jarrow, to bring back jobs to their town. They were not the only group to publicize their plight. The National Unemployed Workers Movement (NUWM) represented unemployed people before benefit tribunals and organized hunger marches, including one of 2000 people in 1932 and national marches in 1934 and 1936. Two hundred blind people also marched to London in 1936. While the NUWM had been refused Labour Party affiliation because of its communist connections, the Jarrow march was organized by Jarrow Borough Council and attracted broad political support. Ellen went neither as their leader nor as their organizer, but in order to demonstrate her support and win them publicity. She had also supported the 1934 and 1936 NUWM marches. Ellen Wilkinson herself wrote a vibrant plea for Jarrow's restoration, *The Town that was Murdered* (1939).

It was in the field of international politics that Ellen, who had travelled in Europe and was well versed in the subject, challenged official Labour Party policy. While her sister, Annie, became secretary of the Manchester Women's International League for Peace and Freedom, Ellen chose a different route to protest fascism. She had joined the newly fledged Communist Party in her youth, retained her membership of the 1917 Club founded to celebrate the Russian revolution, and was still a member of the Communist Party when elected to Manchester City Council. However, she was both too much of a reformist and too much of a rebel to brook Communist Party discipline. The parliamentary road to socialism was Ellen's chosen way albeit, as Herbert Morrison, one of Labour's leading figures, said of her at the 1933 Party Conference: 'sometimes she is a bit of a nuisance to us'.[49]

The reason why Ellen's anti-fascist activities were problematic derived from the European left's division into Social Democrat (or Labour in Britain) and Communist wings. The Third or Communist International, heavily dominated by Moscow, organized Communist Parties globally while the Social Democrats were affiliated to the Labour and Socialist International (LSI). Communists, in their 'Class Against Class' phase, had been hostile to social democracy from 1928. From 1933, in view of the gravity of the situation, the two Internationals discussed collaboration; some European parties entered into United Front (Social Democrat and Communist) and later Popular Front (including Liberals and Radicals) agreements. In France and Spain, Popular Front governments were formed in 1936. Such collaboration was unacceptable to many Social Democrat parties and in particular to the British Labour Party. Communists were blamed for the backlash which contributed to fascist victories; the 1933 Trades Union Congress was told: 'Every time they made a communist they made a fascist'.[50] The Communist Party of Great Britain (CPGB) was small but persistent while the Labour Party presence in parliament had been greatly weakened following its 1931 debacle. In particular, Communist 'Front' groups were viewed with suspicion – groups like the NUWM, which ostensibly had an independent appeal but were suspected of being covers for communist activity and recruitment. These groups, and individuals prominent within them, were liable for proscription. Thus when the ILP entered into United Front work after its disaffiliation from the Labour Party, membership of the ILP and the Labour Party was incompatible.

In 1932, when Ellen undertook a tour of Germany taking with her, without authorisation, an anti-fascist flag from British Labour women, she merely upset protocol. However, the following year, she became a member of the Commission of Enquiry into the Reichstag Fire Trial. This act of arson, allegedly by communists, preceded the March 1933 elections that brought Hitler to power. Membership of the commission included communists and its activities were therefore suspect in the official Labour mind. Ellen was later able to persuade the Home Secretary to allow the defendants entry to Britain. As the international situation deteriorated with annexation of Austria by Germany in 1934, the success of far-right parties in Central and Eastern Europe and the outbreak of the Spanish Civil War in 1936, Ellen's nuisance value grew. She visited Spain in 1934 and 1937, joined the all-party National Joint Committee for

Spanish Relief and was a member of the Labour Party Spanish Campaign Committee.

Ellen, like NUDAW, was in favour of both United and Popular Fronts and a formidable speaker in their favour and against proscription. She joined the pro-Popular Front Socialist League in 1937. She remained on the executive team of the suspect Labour Research Department until the Russian invasion of Finland altered the political stakes. Typically, she helped organize a Popular Front National Emergency Conference on Spain in 1938, chaired by Gilbert Murray, attended by 1205 organizations and 1806 delegates, including ten MPs representing all parties. Unlike other prominent rebels, such as Aneurin Bevan and Stafford Cripps, both briefly victims, Ellen was never expelled from the Labour Party, although she came close to the edge. It was a measure of her political intelligence that, despite the openness of her position as a Labour Party rebel and the vehemence with which she expressed her views, she remained one of its stars.

As Minister of Education in the 1945 Labour government Ellen had her greatest single achievement when she engineered the raising of school-leaving age to 15, despite the shortage of buildings in war-damaged Britain and the need for 13,000 extra teachers.

Apart from her book on Jarrow, Ellen wrote novels, including *Clash* (1929) (which centred on the 1926 general strike), a 1938 autobiography *Myself When Young*, fundraising and propaganda pamphlets such as *Terror in Germany* and *Feed the Children*, and, as 'EW' ('East Wind') articles for *Time and Tide* and other feminist and left journals.

Irene Wagner: the menace of fascism (Germany 1930s)

The reason why I was called Irene,[51] is that my parents didn't know if I was going to be a boy or a girl and they weren't prepared for any names, so on the day I was born the Kaiser made the first peace offers to the Allies and my parents said, 'Aha Peace, in Greek, Irene'. I remember the terrible upheavals and the end of the War. In my first years at school, there were still tremendous shortages and the English Quakers moved into the school with bags of cocoa and large rolls, of a type which I had never seen before, they are called 'baps'.

In my secondary school I very soon got involved in local politics. From the age of 11 onwards, my Father, who was very active, took me to the meetings of the Democratic Young People... this school I went to was co-educational and my parents decided it was better for me to go to a girls school... it was a completely different set of people I was with; they were the daughters of local councillors and bank managers, and not until 1933 and the Nazi arrival did I really know who in that school was on my side. The tragedy of it all, of the politics of Nazism, were brought home to me quite early on in 1933…a girl who was in a parallel class to mine, her father was a trade union official and he suddenly disappeared and the girl came round to my father and said 'Look you knew my father, could you do something'. My father was very exposed of course with the Nazis and he was very surprised that he was not being collected…but so far, so good. It wasn't about more than six months after that, when this father of the girl was returned to her mother in a tiny box and the box was about 5 inches by 5 inches and in it were the ashes of the man who used to be the Trade Union leader, and that was the greatest shock to my system because I *knew* that although I knew I was Jewish, I knew the Nazis were going to eradicate Jews altogether, but we were well established in the town (for a long time my family has lived in South West Germany and Saxony). I thought that nothing could happen to me and it wouldn't be so bad. It dawned on me then, like it dawned on everybody else, that this was really the end of democracy.

I went to one meeting…where Hitler was speaking in the local permanent circus and a circus indeed it was, because most of the audience were women and the hysteria gripped them when Hitler appeared. It was very much an eye opener to me. I was terrified and I tried to get out and people wouldn't let me get out, this was Hitler and you couldn't dare to get up and out, so I sat there and I got more and more frightened. If I could have I would have 'peed' in my pants but I didn't and I watched these women and they became more and more…irradiated I suppose…. The light of Hitler shone upon them and it was really very frightening so if somebody asks me later on who contributed mostly to the success of Hitler, I would have answered without hesitation, the women, the women of Germany have sold Germany to Hitler.

During that time I went to Czechoslovakia. Our town was only about an hour's train journey from Czechoslovakia, and I used to go there to see my cousins who had emigrated very quickly after 1933, being members of the Communist Party…and there I would sort of make contact with socialist friends and come home with literature to distribute amongst hungry socialists for news…The way I did that, was at that time you still used to wear knickers with the elastic round the waist and round the legs, and I would stuff these absolutely full of socialist papers and I would buy a lot of fruit, and the fruit used to be always sold in newspapers, and I saw to it, that it was always sold in the German speaking Sudetan German newspapers. Well one day I remember at the border when I didn't come by train but by bus, because it was cheaper, they hauled everybody out of the coach into the Customs house and you can imagine how difficult it was to walk with knickers full of newspapers. You didn't expect to walk until you got on the train, into the loo where you could take them out and put them in a safe place, in a suitcase... walking was a nightmare because there must have been a hundred steps up a hill to the customs house, but in the long run I managed, still clutching my plums to my bosom and the plums soaking through the socialist papers but nobody really minded a rather smallish girl and they let me go down to the bus again. I really was in a state... when I arrived home and told my father and gave him the papers... He nearly hit me because he didn't know what I had been doing and secondly the danger of being put into a concentration camp and forever disappearing was getting greater and greater and this wouldn't have helped, and so he wouldn't let me go after that – that was it... It was only with my father and mother that we used to go for Saturday and Sunday trips to friends of ours who had a house very near the border, we would walk across the border and write our letters and make arrangements to emigrate to America.

This was the great thing because my father helped a lot of people out of Germany, then we would get letters from these people 'we can help you'... A person who had a factory and he had to hop it because he was Jewish, he hopped it to New York, and my father said to him, well he would take his offer.... And so we went on still reading the papers, still cutting bits out and coming back with the bits of news for our friends and so we prepared eventually to get out....

And then one day there was a knock-knock on the door and friend of mine who used to be with me in the Young Communist Organization said 'whatever happens, I don't think you will get away because somebody is on his way to question you', and sure enough he was hardly out of the door, up through the top floor and the roof when the Gestapo came – it wasn't the Gestapo it was the criminal police... they had to ask me several questions and could I accompany them, my mother nearly had hysterics... but the policeman was very kind so it was a good job that someone asked him to interview me... I got to the police station and they locked me up and they took my finger prints and I was very frightened.... A nasty piece of work with glasses and duelling scars asked me questions about my activities at school and what did I do at the technical university (which I was kicked out of in the end) and what my political activities were... I said I was an utterly apolitical person… 'What with a person like your father who has always been a good liberal and one hears'… they finally kept me overnight and I heard what they do, torture and so on, however they didn't. In the end it was again my friend who talked to this person and said I was not really politically active and we were getting out anyway… In the end I started packing my things because I was getting out earlier than my parents… talk about German efficiency, the Gestapo told me that there were only certain things I could take out, like personal belongings but nothing of value. I had a friend who was a chemist and she wanted to have some platinum melting pots taken out of Germany…. Well, I noticed that the gramophone that I was taking out was sealed… in such way that if I lifted the lid all the string with the seals would slip down and I could put things into the hollow places, so I slipped all those platinum melting pots in that… Somebody wanted a diamond ring taken out and I put the ring into a jar of cream unbeknown to my parents… I had a visa to go to America and the quickest way was to go to Hamburg, so we booked a ticket for me to go from Hamburg to New York, but I was supposed to stay for a little while in England and I had a visitor's visa to stay with relatives…. that was in 1938….

Here I was with my gramophone… I had to put it all on the table and there were the SS guards and Gestapo and I was getting hotter and hotter and then they said 'what's this here' and I said 'it's a gramophone' and they said 'open up' and I said 'no, I can't the Gestapo sealed it'. 'Oh, why didn't you say so, go on'. So I got onto the ship, an American boat… And I knew I was safe… I had the normal reaction to stress…. I was terribly sick… then we set sail and I was even further sick because the North Sea was very choppy… and I had visions of someone grabbing my gramophone. I arrived in Southampton very happily… it was a really ghastly day… rainy, November, foggy… and then I arrived in London and my new life started.

Irene Wagner: socialist London at war

When I had made it to London,[52] I stayed first with my father's sister; she was the widow of an Irishman who died in Internment in Germany during the First World War. Her two sons, one a civil engineer the other a physicist, were well established in England, I looked for a job, but the only one the immigration authority allowed me to take up was an au-pair job with a dentist. His wife and mother worked me to the bone. Then I managed to crush a toe under a falling piece of furniture and left. I found refuge with my mother's sister who lived in England as a refugee herself. She was married to the famous architect Mendelsohn, one of the Bauhaus lot, who had to leave Germany in 1933 because he was a communist. There was a job going with the Jays: young Peter was already there, the next one, to be called Martin later, was under way and I was supposed to relieve the expectant mother by more or less taking over the running of their large Hampstead house.

It was by now the summer of 1939. My parents had also got out to England a few months before. Then war broke out and I was somewhat apprehensive about what would happen to me. Peggy Jay and the children moved to the safety of Oxford and in moved a motley crowd of geniuses. There was Thomas Ballogh (he and Nicolas Caldor formed later the famous 'Hungarian twins' who, as economics professors, advised the 1964 Labour Government). Douglas Jay, then a journalist on the Daily Herald, made use of my German background for his editorial work. For them, and some more highly intellectual (and very difficult) people I cooked every day pretty horrible breakfasts, which they did, however, survive. There were also a number of ladies in 'occasional residence' and, in all, it was quite good fun.

Though I was, after all, an 'enemy alien', the Red Cross accepted me for a training course and I learnt first aid. My boyfriend from Germany had also arrived, but everything was somehow different now, and we no longer got on very well. Peggy Jay, having popped her baby, was back in the house. She egged me on to go out and acquire a social life. Ruth Dalton (a close friend of Peggy's) had 'such a nice young German' staying with her, just the right man for me to meet. I thanked her politely but firmly. At that stage, I was so conscious of being a refugee that I abhorred any contact with anything connected with Germany. Anyway, the young man in question was only staying at the Daltons in between his tours of duty as an auxiliary fireman.

In the end, Peggy persuaded me to go to a Fabian Dance on Leap Year Day 1940. The place was full of Labour notables. There was Margaret Cole; the only information about her I was given was that she wrote thrillers. There was also Harald Laski: 'fearfully brilliant'. Peggy Jay sailed in with a young man in tow. He wore a black suit, patent leather shoes and was the aforementioned German fireman. 'Meet Dr Wagner', said Peggy and to my horror the young man bowed stiffly and clicked his heels. I was horribly embarrassed, but then we danced and things got better. In the course of more dances and several whiskies, I found out that he had been to school in Danzig, where the war had started and where I had some relatives whom he knew very well indeed (particularly one female cousin of mine!). He walked me home all the way from Burlington House to Hampstead Heath.

Gyuri (Hungarian for George) had been up to the neck in the resistance; Hugh Dalton had got him out just two weeks before the war broke out. He described himself as 'Hugh's tame German'. Relations took their natural course and my continued residence with the Jays was getting somewhat problematic. So I was invited to move in with the Daltons. Meanwhile Hugh Dalton, who had his own ideas about how my Gyuri could better aid the war effort, had got him into something terribly hush-hush, and he disappeared from view to a place nobody was supposed to know about. Of course I found out in no time from the various geniuses in the Jay household, all of who were now doing frightfully important and high-level jobs.

At any rate, my man turned up once a fortnight and was thinking of finding a little love nest for us somewhere, say in Chelsea. This was where Ruth Dalton intervened kindly but firmly (and when Ruth was firm, that just was it). 'The Foreign Office' (which provided, at that time, the official cover for the outfit Gyuri was in) 'will not allow their people to live in sin'. So, Gyuri proposed and I said yes.

Everything, so far, had moved very suddenly. Then came the hitch. In view of Gyuri's work, I had to be cleared by MI5, and that took some time. Meanwhile the war had heated up considerably and I was moved out of the way to the Dalton's Wiltshire house, I was 'cleared' at the beginning of June and got permission to travel to London to marry.

On 7 June 1940 we married at Caxton Hall. It was hilarious. The registrar asked Gyurl why the hell he was not in internment. That was quickly settled. Then he asked me for my parents' consent to the marriage – I had made myself a smashing dress of dusty pink, and looked about 15 in it. In fact I was 23. Hugh Dalton, one of the witnesses, stormed in late from a cabinet meeting and roared at the registrar to … get on with it, as Mr Churchill was waiting. Hugh's whisper was known to burst windowpanes and his roar reduced the hapless official to a jelly. He mispronounced every name he had to read out. But it was achieved. The wedding ring – very thin – cost 12 shillings and 6 pence. Gyurl paid 10/-, Ruth 2/- and I 1/6 pence. Later on our wedding day, my brand new husband was whisked back to duty, because something dreadful had happened in France. And that was that for the next five weeks.

After a while, I was allowed to move to digs somewhere not too far from where he was. I was terribly bored and only too glad when Dora

Gaitskell, who had gone to ground somewhere nearby, asked me to walk her children in the park.

After six months of marriage, I was allowed to live with my spouse, and some months later, the hush-hush people farmed out some work to me. Ultimately I joined them full-time. What did we do? Well, I can only say it had something to with the Nazi war machine and that my training as a librarian was quite useful. Now, at 70, I am still bound by the old secrecy obligations. Some of the big wigs in our place have published memoirs. Small fry like us have to keep mum – and refer to those fine contributions to British historical fiction, which our betters were allowed to publish.

Sometimes we went to the local hotel/pub in the evenings, as there was nothing else to do. There were a lot of people in uniform there, some pretty high ranking ones among them, mostly also from some unmentionable outfit. At first we sat quietly by ourselves. One day, the landlord asked us 'Where are you from?' Gyuril answered, 'If I were to tell you, would not sell us any drinks'. When the publican insisted, Gyuri told him that we were German 'Where are your hairy wrists?', came the reply, a reference to rumours that the Germans were dropping parachutists, disguised as nuns, but easily recognized by their hairy wrists. One day came the breakthrough, a fierce controversy about some problem relating to Germany had broken out in the pub around the open fire where, naturally, the brass hats were sitting. 'Why don't you ask them?', asked the landlord, 'they are Germans'. There was a momentary hush of horror. Then the gentlemen in question put two and two together, assumed we were 'from that other place', and asked us to join them. Now we were 'in'. Whenever we entered the pub, they called out 'make room for our Huns'.

There was a group of dedicated German and Austrian socialists working together in our organization and we spent much of what leisure we had discussing what we would want to happen at home, once the war was won. When the war had taken a turn for the better, the powers above decided that most of our organization should move to London. So we got orders to get ourselves accommodation in the metropolis. But it was of course still all very hush-hush. Officially we did not exist. We were not supposed to figure on any list of residents and our (compulsory) telephone was ex-register.

We were lucky a woman in our outfit was getting married and we took over her flat in Bloomsbury, where we are still living after 44 years. We got a few bits of utility furniture, found one or two other things here and there and organized a fine collection of orange boxes for the rest of our needs. God knows where the oranges had gone; we never saw any during the war. Work went on as hectically as ever, I was now running one side of my old man's section. Come the V1s and V2s and we had a lot of them in Central London. One day, a particularly nasty 'doodle bug' exploded just in front of our place of work literally minutes after we had gone out for lunch. We rushed back and found a pretty horrible mess of men and matter all over the place 'doodle bug' was an American term for the flying bombs. In the last stages of the war, we had a lot of contact with our Yankee opposite numbers. Some of them became good friends. Nearly all of these were members of 'Americans for Democracy', a political group that was as near to Labour thinking as was feasible for them. All the Americans we had contact with thought very highly of their own knowledge and activity in our joint field. Most of them had no very good reasons for this self-esteem.

We also had some (very reliable) German prisoners-of-war working for us. One of them turned out to be the godson of an aunt of mine who was living in Finchley. After a lot of difficulties and with some slight disregard to rules, I managed to engineer a meeting between my aunt and our German and there was a very happy reunion indeed.

Politics, while we were still 'somewhere in England', was restricted to long discussions during off-duty periods. London was different. Meetings were held all over the place. The wartime 'political truce' between the three parties forming the wartime coalition government was of course a great hindrance to the Labour Party. It was quite clear that the country had moved as a whole to the left. So, like many other socialists, we were attracted to the Commonwealth Party, which was organized by Sir Richard Acland. Here we could hear and say, and do, what the Labour Party would more or less painfully merge with the Labour Party once the war was over.

When the war came to an end, we had decided to stay in Britain and our daughter was 'en route'.

9. The Second World War and after

This section examines the effects of the Second World War in changing the nature of women's participation in the Labour movement, due
to their increased participation in the labour force and the growth
of women's trades union membership.[53] It shows how the Labour
Party perception of women workers changed during the course of the
war. The wartime role of the Standing Joint Committee is considered
and the reorganization of Labour women in the post-war period. The
equal pay campaign, in which the SJC was involved, is considered in
detail.

When the Second World War started, Labour Party leaders were initially of the opinion that women would remain constituency stalwarts
and replace the young men who had been conscripted; James Middleton wrote that women's constituency work would be very important
'while the young men were away'.[54] These hopes were foiled: on the one
hand, because bombing, evacuation, the conscription of agents and the
lack of elections around which to focus, weakened constituency organization; and on the other, because the women were conscripted into
the workforce. Labour Party membership fell from 400,000 in 1939 to
219,000 in 1942. Nevertheless, the Labour Party decided against factory organization, leaving the field clear to the Communist Party, which
focused its organization in the workplace. Some of the newly unionized
women thus found their first political home not in the Labour Party,
but in the Communist Party. This was recalled as their experience by
several of the women members of Labour Heritage, who began work
and began political life during the war. Ann Leff's tale was familiar; she
was recruited from the furnishing trade to the manufacture of wooden
aircraft, became active in her union and joined the Communist Party;
she joined the Labour Party in 1956.[55] Communist Party membership
rose to 25 per cent of that of the Labour Party in 1942.

The trades unions were hardly welcoming towards their new recruits.
Both the AEU and the TGWU at first refused the inexperienced women
workers and thereafter had little success in achieving equal pay; from
October 1938 until January 1942, men's earnings rose by 41 per cent
but women's by 35 per cent; women earned roughly half the male
wage and girls a third.[56] Although workplace nurseries were opening at an unprecedented rate by 1943, child care provision remained
unsatisfactory, despite the protests of Labour women MPs.[57] Registered
childminders, rather than trained nursery nurses, provided the staffing
in the new nurseries. The TUC maintained that children under two years

old should be with their mothers. Nonetheless, women's membership of trades unions did rise (see Table 1).

Ernest Bevin, previously leader of the TGWU, became Minister of Labour in 1940, joining the war cabinet in October of that year. His attitude to women workers illustrates the way in which Labour's previously reluctant male trades unionists accepted women workers when the need arose. In 1940 Bevin maintained that a 50–55 hour working week was ideal for wartime production but that women could work 60 hours to finish a special job.

In March 1941 Bevin required women of 20–21 years to register for work, which might be in industry, civil defence or the women's voluntary forces. By August that year, all women up to the age of 30 were required to register and those over 30 to volunteer. In September, Bevin demanded another 500,000 women for the WAAF, ATS, civil defence, nursing and industry, for aircraft production, electric cables, engineering, the Royal Ordinance, radio and transport.[58] The National Service Act of 18 December 1941 enshrined these demands in legislation. By 1943, the legislation was extended to women aged 19–51 years, with exceptions for reserved occupations; married women with children under 14 years and husbands in the forces; and pregnancy. By 1944 however, Bevin had started to shed the workforce of its female members.

Labour Party publications illustrate the way in which ideas about the female labour force altered with the demands of the war. In the early days, heavy industry unions were reluctant to accept women, fearing that men's wages and conditions would be endangered by the presence of the lower-paid and unskilled women. There were adverse reports about the working conditions of the female labour force in France, including poor conditions in factories and the use of girls under 16 in Paris soup kitchens, sweated work and punishment for absenteeism. After the French surrender and the British alliance with the Soviet Union, reports praised the prowess of the Soviet female labour force, women working in factories, the railways and the metallurgical industries.[59] The Communist Party made the most of this publicity; its delegates asked at a public meeting why women railway cleaners were not trained to be drivers, while the Communist press claimed 'Our women are strong and wise', with examples of guerrilla heroines tortured to death, killing fascists by the hundred and leading Red Army battalions.[60]

The SJC continued operating during the war, giving advice for instance on rationing of food and clothes, the care of homeless children, nurseries and family allowances. It was successful in gaining the

Table 1 Trade Union Membership of Larger Unions, 31 December 1942

Union	No. of Members		Union	No. of Members	
	Men	Women		Men	Women
Miners	599,241		Plumbers	27,340	
ASLEF	65,059		Woodworkers	164,000	623
NUR	358,927	35,217	Wood Cutting	21,029	
Seamen	48,549	744	London Comps	13,275	
TGWU	506,000	300,000	Typo. Association	38,986	
Boilermakers	83,293		NATSOPA	22,493	5,278
ETU	108,074	4,592	Card etc. ops.	7,344	29,379
AEU	645,203		Printers	30,468	29,886
Blastfurnacemen	19,274	775	Sheet Metal Workers	25,000	
Enginemen	38,450		Boot & Shoe	56,547	30,556
Foundry Workers	41,021		Bakers, Confects	21,026	3,382
Dyers, Bleachers	35,984	27,106	NUDAW	152,756	100,800
Tailors & Garment	27,450	81,960	Shop Assistants	22,535	40,031
Weavers	12,408	60,000	NUPE.	69,500	9,000
Bank Officers' Guild	21,444	7,872	NUG & MW	463,528	257,138
Clerical & allied	11,613	17,809	Society Of Painters	44,268	345
Fire Brigades Union	78,000	7,000	Agricultural	66,000	5,100
Iron & Steel Trades	93,383	11,168	Total*	4,804,866	1,219,543

*not all unions are shown

Source: Labour Research Department *Fact Service* no. 208, 1943.

inclusion of the category 'housewife' in the Personal Injuries (Civilian) legislation.[61] The SJC provided evidence on housing for the Ministry of Health in 1942. The usual exhaustive and participative method of enquiry was undertaken; questionnaires were sent to affiliates, with a separate form for the views of women under 30. These were individually completed, but also discussed at branch meetings. Summing up the responses, the SJC emphasized that a variety of housing was needed and that the universality of family units should not be assumed:

> We believe that the majority of women prefer a home...for family life...some women with families (who) prefer a flat; and there are many people who find a modern flat the most convenient type of home, eg. childless couples, people who do not want a garden, single people.[62]

Not only was this advice passed to the relevant government committee, but, the SJC succeeded in placing its nominees thereon.

Using a similar methodology, the SJC received reports on evacuation from a wide rage of affiliates: included were resorts such as Blackpool and Southport; town branches such as Birmingham, Islington, Salford, Newcastle, Gateshead and Northampton; more rural areas, for instance Cheshire, Wilmslow, Ulverston, Dalton, West Cumberland, Suffolk, Norfolk, Sussex and North Wales.[63] Its geographical range, in addition to its contact with women as workers and consumers, allowed the SJC to consider evacuation from the viewpoint of both evacuee and host. Affiliates were asked questions about schooling, hospitals and other facilities in their area. Both organizers of evacuation and schoolteachers were asked their opinions. The resulting report was delivered to the Ministry of Health.

The rise in numbers of older and married women in the workforce was sustained at the close of the war. Recognizing this, the Labour government asked for advice on reinforcing legislation on the closing hours of shops, which had been relaxed. The Home Office was especially concerned with health and safety at work and the hours worked by young people.[64] The SJC 'three-winged' approach was particularly apt in this case, enquiries being made of consumer – Co-operative; shop worker – trades unions; and Labour Party women, plus the Women's Public Health Officer's Association. Three hundred replies were received. The shop workers' union NUDAW suggested amending closing hours from 8.00 p.m. to 6.00 p.m. and opposed Sunday opening, aiming at a

40-hour, five-day week. Evidence was given to the relevant parliamentary committee, the SJC being able to refute authoritatively the need for late hours and insisting on Sunday closing.

Turning to its own field, the SJC noted in 1943 'the widespread desire among women members of the Party to have more women candidates and more women Members of Parliament'. The SJC acknowledged but refuted prejudice within the Party that women attracted less electoral support, claiming that war was doing away with old prejudices and suggesting a list of potential industrial and professional women candidates, the former to be included on both general (B) and trades union (A) listings. The SJC called for training and for propaganda within the party on the necessity for women candidates, including the use of women speakers in national campaigns, plus a special fund earmarked for women candidates' expenses.[65] The Second World War did raise the profile of women MPs; 24 women were returned at the general election of 1945, 21 of them for the Labour Party. Amongst the pre-war faces were Ellen Wilkinson, now a government Minister, Bessie Braddock, Jennie Lee, Clarice McNab Shaw, Barbara Ayrton Gould and Lucy Middleton, third wife of James Middleton. Barbara Castle joined the short list of luminaries.

The large growth of women in trades unions continued, in total, after the war. Despite a dip in the numbers of women in general labour, transport and engineering unions, the figures for 1950 were around three and seven times higher, respectively, than those of 1939, whilst women members of local government unions had nearly doubled in number. The Labour Party was able to capitalize on this to win recruits so that women's wartime experience contributed to the vitality of both the industrial and political wings of the Labour Movement after 1945. Indeed, as had been their traditional practice, women active in the Labour movement were reluctant to distinguish between their trades union, political and consumer membership. For instance Mrs Shaile, chairing the Labour Women's Conference in 1945, said:

> We have the woman wage earner from the Trade Unions, the woman with the basket from the Co-operative Guild and the woman politician from the Women's Section of the Party. These three together are a mighty force and represent the true unity of the Workers' Movement.

Similarly, Dame Anne Louglin told the Labour Party conference (1951): 'when I hear people talk about trade unions and the Labour Party as if

111

Figure 1 Labour Women Members of Parliament, 1945

they were something separate it leaves me a little puzzled because to me the movement is indivisible.'[66]

Women interviewed for Labour Heritage have recorded intense activity from 1945. For instance, Joan Davis, later Labour Group leader of Epping Forest District Council, remembered:

> At the 1945 General Election we started to get really involved in the local Labour Party...when you are fighting your first General Election as a newcomer to politics it is quite exciting.

Joan shortly became, at the age of 22, the youngest and first woman vice-chair of North Kensington Labour Party. Bertha Elliott began her career as a Labour Party agent at this time, appointed from a shortlist of six, the only female candidate.[67] The growing strength of women's Labour Party membership was shown by the steady increase in women's sections that was reported by Mary Sutherland year by year. In 1945, 243 women's sections were formed; by 1947, 473 new women's sections had been formed; two years later the total stood at an unprecedented 1843; in 1950 the total was 2140.[68] This growth was mirrored by an increase in Regional Women's Advisory Councils. Mary Sutherland reported that more women's sections were planned and the importance of women in electioneering was generally acknowledged.

Regional and district women's committees sought to reach the grass roots by an impressive array of educational opportunities.[69] Women assumed engagement in all aspects of the Labour Party programme as the range of subjects raised by women speakers at Labour Party conferences from 1945 to 1951 shows. It cannot be claimed that such speakers were representative of rank and file women, their attendance at the annual conference in itself marking them out as extraordinary; however, it can be seen that these very active women chose not to emphasize gender issues. It is especially interesting that there was only one speech on the issue of a women's department in six years, but 38 on party organization and the manifesto, the highest number of speeches by women. There were three speeches on equal pay but 14 on the economy, prices and profits. The party organization issue was, of course, a catchall and several of the speeches were about women's involvement; nevertheless, it seems clear that women were claiming inclusion across the whole range of the Labour Party programme. Thirty-five speeches were about social welfare; Ellen Wilkinson's position as Minister of Education (until her death in 1947) is, perhaps, reflected in the interest on that subject. International policy was the next largest grouping. The SJC had helped to inaugurate the International Friendship and Freedom fund in 1943, in order to assist women's organizations of Labour and Social Democrat parties, which had been suppressed. It continued to be represented on international bodies when these were recreated.[70] However, the internationals were not as active in the post-war period as they had been in the 1930s.

The SJC claimed two-and-a-half million members at the close of the war. However, despite its continued wartime activity, the growth of women in the workforce, and their heightened political awareness, all of which would have seemed to call for greater SJC activity, the SJC lost some of its status at the close of the war. Problems had arisen over representation on the Women's Voluntary Service (WVS) national committee, which led to complaints from a Conservative WVS member that the Labour Party was privileged. A groundswell of such complaints seems to have ensued. Mary Sutherland was forced to defend the SJC to front-ranking Labour politician Hugh Gaitskell, denying that it promoted party appointments and insisting that it worked rather to determine policy on behalf of, secure representation of and campaign for working women, electing its own officers and advising the Labour Party at the latter's request. This was broadly true, but disingenuous, belying the close links between the SJC and the Labour Party. Further, Mary Sutherland stated that the SJC had no authority to deal with women's organization within the party, despite providing the president of the women's conference.

Trades union women already had their own National Advisory Committee. The energy generated by the women's councils caused Mary Sutherland to propose the creation of a National Labour Women's Advisory Council in 1951. This was originally to meet three times a year, to consider 'questions connected with the organization and work of women in the Party'.[71] In addition to its eponymous role, the National Labour Women's Advisory Council took over education and propaganda work for women and the chairing of the Women's Conference. It was also to give advice where necessary to the SJC. Party secretary Morgan Phillips was of the opinion that the Labour Party had been strengthened by this move. Indeed, women's sections continued to attract members and a network of women's committees and federations at constituency level and regional Women's Conferences developed. To accommodate this growth of women's organizations and the expense they incurred, the National Women's Advisory Council changed the Women's Conference to a biennial event and arranged that constituency women's sections elected the delegates thereto. This was promoted, with some justice, as a more democratic arrangement but in fact marked a decline whereby the Women's Conference became of little importance. The SJC constitution was reviewed in February 1953 and it was renamed the National Joint Council of Working Women's Organizations (NJC). Its independence and its close relationship with the Labour Party were maintained, but it was overshadowed in that relationship, to an extent, by the existence of the National Women's Advisory Council. However, women remained 42 per cent of Labour Party membership from 1951 to 1970 and women's sections and councils continued to attract members.

It is commonly held that women were swiftly manoeuvred, by direct action and by media pressure, out of the workforce and back to the home when the war ended. However, as the trade unions' membership figures above indicate, this was not the case. As conscription ended, many younger women did indeed leave employment; but the older, married women workers, often on part-time contracts, were valued and were encouraged to remain working. Women were quick to spot any attempt to exclude them from employment; in 1946 the TUC debated the abolition of female employment in the metal polishing and foundries trades, Florence Hancock of the TUC General Council firmly stating: 'if a job is bad for women it is bad for men also'. That year the Women's Consultative Committee, which had advised on women conscripted to industry and the armed forces was recalled 'to advise the Minister on questions relating to the resettlement of women in civilian life'.[72] Alice Bacon represented women Members of Parliament; Dorothy Elliott, the National Union of General and Municipal Workers; Florence Hancock, the Transport and General Workers' Union; and Mary Sutherland, the Labour Party. There was also a recruitment drive for the Women's Land Army to compensate for the end of female conscription.[73] In 1948 the government campaigned in districts with a shortage of female labour, successfully recruiting 17,000 women directly into employment and gaining 114,187 women volunteers.[74] Anabel Williams-Ellis (author), discussing for the Labour Party 'Is Women's Place in the Home?', gave the opinion that, for the first time ever, the government of the day wanted maximum production and full employment so that there was no need for working men to fear competition from women. She took account of working people's struggle for acceptable working conditions, an understandable motive for caution about women's labour force participation, and noted fears that women would become 'hardened, coarsened and de-feminised and therefore unattractive if they work outside their home'.[75]

A notable characteristic of a part-time Labour force is that it is under-paid. Having spent so much effort promoting the image of women as worker the government failed to follow through with measures to make the role attractive. Both the TUC and the LP were officially opposed to bars on married women's employment and the government removed the bar for its own employees. However, no action was taken on the marriage bar outside the civil service. The 100 per cent grant to local authorities for nursery provision was replaced by a block grant for welfare services, which the TUC estimated would mean halving the nursery grant. Women repeatedly asked for day nurseries and nursery schools; seven motions were forwarded for the 1946 Labour Women's Conference; four, including one from the Socialist Medical Association in 1947. However, at Labour Women's Conference there was less support each year as women delegates expressed solidarity with a Labour government facing economic crisis.[76] The 1946 motion was carried unanimously; the 1947 motion lost; a composite including demands for part-time work, meal centres and placing food orders was not discussed in 1948 because of a procedural device, moving 'the previous question'.

In the equal pay campaign, the Clerical and Administrative Workers' Union, which had grown so fast during the war, was to the forefront. Resolutions on equal pay were put to the Women's Conference every year until 1949. The government refused both legislation and action in the civil service, whilst accepting the principle. The women's leadership again chose not to embarrass the government; SJC representatives, who had given evidence to the Royal Commission of Equal Pay (1944–1946), succumbed to pressure in 1948, recognizing the government's economic difficulties.[77] On this issue there was a rebellion at the Women's Conference but the majority decided on party first. At the TUC women's persistence was better rewarded. The TUC had regularly supported equal pay resolutions, although some women trade unionists were sceptical about the extent of TUC commitment.[78] In 1947, the 'weak and unconvincing attitude' of the General Council was protested and the blame laid 'not so much on their sex as their antiquity'; in 1950, when there had still been no action, the General Council plea 'to withdraw your legitimate claim in the national interest' was overturned by Congress. The following year the General Council itself lost patience with the government's latest argument, that equal pay ought to be evaluated in relation to social services, reiterating that equal pay was a wage claim demanding immediate action.[79]

On the only occasion when the equal pay demand was pushed to a card vote at the Labour Party conference and won (2,310,000 for; 598,000 against) the leadership had already entered the caveat: 'it will…continue to be the function of government to plan legislation in the circumstances as they find them.'[80] The SJC commissioners had found that where piece rates were paid without gender bias, there was little difference in men's and women's earnings. The problem was demarcation of jobs by gender. In addition, as Amabel Williams Ellis wrote, 'wage rates…have largely been determined by the relative strength of the contesting parties in the process of collective bargaining.'[81]

The change in the nature of women's participation in the labour force, caused by the war, inevitably changed women's involvement in the Labour movement. Women's presence in the traditionally male preserve of heavy industry, women working alongside men, and the growth in numbers of the clerical and administrative unions made an impact on the masculine image of the trades unions. The growth of women's sections, regional councils and finally the National Women's Advisory Council similarly altered the image of the Labour Party. Half of its membership was female and these women were responsible for their own organization. The SJC was affected as it lost its advisory role to the Labour Party and its management of the Women's Conference. However, the Chief Labour Party Woman's Officer and the SJC/NJC secretary remained the same person, so the diminution in the SJC's role should not be overstated. During the war, it had confirmed its ability to contact a wide range of women, both geographically and professionally, as housewives and consumers, and had continued to give evidence to government. Its record was good.

However, there were signs that gains in women's Labour movement presence were relatively fragile. As part-time workers, many women remained low paid; nursery provision diminished, affecting women's ability to work; and the campaign for equal pay was shelved in the face of the government's economic difficulties. The Women's Conference became a biennial event. During the war, it had been seen that Labour Ministers' perception of women as workers was opportunistic; women were called up when needed and discharged when surplus to requirements; this attitude to women workers came to be called that of a 'reserve army of labour'. There was need to guard against a similar perception of women as Labour movement reserves; and it was women who needed to mount the guard, to struggle for their place in the Labour movement and labour market; their conditions of work and of domestic life, none of which had fundamentally changed.

Part III

The Second Wave: The National Joint Committee

From the 1960s, women in the Labour Party continued their traditional campaigns on behalf of working people, bringing to their arguments a new emphasis on the need to fundamentally change attitudes about women's place in social, political and economic life. They were both influential in bringing issues to the fore and themselves influenced by what came to be called 'second wave' feminism. The term second wave (a phenomenon following the first, suffrage-centred wave) illustrates the opinion, once commonly held, that the appearance of a sizeable feminist movement at this time was a sudden development. It is now more generally accepted that the continuity of feminism was underrated and that the second wave feminist movement was a natural and relatively gradual development from currents of feminist thought throughout the 1950s and 1960s. Of course, the SJC, now renamed the National Joint Committee of Working Women's Organizations (NJC), was never isolated from these social trends, and as has been shown: 'By the late 1970s, most of the demands adopted by the inaugural women's liberation movement conference meeting at Oxford in 1970... had found their way into Labour's policy discussions'.[1]

We may now go further, thanks to Hilda Smith's papers, and view this period as one when goals were won by Labour women, when their achievements were possible because it was relatively easy to lobby: the sixties and seventies were distinguished by the presence of Labour Governments or strong Labour oppositions which had the expectation of office. Thus the campaign for equal pay continued through Labour and Conservative governments and legislation was finally introduced by the Wilson government, despite having been banned from discussion for the previous three years at the Labour Party conference, under a rule that forbade reintroduction of defeated policy resolutions. The

Equal Pay Act was passed in 1970 and its provisions took effect in 1975. The introduction of Employment Protection (1975) and Sex Discrimination (1975) legislation by the 1974–1976 Wilson government completed statutory protection for women. At first, when tribunals operated with minimal intervention by the legal profession and before case law accumulated at the Employment Appeals Tribunal, these acts were successful in challenging decades of discrimination.[2] In addition, the Health and Safety at Work Act, then introduced, reinterpreted the longstanding protection debate by making safety everyone's responsibility, employer, employee and the wider community. Trades union organizing positions had tended to be held by workers with some longevity of service and seniority, whose ad hoc absences on trades union work were, to some extent, condoned by their managers. As these Acts called for greater trades union activity, whilst providing time-off for trades union and safety work, their effect was to open up trades union organizing positions to a broader band of workers, including women. Finally, in 1967 the Abortion Act was passed, following a private member's bill.

The second-wave feminist movement that began to coalesce in the 1960s owed much to its grass roots and was marked by suspicion of hierarchy and leadership. Theory and action were strongly allied. The theory of sisterhood, women prioritizing and acting together with other women, and thus the creation of a discernible women's movement, distinguished second-wave feminism. The approach to sisterhood was to engage in consciousness-raising, whereby small groups of women would jointly discover and reflect on disadvantage hidden by its acceptance as the norm within a male-dominated society. In a sense, second wave feminism was the inevitable outcome of the discovery that enfranchisement had done little to change women's lives. On the one hand, women remained underrepresented politically, in central and local governments and on the other their disadvantaged status in society and the family continued. Equal pay remained a goal rather than a reality, so that, even when legislation took effect, financial autonomy was impossible for many women. The separate sphere ideology, if modified, remained extant as women continued to bear the burden of domestic and child-care duties. The public sphere remained not only male-dominated, but was an arena in which women's domestic subordination was not challenged. The catch phrase of the second wave became 'the personal is political', a statement both of this political failing to address women's position and the importance of domestic and sexual equality.

One group of traditional issues addressed was the demand for equal access to education and employment, extended to include equal pay and conditions of work. A second group made a greater, and now explicit, challenge to social and sexual gender identities: equal child-care and familial roles for men and women, women's right to choose abortion and contraception. Lesbian feminists insisted on the recognition of sexual orientation as a major determining factor of experience and understanding. Meeting the challenge of lesbian feminism included retheorizing heterosexuality, so that sexuality became one of the major issues for later second wave feminism. A sustained critique was made of traditional perceptions of sexuality that had differentiated male and female sexuality, extending stereotypical male and female gender roles into sexual behaviour. Third, a women's peace movement developed, particularly around the US Greenham Common cruise missile site in Britain. This protest, huge for over a decade, international and with women living at the base, at its height made Greenham synonymous with feminism in Britain. Fourth, feminists demanded a woman-centred education so that, starting with community classes, Women's Studies gradually became established in universities. A robust exploration of feminist theory developed. Second wave feminism provided much of the vocabulary for the understanding of gender issues, for contemporaries, in order to look back at the past, and for the progression of theory in the third wave. 'Feminists/ism' entered the common political vocabulary and the term 'gender', was used by feminists to distinguish the social construction of womanhood from a female's biological sex. Major second-wave theorists included those drawn from both French and American traditions of feminist thought, but second wave feminist ideology was partly a joint discovery made by women. It thus owed little to male theorists, so that for some second wave theorists a male feminist was an impossibility.

Alliances were however, as always, made with other mixed male and female groups and schools of thought, which contributed to feminist thinking. Recognizing these alliances, feminists were described as liberal, radical and separatist, Marxist and socialist. Liberal feminists carried on the tradition of seeking an end to discrimination against women in education and employment. Radical and separatist feminists opposed alliances with mixed (male and female) groups, insisting on women's need to find their own solutions to oppression, separatist feminists believing that, in order to do this, women must live apart from men. A lesbian lifestyle was advocated, not necessarily a sexual, but a woman-centred experience. The difference between men and women as social, psychic and sexual beings was emphasized and women's characteristics valued, so that the label 'gynocentric' was sometimes applied to radical feminism. Marxist feminists, engaged with left politics in uneasy alliance, challenged not only male preponderance in and control of political action but male understanding of Marxist theory. The role of the female in nurturing the male worker while herself undertaking menial and low-paid jobs was asserted as an amendment to the Marxist understanding of capitalism. Socialist feminists followed much the same line while questioning the centrality of Marxism to either the left political or socialist project, seeking rather to add gender to the gradual approach to a transformation of society. *Beyond the Fragment: Feminism and the Making of Socialism* was a good example.[3] The sisterhood that characterized second wave feminism co-existed with occasional alliances made with Labour movements as it drew on similar ideas of the need for collective action and joint consciousness of disadvantage.

These labels were a product of the belated recognition, indicated above, of feminism as a substantial political ideology and movement. They should be treated with caution as an attempt to categorize feminism and incorporate it within contemporary political philosophy, rather than as terms that were adequate to describe the totality of feminist thinking or activity; it was rarely that one woman remained committed to one grouping over time. However, second wave feminists did use these terms for self-description and although the labels came to be jettisoned as misleading, they were powerful influences.

The year 1979 marked one of the great changes in British politics: the start of Margaret Thatcher's premierships and of two decades of Conservative government. The NJC could no longer operate in its original style, when it relied on the parliamentary lobby and links with a Labour Party that, if not in government, formed a government-in-waiting in opposition. The Labour Party moved to the left and was more open to ideas from other oppositional groups, including feminists. Feminists were equally open to the chance of pursuing political goals through alliance with the Labour Party. It is generally accepted that there were two main periods of feminist/Labour Party interaction, 1979–1983 and 1983 onwards (the watershed being the loss of a second election to Margaret Thatcher).[4] In local authorities that remained under Labour control, notably the Greater London Council, measures such as equal opportunity programmes were initiated, the fruit of such alliances. The NJC, deprived of its former and reasonably successful method of operating, turned to new alliances, and its members began to call themselves feminist, discarding their former reluctance to accept this label.

Feminism, however, was developing. Political expressions of feminism had in common that they posited women as a group, disadvantaged and subordinated by men as a group. The base of such theory began to be perceived as inadequate, because it failed to comprehend and account for the differences between women. As ancient philosophers had described an 'essence' of mankind, so feminism had conjured up an 'essence' of womankind. Dismantling this theory in favour of celebrating women's difference from each other was thus called 'anti-essentialism' and encouraged an understanding of how factors of class, race, age, location, disablity and sexuality impacted on women's lives. NJC women, of course, together with their forebears in the SJC and Women's Labour League, had a good understanding of class difference. They were also aware of the difference caused by location; Lisbeth Simm's pre First World War account of the mining villages, reports of distress in South Wales in the 1920s and studying the impact of evacuation in World War Two were all examples. Also noted had been the effects of age on women's participation in the labour market. However, the effects of race, sexuality and disability had been less appreciated.

One problem of anti-essentialism was that it problematized sisterhood as a basis for feminist consciousness: some feminists, therefore, regarded an emphasis on difference as a betrayal of women's new-found collective strength. In practice, two of the biggest collective women's campaigns developed in these years, that on abortion and the anti-nuclear protest at Greenham Common. Neither campaign was free of controversy and at Greenham Common the separate sites, for example for lesbian feminists and for Christian feminists, gave physical representation to the recognition of difference. Meanwhile, on 13 July 1979 John Corrie's Private Member's Bill to amend the 1967 Abortion Act had its second reading. The purpose of the amendment was to restrict the grounds on which abortion could be granted and to reduce the time limit from week 28 to week 20 of pregnancy. It was on this issue above all that second wave feminism mobilized, women of different politics and lifestyles combining behind the National Abortion Campaign in a way that had not happened since the days of the suffrage movement. Debate around the issues of essentialism reached their zenith in the third wave of feminism, which flourished in the 1990s and is examined in the conclusion.

10. The National Joint Committee from the 1960s

In the 1960s women accounted for nearly half the Labour Party membership.[5] The extensive network of women's local and regional committees that had grown up in war, and the National Labour Women's Advisory Council remained extant. The Labour Party women's officer continued to head both the NJC and the NLWAC; this was Mary Sutherland until her retirement in 1960. Sara Barker replaced her, followed by Constance Kay and then Betty Lockwood, who went on to become first head of the Equal Opportunities Committee. Joyce Gould took over in 1977. The NJC continued to represent women in the trades union, Co-operative and constituency party wings of the Labour Party. In its own words in an article submitted for *Women in Council* (1967) '(the NJC) has continued to carry out work on social questions and improving the lot of women at work'.[6] The article specified the giving of evidence to 'numerous' Royal Commissions and government committees, suggestions of women's names for the Consumer Consultative Committee, carrying out enquiries into aspects of social services, submission of memoranda and the sending of deputations to Ministers and government departments. This section considers the some of this work, concentrating particularly on the related campaigns for women's education, training and employment. The first NJC acknowledgement of what it dubbed 'Women's Lib' is recounted, and the first meeting with Margaret Thatcher.

In contrast to the Chief Woman's Officer/SJC secretary's involvement with changes in women's organization within the Party during the war years, the NJC leadership at this stage took no direct part in the contemporary debate about change in women's organization. While some women were content with the structure of women's representation within the Labour Party, others expressed disquiet. The chief concern was the role of the Labour Women's conference, its confinement to a four-day agenda and its restriction to 'women's issues', usually those relating to home and children. In addition, the five reserved seats for women on Labour's national committee were protested, the demand being reiterated that this number should be increased and that voting for these women should be confined to women delegates. It may be that the NJC leadership, satisfied with the numerical strength of women's Party membership, did not choose to engage in this debate; or that the changing secretaries did not have the powerful voice that Mary Sutherland's long service had given her.

The NJC's contribution to raising women's profile in public life was to continue to press for women's representation on public bodies and to identify women as workers. For example, in 1965 three names were submitted for Regional Health Boards, both directly to the Minister of Health as part of panel suggested by Women's Groups in Public Welfare. A list of names for Hospital Management committees was also provided.[7] In the same year, an NJC nominee was accepted for the Post Office Users' Council and the NJC notified the Postmaster General of its desire to be represented on the forthcoming nominating body for the Viewers' and Listeners' Council.[8] In the growing number of campaigns initiated and supported by the NJC in this period, the awakening feminism of its membership was illustrated. For instance, the twentieth session of the UN commission on the status of women was held on 2 March 1967 and adopted a new draft declaration on the elimination of discrimination against women.[9] The text, to the effect that discrimination was fundamentally unjust and constituted an offence against human dignity, was discussed by the NJC at meetings of women's organizations in London.

The NJC continued to use its traditional method of research, using all three wings, the trades unions, Co-operative and Labour Party affiliates. A good example was the handling of the prices and incomes issue in 1965.[10] First a women's conference was held (14 October) at which George Brown, then Secretary of State for Economic Affairs, spoke. This was followed by a sample survey conducted by Labour Women's Sections visiting one hundred houses from different income groups in each constituency, covering 14,265 households across the country. In addition, trades unions with women workers were asked to give views and English and Scots Co-operative societies made enquiries of shoppers in Co-operative stores. The resulting findings, reported to George Brown, were that merely 395 households preferred the 'giveaway gimmicks', the large majority favouring improvement in quality or price reduction: 'housewives prefer price to be related to quality and weight'. Also in 1965 evidence was given to the Commission on public schools, which inquired into the best way to integrate public schools and the state school system.[11] The NJC received 1076 replies to a questionnaire submitted to Co-operative Guild branches, Labour Party women's sections and the TUC and gave its opinion that there should be a single state system for pupils aged from 11 to 16, that direct grants should be stopped and independent schools transferred to local authority control. Boarding schools should be available for all children who need them and there should be equal opportunities for boys and girls.

The major way of influencing policy, however, continued to be lobbying parliament. Following recommendation by the International Labour Office, the NJC lobbied the Minister of Labour for improvements in childcare for working mothers.[12] It also sent a deputation to the Minister of Housing and Local Government, asking that he raise with local authorities the provision of indoor and outdoor play spaces in future housing plans. On 6 May 1965 Shirley Williams MP spoke on the financing and purpose of nursery accommodation and pre-school playgroups in an Adjournment Debate of the House of Commons. The NJC also lobbied for inspections and a code of standards for nurseries, grants by local authorities in order to provide some free places, and provision for children in high-rise flats and council estates. Echoing its submission at the close of World War Two, the NJC gave evidence in 1965 to the Home Office committee on retail trading hours.[13]

During the 1960s there was much debate about the revision of social services, where the responsibility for provision lay and how the services should be organized. This in turn led to consideration of familial and gender roles, and of childhood and the need to protect children. The NJC took part in this debate. It provided information in 1966 for the White Paper on the Child, the Family and the Young Offender,[14] and gave evidence to the Seebohm committee on Local Authority and Allied Social Services.[15] Here, the NJC's opinion was that it was not so much new legislation but more imaginative and ambitious use of existing powers that was needed. The NJC was in favour of encouraging voluntary service and agreed with Seebohm in wanting coordination at local and national level, believing that social services departments were too watertight. At that time the separation of children's, mental health and welfare departments meant that one family could receive visits from several social workers. The NJC suggested a local authority coordinating committee and housing all social services in one local building. Its demands included domiciliary care for the elderly, play areas for children and recruitment and training of married women on higher pay and with better working conditions. Finally, its opinion was that social service duties should be mandatory, not permissive. The NJC was ahead of its time in some of the 1970 evidence it gave to the Finer Committee on One Parent families.[16] The NJC reiterated its particular interest in working women; the problem facing the committee could, in its view, be handled by better provision for all working mothers, so that the child of a lone parent was not differentiated. The NJC thus asked for support services for mothers, to whom work gave not just money but also social contact; there should be nursery provision, including workplace nurseries for all working mothers. A fuller use of school premises should be made and emergency peripatetic care should be available to cover sickness. These goals would be assisted, in the NJC's opinion, by a greater availability of part-time work that was skilled and carried promotion prospects. Family Allowance should be available for the first child in a family. There should be supplementary benefits for working single mothers and maternity benefits for all mothers, whatever their national insurance position. Maintenance should be paid by the state, which would collect from the absent parent. Sex education should be available in schools, family planning should be free and there should be a school counselling service.

Another major issue of the time was revision of health services, including the question of private provision. In 1970 the NJC submitted evidence on the government green paper on the future of the National Health Service (NHS), to the effect that health should be the responsibility of democratically elected local government agencies.[17] Should the government be adamant on local authority reorganization, it should create broadly based new Health Authorities. These should reflect the pro-rata strength of local political parties; the danger was that should the new health authorities be composed of one-third local authority, one-third professionals and a final third nominated by the Secretary of State, the local authority third would consist merely of its ruling party. The Secretary of State's third should include trades unions and women's groups. District committees should also be broad based and have executive and financial powers. In the NJC view, it was a mistake that the green paper did not include the Occupational Health Service; this, with a bias to preventive medicine, should be an integral part of the NHS. Health centres should be comprehensive, including not merely general practitioners but dentists and opticians. On finance, the NJC submitted that a greater percentage of national wealth should be devoted to the NHS; the NJC was opposed to hotel charges, fees and means tested benefits: 'A centrally financed NHS is the only way to achieve an even distribution of resources between regions and different client groups, and this should be achieved by direct taxation'.[18] Local authorities should sponsor Co-operatives to dispense drugs. Overall, the emphasis should be on preventive medicine.

In a comprehensive 1977 document recording its proposed evidence on health care for women for submission to the Royal Commission on the NHS[19], the NJC reiterated its demand for a preventive health care policy: '...aimed at a drastic reduction in the dependence of the community on doctors and hospitals and on drugs and alcohol'. It called for greater NHS awareness of the growing economic role of women in families. Focusing on the operation of social and economic factors on poor health, the NJC asked for greater resources to be devoted to deprived areas. The NJC maintained that the NHS should be financed from tax and be free at the point of use, and that private insurance could not meet health needs: 'There is a real danger that those who pay the largest premiums will determine where services are located and the future pattern of the development of the health service'. Ahead of its time, the NJC document called for the abolishment of cigarette machines and advertising, aiming for an end to smoking in 10–15 years. The NJC proposed that patients be involved in running the health service and reiterated the need for cooperation between the various services at local level. Among other measures, the document opposed over prescription of tranquillizers for women, arguing that their disadvantage in the labour market affected women's judgement about themselves and their capacities, while at home they were expected to subordinate themselves to husband and children. It supported the Women's National Cancer Control Campaign, asking for breast and cervical cancer screening; at that time merely three out of ten women benefited from cervical cancer screening which, in the NJC's opinion, was useful for discovering and allowing the treatment of minor gynaecological conditions. The NJC also demanded health education aimed at young families and children in school. The NJC called for more effective sex education in schools and a better family planning service, noting there were about 100,000 abortions per year in Britain. Ten years after the passage of the 1967 Abortion Act, the NJC found that its implementation was patchy and demanded that general practitioners who remained opposed to giving advice should be obliged to refer the patient to an alternative doctor. The NJC asked for more home births, stating that hospital births were disruptive of family life. In 1979, some of these views were repeated when Alf Morris, Parliamentary Under Secretary of State, Department of Health and Social Security, addressed the NJC on the Chronically Sick and Disabled Persons Act; concern was expressed about mobility allowances.[20]

The NJC was able to pull together many of the threads of its campaigns when, in 1974, it gave comments on the Labour government white paper on equality for women. This was warmly welcomed and included many NJC recommendations. The NJC wanted legislation as soon as possible, believing it important that the Equal Opportunities Act (which was to become the Sex Discrimination Act) should come into operation at the same time as the 1970 Equal Pay Act.

The NJC's opinion was that gender-biased attitudes were formed in the pre-school period, partly by children's books and asked the minister to speak to publishers: 'The committee has always held the view that entrenched attitudes are not only amongst the most pernicious obstacles to achieving equality but will be the most difficult to eradicate'.[21]

Heralding what was to become Women's Studies, the NJC advised that Liberal Studies should include work on the status of women and girls. Attention should be paid by policy makers to nomenclature, so that rather than 'marriage', 'marital status' should be cited, thus encompassing widow and divorcees. On the one hand, there might be need of positive discrimination to improve women's status, but on the other there should be no exemptions to the act, the burden of proof of the necessity for any exemption lying on the employer. Other recommendations included automatic joint tenancy or ownership of the marital home, making known the government's views on taxation and operation of the existing legislation to improve pensions. The proposed Equal Opportunities Commission (EOC) should be well funded.

When the EOC had been created, the NJC commented on its various reports. In 1977, the NJC commented on the EOC report in favour of quota representation, which in the NJC opinion was not in the long-term interest of women.[22] The Sex Discrimination Act barred quotas except for trades unions and political parties. The NJC was not sure whether to support EOC in this, foreseeing difficulties in some trades and where incentive bonus schemes operated. It also queried whether quotas should apply to women only or whether minorities should also be covered. In 1977 the NJC again reiterated to the EOC its long-held position in favour of protective legislation.[23] The appropriate government minister was informed that the NJC favoured different hours of work for women and young people; the NJC maintained that six consecutive hours of work alleviated merely by ten-minute intervals was too long for anyone. Equal pay should be achieved before protection was removed. The NJC showed awareness of the feminist position that protective legislation was based on a perception of women as second class citizens who, while the essential component of family life, were cheap labour, but pointed out that the regulations currently applied merely to a minority of women. As the domestic and child rearing functions were being extended to men, so should protection be extended to all workers if its function were to preserve family life. On grounds of physical capacity protection should also be extended to men, whose strength diminished as they aged. In 1978 the NJC discussed the EOC document on retirement ages and reiterated that all workers should all retire at 60 years of age, with an increase in pensions to the national average wage.[24] The NJC was of the opinion that there should be priority retirement before the age of 60 in hazardous industries and a system of gradual retirement, reducing days worked per week, for everyone. In 1978 the NJC reviewed criminal, civil, industrial and welfare law, and women in judiciary.[25] Renee Short MP was asked to put question in the House of Commons on young girls in prison. The NJC asked the Home Office for statistics on sexual offences, which had been reported as decreasing, and for further information on the facilities for young children in prison.

On the related issues of education, training and employment, the NJC showed itself alive to the feminist issues of the day while pursing its longstanding campaigns around health and safety at work. Without education and training, women could not pursue careers, which would make them financially independent. Thus they might fall into poverty, from which arose many of the evils of women's poor health; they might be dependent on their husbands, reinforcing the ideology of women's domesticity, casting them in the role of childcarer and house cleaner, unfulfilled and outside of public life. Paid work was the key to improvement in the condition of women and the NJC had always represented working women. Unequal education started at school, with a different curriculum and different exam results and continued into workplace training. In 1971 the NJC prepared its notes for a campaign for equal opportunities to compliment the 1970 Equal Pay Act.[26] The basis for the campaign was first stated. Unemployment was then, in the NJC's view, worse than at any time since the Second World War. Despite the fact that men formed the majority of the population below 40 years old and would need to be able to run their own home, traditional attitudes to women and their role in the workplace were being reasserted:

> ... the continuance of some of the traditional attitudes to women's place in the home has led to an almost impossible load being placed on women, and has acted as a deterrent or barrier to them reaching top positions in any significant number.

All sorts of institutional arrangements fostered such attitudes. In education, for instance, mathematics and science provision for girls was poor while few boys studied 'aesthetic subjects', and home management subjects in boys' schools were almost non-existent. The Department of Education and Science made no provision for domestic science laboratories in boys' schools and recommended LESS laboratory space be provided in girls' and coeducational schools.

The campaign itself was launched at a press conference on 18 January 1972 with supporting documentation published on 21 January 1972.[27] It received radio and television coverage in addition to the national and local press; *Woman's Own*, a magazine then widely distributed, ran a feature; trade union journals also provided coverage. This put the NJC on the map for consultation by journalists and television researchers. The NJC was invited to submit evidence to the Expenditure Committee of the House of Commons and the House of Lords select committee on the Anti-Discrimination Bill. The Labour Party published a green paper *Discrimination against Women* (see above for NJC response to the eventual white paper) and the TUC had held a women's conference on 'Roots of Equality'. Two thousand copies were sent to affiliates. In Scotland, a joint trades union/Labour Party/Co-operative committee began its own campaign. The NJC was encouraged by the response also from education authorities, 11 of whom expressed interest, while six requested notes and others asked to be kept in touch; the Educational Institute of Scotland considered the documentation; copies were requested by 250 Colleges of Education and the National Union of Students published a report. The NJC was Invited to take part in YWCA courses and to meet the London and Home Counties Regional Advisory Council for Technological Education.

All national women's organizations had been provided with documentation and some featured the campaign in their own journals. The National Association of Women's Clubs contacted the NJC to enquire about the campaign. However, while making these approaches, the NJC was conscious that it had its own style of operation and expressed a sense of difference to the wider feminist movement, which it referred to as 'Women's Lib':

> Moreover, our campaign has given a different and more readily comprehensible aspect of the campaign from the one portrayed by 'Women's Lib'... Accepting that women's status is not a new issue as one might gather from the emergence of 'Women's Lib' but a deeply rooted product of western civilization the committee has contended that the subject must be dealt with through the established democratic process of the country.

With some justice, given the campaign's wide coverage, the NJC claimed the success of its own brand of campaigning; however, it was the media's interest in 'Woman's Lib' that made its campaign newsworthy.

The campaign continued the following year when the NJC's report was widely distributed, 8000 copies being printed, and was quoted on the BBC.[28] The Secretary of the NJC and Labour Party women's officer was then Betty Lockwood. Much of the information came from trades union officers, the most prominent of whom was Ethel Chipchase. The NJC encountered its first real obstacle in the reply from Margaret Thatcher, then Secretary of State for Education and Science.[29] This presaged her 1979 government in that it adopted a laissez-faire attitude and insensitivity to women's demands. Margaret Thatcher maintained that the education service should reflect, not lead society; that it could be innovatory only in so far as it anticipated obvious change: 'the place of women in society is a matter determined by the views of that society as a whole'. Thatcher stated that responsibility for the curricula rested with local authorities and the managers and governors of voluntary aided schools. As a democratic safeguard, state interference should be avoided; an independent body, the Schools Council for Curriculum and Examination, developed the curriculum; local attitudes were significant in education; 'You are well aware that there are some very marked differences in attitudes towards the aspirations of women'. She attached O and A level tables, showing that more girls were taking these examinations and more were taking science subjects. On school buildings, the 'Building Bulletins' issued by the government were merely advisory, although Thatcher agreed that the minimum size playing fields did differ for boys and girls: 'I can assure you that an application from an authority which included provision for girls to play football would receive sympathetic consideration from my department.' The NJC rejected Mrs Thatcher's comments: 'In her first reply she seemed to abdicate responsibility'.[30] A reply was also received from Mr C.A. Larsen of Central Training Council, in which he stated that the clerical training board would not be reinstated as the NJC had hoped.[31] His opinion was that existing boards should collaborate, pointing out that 50 Colleges of Further Education ran clerical courses providing basic skills; he advised waiting until the Secretary of State had finished her review.

The NJC continued its campaign by demanding a variety of related measures.[32] These included pressing for full time careers teachers in all secondary schools, a reexamination of training for careers teachers and compulsory block or day release. Parliamentary questions were asked about these goals. The Department of Employment responses, however, were equally unsatisfactory and the NJC continued to push for publication of separate figures on women trained under Industrial Training Boards and for more data generally. The Department of Health and Social Security was asked to review child-care facilities and provision made for working mothers. The NJC gave evidence to the House of

Commons expenditure committee on 5 July 1972 and the House of Lords Select Committee on 14 November 1972, asking for an interim order requiring partial implementation of equal pay by December 1973. The Labour Shadow Cabinet and Parliamentary Labour Party gave general approval and an MP was designated to follow up with parliamentary questions. In the NJC's opinion, its campaign had been a considerable success, a contribution to changing attitudes, and it was decided to continue enlisting support from other women's organizations. At local level, affiliated bodies should carry on and enlist support.

In 1972 the NJC was invited to the House of Commons expenditure committee, expenditure and Social Services sub-committee, to submit evidence on training and employment of women and facilities for working mothers.[33] It was decided the NJC would include a reminder of the comparative educational qualifications for boys and girls, which resulted in girls being concentrated into certain categories of job: 'Industries in which women predominate are those where there is little training, i.e. distribution, clerical etc.' The NJC spoke of the need for reflection on the training needs of girls and women, especially as the government's consultative document 'Training for the future' made no mention of this. The NJC also protested the removal of the levy/grant system which encouraged backward industries to train employees, plus the abolition of industrial training boards, especially in hairdressing, commercial services and clerical work: 'the outlook for women looks bleak'. The NJC stressed the need for careers guidance and a reentry guidance service on job opportunities and training for women coming back after a childcare break; this should be seen as a potential for mature women to acquire new skills; training courses should be organized to suit married women, with a chance of part-time skilled work, flexible hours and, of course, childcare. The second phase of the campaign was approved at the biennial meeting of January 1973. This entailed pressure for support services for working mothers:

> The multifarious domestic responsibilities falling on women largely because of their traditional role in the home, requires an extension of supporting services before women can be fully integrated into the workforce.

Childcare was considered the key for working mothers, single mothers and fathers, and fathers with exceptional domestic commitments; it should be continuous, from nursery throughout school life. There should be an extended home help service, sheltered housing, community amenities, libraries, parks, day nurseries, nursery education, an after school service and a school holiday service:

> maternity should not constitute a break in employment, that maternity benefit should be wage related, and that insurance credits should be available at least during a six month's absence.

In 1973, commenting on an employment policy service report on management attitudes and practices towards women at work, the NCJ found its thoughts on underlying prejudice borne out.[34] The person responsible for policy formation and the person responsible for its execution in 230 establishments with more than 100 employees had been interviewed; of these, only 2 per cent of formulators and 11.4 per cent of implementers were women. As far as the formulators and the implementers themselves were concerned it was found that the people on whom the success of anti-discrimination measures would largely depend were predominately men, older on average than working men as a whole and of a higher educational level. Many of them seemed to have inbuilt attitudes towards the roles of the sexes which would, perhaps subconsciously, affect the ways in which they would approach such measures. Only a quarter of formulators and a third of implementers were in favour of equal pay, having more women in senior positions and more training for women. Yet for senior positions, previous experience and training were thought very important.

In the same year, the NJC made recommendations to the House of Commons expenditure committee.[35] This considered the fourth report on youth employment services, the sixth report on employment of women and the seventh report on employment services and training. The NJC repeated much of its previous evidence plus new advice on youth training, which it believed should be mandatory on local authorities, be managed by the introduction of a national service on higher education and employment opportunities, and accompanied by compulsory day release. For women, the NJC recommended commercial apprenticeship in clerical work, the removal of inequality in training grants between men and women, play areas in employment exchanges and that job centres have a specialist officer for matters affecting women. The NJC also demanded a Department of Employment enquiry into homework and evasion of registration, and that the Department of Employment look at the availability of local labour when considering work permits. There should be no licensing if premises were unsuitable or if there was 'improper business conduct'. Finally, redundancy notice should be increased and public relief work, such as that available in Sweden, should be investigated.

The NJC also contributed to the National Campaign for Nursery Education active in 1974.[36] Here the NJC considered that although society accepted the principle of equal opportunity, children under five years old were still thought to be the mother's concern. The NJC maintained that while some mothers wished to give up work, others wanted to work, part-time or full-time, and others had to work: 'we think women should be treated as responsible adults, free to make up their own minds as to what course they follow'. Such freedom of choice implied adequate provision, which was not forthcoming; few local authorities had day nurseries, rich women had nannies, but most women had to rely on child minders, who were badly paid and poorly qualified. There was need of nursery education, with trained teachers, and space and facilities for play. The 1972 white paper had stated that 15 per cent of day nursery places should be full-time; in the NJC's view this was inadequate and moreover, there should be nursery classes attached to schools and workplace nurseries. In 1974, 91 factories provided places for 2626 children, but these were not subject to any controls. Many hospitals and colleges however, did provide nursery places. The problem could be eased if the working day were fitted to school hours, if flexitime were introduced and holidays increased. A mere 12 per cent of three to four year olds were in state nursery schools. Cuts in government expenditure meant that these were closing down. The NJC launched a petition to the House of Commons for legislation to make it a statutory duty on LEAs to provide nursery education in accordance with the needs of parents.

The NJC recommended that, as in its view teachers often had outdated attitudes, the teacher training curriculum should be widened. In the workplace, there was inadequate information about training; the Industrial Training boards (set up in 1964) did not publish separate figures for men and women, although very few women were being trained. Retraining was needed, whether or not women had had time off for childrearing. Both trades unions and employer institutions should adapt to new patterns of work. The mass media could be powerful in establishing new norms, as could women's magazines. For its part, the government should have a positive policy to provide equal educational opportunities, encouraging girls to consider wider job opportunities, and providing more effective reentry training for women. Government should aim at improving part-time employment for women and men with domestic responsibilities. There should be compulsory day release for all workers under 18 years of age. Nursery education should be extended. Local authorities should take into account the effect of school buildings on the curriculum. The NJC had protested to the government about discontinuing the Hairdressers and Allied Services Industrial Training Board and asked that the Clerical and Commercial Training Committee be reconstituted.

The NJC decided to send this campaign document to the government and the opposition, and to release it to the press. Affiliated bodies were asked to publicise it through meetings and letters to press, and to approach their MPs. In 1974, Margaret Thatcher received a deputation from the NJC.[37] The delegates claimed that the statistics showed little improvement to girls' disadvantaged position in education. Results at O and A levels were becoming closer but girls were still not taking mathematics and science subjects and fewer went on to higher education: 7.5 per cent of boys going on to university but only 4.6 per cent of girls; 1.3 per cent of boys went on to Colleges of Education but 5.2 per cent of girls. The NJC reiterated its demands for a reexamination of the curriculum, which had been promised in Margaret Thatcher's green paper on equal opportunities but had not been carried out, and for training for adult women. Again, the point was made that education should lead, not just reflect current attitudes, to prepare students for the future, not the past. There was also a demand whose wording indicated a closer alliance with the wider feminist movement: 'Women's Studies should be developed throughout the curricula in all subjects and at all levels'. The NJC asked that the Department of Education finance research in women's studies to assist universities, colleges of education and polytechnics, using International Women's Year to focus attention. Whether the NJC meant women's education in general or, less likely, Women's Studies as it developed as a separate academic discipline, is not clear, but the terminology is interesting.

In 1975 the NJC set out its case on 'The Interrelationship of Education and Employment Opportunities', pointing out that there had been little improvement in girls' career prospects since their 1972 campaign.[38] Different curricula still pertained for boys and girls, careers guidance had not improved and girls continued to drop out of higher education. While boys received technical and professional training with day release, girls were still in lower level courses in further education. The effect of the expectation of marriage and domestic commitments still affected girls' and women's careers. This was reflected in lower levels of pay and poor promotion prospects for the female labour force. Homeworking for very low pay continued. Mature women still suffered from lack of training and difficulties of reentering the labour force after time out for childcare. Support services for childcare and care for elderly people were still inadequate. The NJC ran an open forum at Transport House on the subject, expressing its concern for 'the broad mass of women' who left school at the minimum age, not the 'fortunate few'.[39] A hundred and eighty three women from 72 organizations attended. Ernest Armstrong, the Parliamentary Under Secretary of State for Education and Science was the opening speaker: he remarked on the continuance of traditional assumptions of societal roles, reinforced by the media, but suggested there were grounds for hope in developing curricula in middle schools, whilst the reorganization of colleges of education into the university level offered an opportunity for change. Marie Patterson of the NJC and TUC chair then spoke on the changing pattern of the female labour force, two-thirds of whom were now married as opposed to 10 per cent of the pre-war female labour force. The average woman could now expect a working life of 30 years. However, women were still concentrated in a few industries, although there had been breakthroughs, from bus drivers to bank managers. 1975 was a 'vintage year' with the Equal Pay Act now fully operational, maternity leave a right under the Employment Protection Act and a new pension scheme, but in Mrs Patterson's opinion, legislation on its own was not enough – strong trade union organization was necessary. Contributors from the Tobacco Workers' Union, the Socialist Education Association, NALGO, USDAW and the Women's Gas Federation all repeated the NJC general theme with specific examples from their field of work. For example, half of USDAW members were women but less than three in ten were at management level. Liz Chambers of the Pre-School Playgroup Association pointed out that men could not train to be nursery nurses and that there was no career structure for men in nursery teaching.

Later that year the NJC gave its comments on the HMSO education survey on curricula differences for girls and boys.[40] Their recommendations included appointing more women to headships, updating of teaching materials to reflect changing roles, encouraging mechanical training for girls and reading for boys, monitoring play, mixed classes for all subjects and an end to early specialization which would restrict employment opportunities. At work, day release should apply to both sexes with education credits being given, while further education colleges should provide 'catching up classes' for people who had missed out on some subjects while at school.

This report closed the major area of NCJ activity around the issues of employment and education. They had reached government, trades union, education authorities and women's groups, reflected and promoted changes in women's stereotypical domestic roles and covered the field with their usual depth. Overall, the NJC engaged in competent, detailed work, its conclusions were well founded from use of its own wide resources, consideration of government white papers and contact with other women's organizations. It took note of, and sought to further, the changing role of women, who were working more frequently while men were starting to take a greater part in running the family home. Growing recognition of the NJC's work was shown in 1976 by its meeting with John Tisdall, Deputy Head of Current Affairs at the BBC.[41] The NJC had prepared a discussion paper on women in the media, which claimed that the mass media was influential but male-oriented, trivializing and undervaluing women's contribution to society.[42] Tisdall agreed that the programme output was male dominated and that men produced the majority of programmes, but maintained that producers should reflect the attitude of the BBC so that the gender of producers should not affect the contents. He gave a reason for refusing to take action that was to be reiterated to the NJC, that the role of the organization he represented was not to give a lead or influence public opinion but to provide a focus for ideas. In this context, the importance of the insistence of second wave feminists that each person should reflect on their own attitudes becomes apparent. Tisdall's opinion was that women had equal opportunities at the BBC and that young women reporters were encouraged to seek promotion. He showed little appreciation of the realities of women's lives at the time by maintaining that the timing of programmes was not an issue, as women could delay the Sunday lunch if they really wanted to watch something. In the discussion, the NJC spoke of the differences in attitudes of men and women due to their different life experience. Specifically on 'Any Questions', the NJC complained that there was merely a statutory woman panellist and never a woman chair and that the studio audience should be broader. As a result of this meeting, the NJC decided to request nominating rights to the BBC advisory council.

Whilst still shying away from the feminist label, the NJC had been one spearhead of a feminist attack on outmoded attitudes. Their one real set back, in addressing the changing governments of the day, had been their brush with Margaret Thatcher. This was prophetic of the NJC's difficulties with the governments she lead from 1979, when it seemed that all the ground they had gained needed to be fought for once again.

11. The National Joint Committee in the 1980s

In July 1979, the NJC considered its future role.[43] Brenda Dean, of the Society of Graphical and Allied Trades and one of Britian's first prominent women trade unionists, had joined the committee. Labour women MPs represented were Jo Richardson, Renee Short, Gwynneth Dunwoody and Judith Hart. Patricia Hewitt, then of the National Council for Civil Liberties, also joined the NJC. The committee members reiterated their main goal; to forward the interests of working women and assist in their election to local, national and international groups in which women had a special interest. This main focus never changed and the NJC's 1979 statement echoes that of the Women's Labour League 70 years earlier, prioritizing industrial women on the one hand and seeking their election to decision-making bodies on the other. This section continues the NJC history and shows how it became more aware of the wider feminist movement, contributing to the national abortion and peace campaigns. It recounts how the Labour Party became more open to feminist proposals and how feminists, for their part, became more willing to work with the Labour Party.

The NJC stated its determination to submit the views of working women to government and to keep working women informed of matters concerning them where their combined action was needed. In the NJC's words:

> Whilst a Labour Government was in power the committee had direct access to Government Ministers and was able, with comparative ease and speed, to refer to them issues of immediate importance; a change in government has, however, given the committee the opportunity to examine its future and direction.

The NJC feared in particular a price 'free for all' due to the abolition of the price commission; cuts in public expenditure and the removal from local authorities of health, welfare and transport duties; and the privatization of the National Health Service with greater numbers of 'pay beds'. In the longer term, the NJC wished to review the effect of new technology on women's employment and monitor their training in this field.

As the NJC considered that Conservative government policy would call for immediate, accurate response, it decided to grant its officers more power, including the ability to call emergency general purposes committees. The NJC also wished to set up machinery to maximize its receipt of information. It decided to increase its links with outside bodies, with more public meetings, publication of papers, use of the media and the election of women to public bodies, including parliament and local government. It called for stronger links with its affiliates who, between them, had direct access to huge numbers of women workers, and suggested greater regional organization and closer links with trades unions, Co-operative parties and Labour parties at regional level. Finally, the NJC sought to increase its liaison with Labour MPs.

In making alliances with other bodies, the NJC joined the major feminist campaign of the period, that of opposing restriction of the provisions of the 1967 Act, which had extended the possibility of legal abortion. This resolve was new to the NJC, which had remained largely silent on such issues since the SJC's 1920 sub-committee on birth control. The NJC's 1979 opinion was that the current Bill to amend the 1967 Act was 'undoubtedly the most retrogressive of the many abortion bills that had been presented in the last few years'.[44] It immediately supported the National Abortion Campaign and called on all affiliated organizations to mobilize against the Bill. In October 1979 the NJC supported a Trades Union Congress demonstration against the Bill. Letters were sent to Labour MPs and a joint meeting was organized between these, the Labour Abortion Rights committee, and the National Labour Women's Advisory committee. Ten hours of parliamentary time were devoted to the debate and the Bill was finally talked out, to the NJC's delight. It continued to monitor the situation, in 1982 calling on Labour MPs to protest proposed changes to the forms doctors filled out when considering a patient for abortion.[45] The same year, following campaigning within the trades unions by the anti-abortionist groups Life and SPUC (Society for the Protection of the Unborn Child), the NJC wrote to Labour MPs who had helped sponsor the Life leaflet to point out inaccuracies.[46] The NJC at this time also wrote to the Minister of State, Department, Health and Social Security, unsuccessfully demanding the withdrawal of Playtex tampons, which were said to cause toxic shock.

The NJC also contributed to the peace campaign. Margaret Thatcher's 1982 'arms selling' tour alarmed the NJC and, prophetically, it deplored the Premier's role as 'sales representative for exporting weapons of mass destruction to repressive regimes in politically sensitive areas such as the Gulf'. In its view, Margaret Thatcher should be working for peace and disarmament. The NJC protested increased military spending and was opposed to basing Trident nuclear submarines and US cruise missiles on British territory.[47] Calling for a nuclear-free world, the NJC's opinion was: 'Peace is the essential success, if we fail to achieve it in this Nuclear World there will be nothing left to embrace with a family policy'.[48] This was a revolutionary acceptance of the feminist position on peace for organized, mainstream Labour women. Such open support for these issues were prime examples of the way the NJC was prepared to extend its activities and its alliances with the feminist movement.

A more traditional NJC campaign was that on the National Health Service. Evidence had been given to the Royal Commission, whose 117 findings had been welcomed. However, the Conservative government's response had been not to take action, but to issue a further consultative paper, 'Patients First'. This paper went against everything the NJC had worked towards, in its view suggesting a 'sickness service', not the preventative service that the NJC favoured, and aiming to reduce costs. The NJC evidence to the Department of Health and Social Security started by condemning the 1974 changes in the NHS, initiated by Keith Joseph while he was Health Minister, as reducing democratic control and public accountability.[49] It went on to reiterate its demands for preventive medicine assisted by local links between health services and clear management lines which allowed for employee participation. Further, the NJC protested the growth of private medicine:

> The growth of private medicine coupled with the cut backs in National Health Service funds can only lead to a two-tier health care system, with [sic] those with the money to pay will receive the best treatment from private facilities, whilst the NHS will be restricted to caring for the poor, the needy and the chronically ill – who will be ignored by private practitioners as unprofitable. Such a two-tier system would be the end of the NHS as it was founded, and the NJCWWO expresses its absolute opposition to such a system developing any further.

A few months later, the NJC responded to the government's discussion paper on primary health care.[50] Again, the NJC's concern was that the government was concerned with cutting costs, rather than improving care. It also reiterated the need for preventive medicine and comprehensive local services and urged the government to consider the links the NJC had repeatedly made between poverty, bad housing and ill health, holding that the paper did not recognize cause and effect. Specifically, the NJC attacked the proposition that higher car ownership had reduced the need for GP visits, pointing out that the majority of women still relied on public transport. A concern was expressed, new to the NJC, but reflecting the development of second wave feminism, that there was no reference to the needs of ethnic minority women. Perhaps also reflecting second wave feminist campaigns, the NJC called for breast and cervical cancer screening. It called for smaller GP lists, was opposed to capitation payments and protested the restrictions on pharmacies, which it feared would give rise to 'large impersonal stores'.

Among the measures the NJC concerned itself with were child poverty, where it lobbied the government's Home Policy Committee for an increase in child benefit and formed an alliance with the Child Poverty Action Group; single parent's benefits; cuts in widow's benefits; and working for acceptance of the European Community directive which demanded equal social security rights and payments for men and women. The NJC became a sponsor of the newly formed Maternity Alliance, which aimed to extend maternity grants. It also lobbied Labour MPs to abolish the married man's tax allowance, claiming that Conservative government tax proposals rested on the assumption that women stayed at home. Hilda Smith's own resolution, to an October 1982 NJC meeting, was:

> That this National Joint Committee of Working Women's Organisations is seriously concerned at the threat to the welfare state proposed by this Tory Government which will have a disastrous effect on working women and their families.[51]

In particular, the NJC protested the new method of self-certification of sickness, meeting Brynmor John MP, the opposition spokesman on Health and Social Security to raise their concerns about the lack of uniformity in applying the scheme, the lack of confidentiality, the complicated forms and the obligation to pay if a private sick note was necessary.[52]

The major campaign of the previous decade on women's employment and training, in order that they might compete fairly in the workplace, was continued. In view of the recession: 'it will be necessary to ... accept the slogan ' "a woman's right to work", and to evolve concepts and policies which enshrine this first principle'.[53] The NJC stated the need to define 'work': 'cooking and cleaning is work – here we mean paid employment'. It reiterated that, while women formed 42 per cent of the workforce, they were concentrated in a limited number of service and manufacturing industries, using tables from the *Employment Gazette* to illustrate the point. Over 80 per cent of part-time women workers were in the service sector, and the largest number of part-timers were working wives with dependant children. Women as a whole received 72 per cent of men's wage, a decrease from 73.6 per cent in 1977

Table 2 Employees in Employment, Manufacturing Industry, December 1980 (GB;000s)

Industry	All women	Part-time women	Part-time % of total	Men	Total	Women as % of total
Food, drink, tobacco	255.2	88.3	34.6	386.5	641.6	39.8
Coal, petroleum	4.4	0.5	11.4	33.7	38.1	11.5
Chemicals	112.8	19.7	17.5	297.3	410.1	27.5
Metal manu- facture	39.5	8.5	21.5	315.7	355.2	11.1
Mechanical engineering	121.4	25.1	20.7	677.8	799.2	15.2
Instrumental engineering	46.3	10.2	22.0	85.3	131.7	35.2
Electrical engineering	232.3	40.3	17.3	449.5	681.8	34.1
Shipbuilding	11.4	3.1	27.2	133.5	144.9	7.9
Vehicles	78.7	8.3	1.5	594.5	673.2	11.7
Metal goods	119.1	29.0	24.3	343.2	462.3	25.8
Textiles	166.1	32.0	19.3	194.3	360.5	46.1
Leather	15.0	5.0	33.3	17.8	32.8	45.7
Clothing	236.7	41.9	17.7	75.9	312.6	75.7
Bricks etc.	47.5	8.9	18.7	174.6	222.2	21.4
Timber etc.	45.0	11.0	24.4	183.9	228.8	19.7
Paper	160.3	36.9	23.0	344.6	504.9	31.7
Other	90.9	24.4	26.8	172.7	263.6	34.5
Total	1782.2	393.2	22.1	4480.8	6263.6	28.5

Source: NJC 16/8/81, Women's Employment, citing *Employment Gazette*, April 1981, Table 1.4.

(see Table 2). Applications for equal pay under the act had fallen from 1742 in 1976 to 400 in 1978. By 1980 there had been merely ten applications under the Sex Discrimination Act clause which allowed training boards to demand funds to encourage training of women or men in areas where they were underrepresented in the workforce; women formed 0.2 per cent of craft trainees and 1.8 per cent of technical trainees. The NJC argued strongly for positive discrimination in employment, training and education, to achieve equality. Around 200,000–400,000 homeworkers were employed in Britain. The NJC maintained contact with the National Homeworking Campaign and supported a Private Member's Bill for full protection for homeworkers.[54]

The NJC continued its campaign on women's right to work by launching a pamphlet at a fringe meeting of the 1981 Labour Party Conference.[55] There was concern that the government was planning to deal, by order in parliament, with the European directive which stip-ulated that equal pay should be given to men and women for work of equal value rather than exactly the same work (thereby closing the escape route that a man's work was different if, for instance, although largely the same it required additional heavy lifting). Joan Lestor was collecting responses which all interested groups were urged to make.

On unemployment, the NJC went so far as to quote the feminist magazine *Spare Rib:* '...because, as a woman, it doesn't matter that I am unemployed'.[56] Equal Opportunities Commission figures showed that women had a disproportionate share of unemployment; figures for part-time workers, although collected by the government, were not published: 'the methods of collecting, collating and interpreting the statistics of unemployment are based on a wholly masculine concept'. In such remarks, it had become difficult to distinguish NJC rhetoric from that of mainstream feminism. Similarly, newly aware of ethnic differ-ence, the NJC pointed out that black teenagers were at the very end of the dole queue: a South London study had shown that 70 per cent of black girls had held no job since leaving school, compared to 20 per cent of white girls, 30 per cent of white boys and 40 per cent of black boys. The Labour Party and the TUC, in the NJC's opinion, while countering cut-backs, did not treat women 'in a wholehearted way'. The assumption that childcare and home care were female tasks should be challenged and work patterns changed.

The solution proposed by some feminists, that protective legislation should be removed for women, was rejected by the NJC: 'As women and feminists, we must take the argument forwards, not backwards'. This claiming of the feminist ground was a new step for the NJC. Its deep-ened understanding of racism was highlighted when the NJC protested the proposed changes in nationality rules set out in a white paper of 1979. This would affect women engaged and married to foreign nation-als living abroad. As was shown in Part II, European socialist women had argued in the 1930s that a woman should be free to choose her own, or her husband's nationality on marriage, and if the marriage ended the proposed rules were seen as '...racist as well as sexist in character'; again, new rhetoric for the NJC.[57]

The NJC remained wary of job sharing, its dangers being that it would become yet another way of restricting women to the home, while creating problems with pensions and national insurance cover. It was unlikely that job sharing would be attractive to the majority of work-ing women represented in its affiliates, whose wages were not large. It was also a diversion from the campaigns for proper maternity and paternity leave and grants, and from achieving pre-school and holiday childcare.[58] Moreover, given the opportunity to cut the working week presented by new technology: 'It is…important that such a system as job sharing does not become embedded into the employment structure so as to inhibit the movement to a reduced working week for all'.[59]

Its new public commitment to feminism was illustrated when the NJC held a fringe meeting at the 1980 Labour Party Conference, jointly with the National Labour Women's Advisory Council, on socialism and feminism. Jo Richardson and Audrey Wise were among the speakers.[60] The NJC also took part in a November 1980 Women's Action Day organized by two feminist groups, the Fawcett Society (named after the great suffragist) and Women in the Media. The demands were: that fathers should share in childcare; that all girls should be educated for an independent existence; that women at work should have equal opportunities; that women should be encouraged to participate in public and political life; that discrimination against women in the fields of taxation and social security should be ended; that women should have equal rights before the law; that the understanding of women's special health needs should be encouraged; and that the stereotyping of women in the media should be ended.

While the NJC was thus moving to a position where its members felt more comfortable expressing feminist ideas, feminist activity as a whole within the Labour Party was becoming more controversial, women's sections and conferences witnessing lively debate. The 1984–5 miners' strike brought more feminists into contact with the trades unions and Labour Party and vice-versa, through organizations such as Women Against Pit Closures and through women's groups, party constituency and individual initiatives. The tepid support of the Party leadership for the miners' strike was fiercely challenged. The Women's Action Group was formed to pursue strategic goals including the election of the five women Party national executive committee members by the Women's Conference; the right of that conference to submit five resolutions to the Party conference; and women-only parliamentary candidate shortlists. Some feminists found these goals too limiting, while women traditionalists were opposed to positive discrimination:

Women within the party were not a unified group…older, working class women often perceived the language and style of feminism to be patronising and offensive. Those who identified with the feminist agenda tended to be young, articulate and well-educated. They were often insensitive to the experience of other women in the party and lacked the political skills to appeal to a wider constituency of women.[61]

Other women were active in Militant and proritized class activity. The head-on conflicts between the Women's Action Group and Militant, and their joint impact on the traditionalists made the Women's Conference an anarchic, exciting event. The notorious Isle of Bute conference in 1985 was the culminating point when the fire from several entrenched positions (WAG, Militant, pro-miners, vegetarian, punk, lesbian, anti-trades union discrimination, pro-creation of black groups) was directed at the Party Secretary, Larry (now Lord) Whitty, who was denied a hearing. To indicate her differences with the agenda committee Margaret Beckett (already a prominent MP, who would become deputy leader of the Party and then to hold office under Tony Blair and Gordon Brown) spoke from the floor of the conference, rather than taking the platform position to which she was entitled. At the subsequent Labour Party Conference a ground-breaking resolution was taken to engage in the struggle for gay and lesbian rights, although the issue of black groups was avoided.

Among the new faces on the NJC from 1983 were Margaret Prosser of the Transport and General Workers' Union who, although she was not without sympathy for feminist arguments, might be termed one of the traditionalists, and Anne Wilkinson, one of the founders and the secretary of the Women's Action Group. Among the politicians who attended occasional meetings were Claire Short, now on the Opposition employment team, and Peter Mandelsohn.[62] The NJC continued many long-standing campaigns, including protesting against the poor quality of school meals.[63] Other campaigns, while rooted in the NJC's long-term activities, illustrate both the way the committee sought to react to government policy and the way in which feminist ideas were informing Labour Party activity.

NJC work on the issue of youth training was the result of the government scheme to make training for school leavers compulsory against withdrawal of benefit, the first of many schemes to reduce unemployment and the cost of unemployment benefits for young people while providing an inexpensive labour force. The proposals were that trainees, when working, should receive merely 15 pounds per week. NJC members had met with Labour shadow employment ministers and supported the Labour Party alternative proposals, set out in the pamphlet 'Learning for Life'; these proposals were that young people should have a statutory right to education and training, should not be treated as cheap labour, that apprenticeships should be encouraged and that there should be positive discrimination for girls.[64] Once the Youth Training Scheme was operational, the NJC set up a committee to consider how young women were affected. Giles Radice, the Opposition spokesman for employment, attended an NJC meeting; affiliated trades unions were asked for their views; and a pilot study, funded by an affiliated organization was initiated, together with the Fawcett Society, to see what jobs young women were offered under the YTS scheme and to assess the drop-out and rejection levels. In addition the NJC inquired countrywide into the number of women on the Manpower boards, which had been created to manage employment. It also protested a government proposal to have job points in supermarkets instead of fully staffed job centres, and this proposal was dropped.[65]

Other issues of employment considered by the NJC included the health hazards of work on computer screens/VDUs; the effects of radiation and heat from fans was discussed as were the impact on eyesight, back pain and nervous stress.[66] The NJC was also concerned that voluntary and community organizations would employ married women for low wages '...in a kind of "institutionalized secondary labour market" for groups of people "marginal" to the mainstream economic process'.[67] As the NJC explained, short-term, unskilled labour was, 'by definition "FEMALE" employment'. The concern was familiar to the NJC but the wording, as the committee's own quotation marks indicate, was taken straight from contemporary feminist theory. The NJC added that opposition from trades unions to undercutting wage rates was inevitable. To promote equal pay, the NJC urged local authorities to impose contract compliance with equal opportunities directives on their suppliers and contractors using the GLC as an example of good practice.[68] Renewed debate on the issue of retirement sprang from the government's need to respond to a European directive that men and women should have equal retirement rights. The NJC favoured 60 as the retirement age for men and women but were also in favour of flexibility, that people could retire earlier with less, or later with more, pension. The committee also demanded that pensions should be raised, that there should be special provision for early retirement in dangerous trades and that retirement should be a gradual process, the working week being gradually reduced.[69]

The NJC noted that the labour market was changing from manufacturing to service provision, manual to white-collar jobs, resulting in a growing number of working women; this was also a tenet of contemporary feminist theory. The NJC therefore suggested a series of measures. These included workplace nurseries; better employment protection which included homeworkers and gave the right to claim unfair dismissal if this arose from pregnancy; full pay for women on maternity leave; action on the European directive on parental leave for family reasons; improvement and simplification of equal pay legislation; a statutory minimum wage, improved access to training and a mandatory code of practice on discrimination due to marriage.[70] These were all traditional NJC demands, now with a greater emphasis on women as life-long workers who took time out for childcare. The changing emphasis reflected NJC success in contributing to the passage of employment protection, sex discrimination and equal pay legislation. The change was that the NJC no longer spoke of the woman worker, the woman politician and the woman with the shopping basket, but of women in general, expecting that these roles would be interacting.

'This summary of our policy is published as we approach the next general election, against a background of continually worsening conditions for many women' was the first statement of an NJC policy document issued in 1985.[71] Echoing protests against the Poor Law at the beginning of the century, the NJC's opinion was that in prioritizing cuts in public expenditure, the government intended to make being dependant on state benefits 'a miserable and soul destroying experience'.[72] The 1985 document summarized NJC claims, insisting that these be considered by a future Labour government. The NJC had supported Jo Richarson's Private Member's Bill on sex equality, which reflected many of their demands. While their emphasis now remained industrial women, there was a new recognition of grounds of difference between women:

> ...we stand for equal rights. We put the principles of democracy above the demands of privilege, patronage and birth. We believe in positive action against all forms of discrimination, especially those based on age, race, sex or disability'.[73]

Meanwhile the NJC joined the protest by the Women's Gas Federation against the closure of gas showrooms, concerned that this would mean fuel poverty, and supported the Union of Communication Workers in their fight against the closure of post offices. The campaign for Family Practitioner Centres was continued, to include effective family planning advice, ante- and post-natal care, screening and cytology services, and with meeting the needs of ethnic minorities now included in the demands. Similarly, in claiming that benefits should not discriminate against women, special mention was made of young people's right to independent access to benefits from age 16 and of the need for a non-contributory, comprehensive disability income, paid as a right.

A newer issue for the NJC, and one that was admittedly neglected, was that of food. The NJC statement was that women were concerned in food manufacturing and retailing, shopping, cooking and catering. Concerns foreshadowed many issues of the twenty-first century, included diet, catering standards, the Common Agricultural Policy, VAT, nutritional labelling and, of course, the quality of school dinners:

> 'In conclusion, we need a National Food Policy. Norway has had one for two decades. A Labour Government must make this a priority; the benefits will be enormous'.[74]

The NJC again took a fresh approach to its long-standing goal of a better environment. The committee called for more women councillors, but also women architects and building industry workers, minimum standards of safety and training on building sites, greater accountability of building firms and architects, co-operative housing developments and planned units for lone parents, young adults and elderly people. It also asked for well-lit shops. On transport, the NJC called for the design of transport suitable for the elderly, those with children and heavy shopping and asked for women-only transport. Other demands included the extension of the dial-a-ride scheme, buses and 'post buses' in rural areas, more school buses, the redevelopment of the rail network and better links between bus and rail: 'unless public transport is reorganized as an essential community service, many women will remain as they are at present – isolated.'[75] More generally, the NJC demanded control and production of pollution, including noise pollution, protection of biological resources, wild plants and animals, protection of buildings of artistic, cultural and historic interest, and protection of areas of natural beauty. The NJC summed-up: 'Women are socialised to conserve, protect and nurture. For this reason, we are particularly concerned to protect the environment.' This phraseology reflects contemporary feminist concerns with the environment and highlights a feminist controversy; whether women had special attributes and duties towards the environment.[76]

By 1986 the NJC was claiming the right to contribute to Labour publicity; Peter Mandelsohn, director of Labour's Press and Publicity committee attended an NJC meeting and stated that he would welcome an NJC representative, subject to approval by Labour's National Executive. It was decided to send Margaret Prosser to represent the

NJC and to prepare a draft policy statement to send to all affiliates for comment.[77] This step was followed by the creation of a Monthly Journal. This gave coverage to all the NJC campaigns and the first copy reprinted an extract from *Labour Woman* of 1 July 1921, describing 'the dangers against which Government is meant to defend us'; these included disease, ignorance, starvation and disorder. Some history of the NJC was given along with a brief account of Mary MacArthur and Marion Phillips. At present, 'The main purpose of the committee is to research and highlight the needs and concerns of working women particularly during the current climate of worsening conditions'; the NJC aimed to 'coordinate policies for women ... Government cuts in welfare services have made it a priority'.[78]

By 1987, while issues around the miners' strike and Militant were less to the forefront in the Labour Party generally, feminist pressure for change within the party continued to mount and continued to be reflected in the demands of the NJC. Anne Wilkinson became secretary of the NJC, an indication that a more overtly feminist stance had been accepted. It is generally accepted that the 1987 election defeat finally convinced the party to take the women's vote seriously and to pay attention to Party women's views.[79] One may also reflect that after nearly a decade without parliamentary power, the Party had leisure and inclination to put its own house in order. The NJC again set out its policy to remount its campaigns, to continually monitor government policy and to respond, to liase with other organizations representing women: 'above all, we must become a positive, rather than a reactive organisation'.[80] Meanwhile the Women's Action Group was going from strength to strength and Labour women adopted the quota system recommended by the Socialist International and were successful in winning an increase in the shadow cabinet to accommodate women's places. The bid to modernize the Labour Party, promoted by Neil Kinnock and John Smith as Party leaders and continued by Tony Blair, was not inconsistent with feminist demands. The 1989 Labour Party Conference called for 40 per cent of women at all levels of the Party, although women's demands for a staged approach to 50 per cent representation in the parliamentary party was not accepted. Vicky Phillips became NJC secretary in 1989 and that year Hilda Smith said good-bye to the NJC:

> Over the past 60 years we have had an enormous influence by looking at policies and legislation and as working women making our views known. That work is even more important today with

major legislation changing the welfare state in a drastic manner and literally undoing the work undertaken by this committee over the past half-century.[81]

It was a fitting epitaph for the committee, which continued to protest government policy, while the position of women within the Labour Party continued to be an object of discussion and policy change. The NJC finally ceased activity in 1993, when the new Women's Committee of the Party's National Executive considered women's representation within the Labour Party. Claire Short was appointed by John Smith to chair this committee and was successful in pioneering the all-woman shortlist. Although this was later withdrawn following legal challenges, at the eventual Labour victory in 1997 an unprecedented number of women MPs took their seats. With Labour in government, having a large majority, one might expect a new nexus of the relationship of women and the Labour Party. This new situation is addressed in the conclusion.

12. Joining the parliamentary road

It seems appropriate to close this account of women, feminists and the Labour Party with my own experience as a parliamentary candidate, representing Labour for Witney against Douglas Hurd, Conservative Home Secretary and country gentleman, at the general election of June 1987.[82] This experience consisted of three stages. The first was selection, which is like a game of chess, requiring knowledge of the moves, strategy, boldness, concentration and flair. Second, one becomes 'the candidate', a public persona to whom viewpoints are given to voice, a wardrobe is suggested and of whom photographs are taken. Third, the election campaign itself, a whirlwind around Oxfordshire, closing with election day, which seemed to last five minutes and five years all at once. Sue Stewart was the agent for Witney and Maggie Norris was the constituency Women's Officer; these two gave invaluable support, advice and friendship. My main hindrance was the ancient, yellow Austin Allegro, which I drove.

The Labour Party selection process is undertaken by constituency parties, which are comprised of various local and trades union parties and other groups such as women's sections and young socialists. It is the constituency that chooses its candidate from an approved list, subject to party acceptance. Both local and constituency parties at this time, as the previous section suggested, were driven between left and right wings of various types, feminist and ethnic group pressures. In addition, there were the discords common to any group of adult people sharing an interest but not necessarily a lifestyle or background; if there were disruptive personal and sexual relationships, these were made worse by the habit of holding meetings in members' homes. As was written of post Second World War Manchester and Salford: '...the party as a whole estranged fringe supporters and new recruits by creating the appearance of a private club run by close family members. There were...long-standing feuds'.[83] Thus, selection as a Labour Party, probably any party candidate, is a complex process and the outcome may be a compromise, rather than the choice of the most suitable candidate. The Labour Party at that time had 'A' and 'B' candidate lists, the former with trades union backing. The first step was to get onto the list, not very difficult in the case of the 'B' list. I was invited to compete for Luton, Coventry and West Hertfordshire, all far from my home in Wiltshire; for Swindon, where I was defeated and tactical voting to exclude left- and right-wing favourites led to the selection of a very pleasant and competent woman from outside the area; and Witney which, having learnt my lessons in Swindon, I won. Altogether, from 633 candidates listed in the candidate directory, 90 women candidates were selected and 14 black and Asian candidates.

I had blotted my copybook in Swindon. This was not unusual for a woman candidate; as Pam Tatlow has written:

> If women were local, they had invariably committed some political or personal misdemeanours which prevented their selection as Members of Parliament. If they applied from outside, they were carpetbaggers and capricious, clearly unable to be elected on their home ground.[84]

In my case, my misdeeds arose through involvement in the miners' support group. It was my husband who had first materially supported the miners' cause, giving them the use of a room in his trade union office. The support group contained Communists, the Labour Party, anarchists, the Socialist Workers' Party, the Workers' Revolutionary Party and others of no party. Importing feminist ideas, I had proposed that the chair of the group rotate, which was accepted and worked reasonably well; this, however, meant that Labour, the biggest party, could not command the chair. The meetings were acrimonious with heated discussion about slogans, processes, philosophies and personalities. The favourite Workers' Revolutionary Party slogan at the street collection was 'Don't let Thatcher starve them back', delivered very loudly in monotone, which the miners at the street collection found horribly embarrassing. (Indeed, the miners, proud people who were in difficulties through no fault of their own, generally disliked and avoided collections). The WRP slogan was duly banned and the collectors usually consisted of three Communists, Ted and Ivy Poole and Angela Tuckett,[85] and myself. Angela's accordion was used effectively to dissuade drunks and other hecklers.

The point of principle disputed was whether we sent to our three collieries a fixed sum each week or money as it came in. The collectors wanted a commitment to 1000 pounds per week, which was eventually agreed, while the Labour Party wanted to send more when the collection was good, which usually coincided with Labour Party initiatives such as meetings addressed by Tony Benn or Dennis Skinner. More money was therefore also more publicity for the Labour Party, to which the other groups objected. The practical point, which was eventually conceded, was that it was much easier for the miners' centres to cope on a fixed budget per week than on occasional donations, however good these might be. Not only were the miners on strike, but in Swindon the rail works, which dated back to Brunel and were now large employers, were also under threat. In addition to the regular Friday street collections in the town centre, occasional collections were taken at the rail work's gates and support group publicity linked the two causes. A special leaflet was written to address both groups but the Labour Party had added a paragraph calling on rail workers to vote Labour in forthcoming local elections. To this the Communists and other parties objected. In the chair at the support group meeting to discuss the leaflet, I supported the objection, because the support group, and in particular the collections, could not manage without the Communists.

When selection started, I won nomination from some local groups and from the Transport and General Workers' Union and awaited the

Labour for action in Ashton Keynes and Leigh

TRANSPORT — buses should run into Cricklade, Cirencester, Malmesbury and Swindon for work and shopping. The last bus leaves Swindon for the Leigh at 4.20 pm. That is not a public service.

STREET LIGHTS — we need to make our streets safe for children and for women to walk in without fear of attack or accident.

VILLAGES — our villages will die without basic services. Vote for your village to survive.

If you live in LEIGH or HILLSIDE you have two votes on June 7th — one ballot paper for parish and one for District elections.

Christine Collette is your Labour Party candidate at both elections

VOTE COLLETTE
VOTE LABOUR ON JUNE 7th

CHRISTINE COLLETTE lives in the Leigh.

She was a trade union elected official (National and Local Government Officers Association) for five years, representing 2,000 people and a delegate to area and national union committees.

She had worked for local government for twelve years before that. Now she is a mature student.

Christine has been active in the Labour Party in London and Oxford before coming to Wiltshire and stood for selection in the last general election for Oxford West.

She is a founder member of Labour Heritage and represents the South West on its National Committee.

Figure 2   1983 Candidature for Local Council

selection interviews. Meanwhile, I was delegated to the Labour Party annual women's conference by my local party. The selection interviews were called for this conference week. Appealing to Labour Party head-quarters, I managed to obtain a second meeting of the selection group at a later date. My candidature reached the final round of balloting and then was defeated.

The Swindon experience was useful. I had learnt how to address a selection meeting, what questions were likely to be asked, what fac-tions might be present. I was confident at the Witney interviews and won selection. Thereupon started a strange, two-year period of waiting for the election to be called. I attended local, trades union and con-stituency meetings in Witney; but I had become labelled; I was 'the candidate'. Used to arguing my point, I found the meetings went silent when I spoke; no one openly disagreed. My opinions were meant to be Labour Party policy; I had lost the right to differ. Detailed, close-typed information packs and glossy brochures came to me personally about education, hospitals, housing and such, outlining policy but also advis-ing on its presentation. A defining moment was a motion to affiliate to the League Against Cruel Sports. My husband had been an officer of the Agricultural and Allied Workers' Union and I was reasonably well-informed about rural working conditions; I argued that in the case of many of the League's objects, we needed to know much more about the effect on the workforce before we decided our position; also, we were a Party; I felt it was for the League to affiliate to us, not the reverse (my husband, it should be said, disagreed with me totally). My argument was received with the usual moment of silence, but thereafter I was deemed to have betrayed that part of the left-wing alliance that had voted for me.

Two years ensued of driving through Wiltshire and Oxfordshire, in the Aggro whose favourite trick was to blow a fuse so that there were no rear lights when returning on the M4. The brochures multiplied. I met a man who had fought in the Easter Rising of 1916, left leaflets at Richard Branson's house in Kidlington, found the thread for the knots of the local disputes. I had no money, I was a student without a grant and ran a stall at antique fairs to pay my way; the Irish connection, who ignored the blood sports *debacle*, insisted I should not be out of pocket because of my candidature and my petrol receipts were paid. Most dif-ficult were the meeting times, usually 7.00 p.m.; I would leave college but, in Oxfordshire between 5.00 and 7.00 p.m. there is nowhere to go; public houses were not open and tea shops were shut. A highlight was Gerald Kaufmann's visit in November 1986; as shadow Home Secretary, he was scheduled to voice opposition to Douglas Hurd in Hurd's own constituency and was due to speak with me at a public meeting. The Labour Headquarters told me, on the evening before his arrival, that I should pick him up in Oxford after lunch and entertain him for the afternoon. I rang the constituency officers, who had nothing to suggest, until a young man who was a squatter in a remote cottage; said 'bring him to tea'. So I met Gerald Kaufman at Brasenose College and drove him to a squat, where we sat on cushions and ate curry until the meeting. He was very polite and entertaining, and an excellent speaker. It was the one meeting at which I could speak without restraint, relieved of the burden of Labour Party policy explanation, which was in far more capable hands. The second most interesting meeting was a Labour Heritage one, at which Florence Davy[86] spoke. Here it was possible to discuss gender and sexual politics and some of the divisions in the constituency were healed.

When the election was called for Thursday 11 June, life changed gear. Sue Stewart arranged for local personalities to sign my nomination, trades unions and other groups provided funding and the Co-operative Party made their offices in Witney available, which was a huge bonus. I had my hair done but never attended the grooming and make-up sessions that nearly-new Labour organized to customize its candidates. Photographs were produced for our leaflets and these drafted. We always had two goals: to do as well as we could in Witney and to make sure that Andrew Smith, who had a real chance, was elected for the neighbouring Oxfordshire constituency. In this latter goal we were successful and Andrew went on to hold government office.

The campaign started in earnest at the Levellers Day celebrations in Burford, held annually to commemorate the soldiers shot by Cromwell in the churchyard for deserting his New Model Army. The speakers were Dennis Skinner and Roger Woddis, Andrew and I and a visiting Russian who could only manage 'the sky is blue' and such, but nevertheless conveyed his support. At later meetings I met, among others, Bruce Kent whom we joined briefly on his Long March from Faslane to Burghfield, Jack Straw, Melvyn Bragg and Denis Healey – the committed, the strategist, the publicist and the politician. Denis Healey, in particular, had a huge personality so that he seemed to be surrounded by an *noli me tangere* aura. Clare Short sent me a 'good luck' message. To the offices came Pamela Jay, who was a stalwart worker, and descendants of Stafford Cripps and William Morris. We canvassed hard throughout the constituency, most local canvassers going to Oxford to work for Andrew Smith in addition to their Witney tours of duty. Towns were relatively

Your Labour Candidate for Witney

Christine Collette

Christine says:
'It was Labour women who first campaigned nationally before the first world war for free school meals and medical inspection for children, for improvements to the homes and the health of the people.
It was under the 1945 Labour government that poverty, homelessness and sickness were tackled and we were set on the road to higher living standards. The Tories are intent on running down our welfare state.
The next Labour government will invest in society, restore the people's right to prosper and give them more say in the running of our social services.'

Vote Labour
Vote Christine
Collette

Published by S.Stewart, 37 Woodfield Drive, Charlbury, Oxford, OX7 3SE
Printed by Dot Press (TU), Thames St, Oxford OX1 1SU

Figure 3   1987 Candidature Photo

easy, but in rural villages it was less easy to distinguish Labour supporters. In the shadow of Blenheim, agricultural workers did not advertise their political allegiances; one man told me straight that he would not vote Labour 'because his Lordship wouldn't like it'. (This came as no surprise, because I had seen in Wiltshire people literally doff their caps to the Conservative MP Roger Needham, who had renounced his title to take his seat in the Commons.) Judging from the volume of papers I collected on various subjects, including drafts of speeches given at public meetings, I gave priority to the issues of defence and rural policy. The former is explained by my research at that time into Labour Party international policy, women's activity at Greenham, and the presence of an RAF base in the constituency. The latter interest sprang from my involvement in the Agricultural and Allied Workers' trades union (whose delegate I was to the Labour Party Women's Conference in 1986 and 1987) and by living in a rural community.

The glossy brochures arrived thick and fast accompanied by Election Briefings from the Policy Directorate covering the national campaign themes and Campaign News leaflets from the Campaigns and Communications Directorate. Looking back, I am amazed at the amount of information, detailed national, regional and local budgets for education, health, social services, defence and such. My scribbled notes for speeches show that I had read and reflected on these and could illustrate my points with examples of, for instance, availability and standard of housing in Oxfordshire, school costs, transport provision and costs. In the final fortnight, a useful thick pamphlet arrived that contained official Labour policy on any possible question that one might be asked, whether it be Northern Ireland, South Africa, gas privatisation or any number of national and international issues. My schedule for the final three weeks shows the themes 'Jobs' for Wednesday 20 May; 'Defence' for Saturday 23; 'Rural' for Thursday 28; 'Services' for 4 June. All local Labour candidates were invited to a meeting on 23 May at Oxford Town Hall. We were briefed by Bragg and Healey and called up onto the stage. The other candidates were groomed like models entering banking. I looked like someone who drove an Austin Allegro whose rear lights failed. On 7 June, there was a debate with the three Witney candidates (including Liberal Democrat) in St Marys Church, Witney. Douglas Hurd was protected by Special Branch then, and whenever our paths crossed during the election, with attendant helicopters. As employment in the constituency included textile production, I had learnt all about the relevant World Trade Agreement and was surprised to find that I was the sole possessor of this knowledge. It

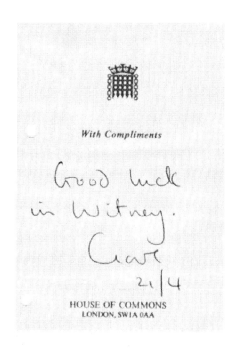

Figure 4 Notes from Claire Short and Neil Kinnock, 1987 election

seemed that every existing association wrote to ask my views on and support for their policies, for instance the National Campaign for the Nuclear Industry at Sellafield, the Nuclear Energy Information Group, the Peace Tax Campaign, the Ramblers Association of Oxfordshire, LIFE, the Open University, Oxford Animal Rights, Friends of the Earth, Johnson Matthey (makers of autocatalysts which reduced car pollution), Oxfam, Stop the Flying at USAF Upper Heyford, the World Development Movement, MIND and the Disablement Income Group.

On 8 June Neil Kinnock sent a letter to all candidates:

Dear Comrade

It has been a great campaign. We have won the battle in the media and on the ground and we are going to have a great result on

Thursday. The professionalism and approach has been far superior to that of the other parties.

Our candidates in the front line have done us proud. Thanks for everything.

Best of luck on Thursday.[87]

On election day I was escorted throughout by Howard Latham, son of a former Labour MP. We started in the small hours and toured markets, in one of which Howard nearly had a fight with a vociferous and threatening heckler, visited the polling stations, gate crashed a reception for Douglas Hurd, who was still surrounded by Special Branch. We lost the seat but won a 4 per cent swing to Labour, no mean feat in 1987.

Douglas Hurd, Conservative 33,458 = 57.55 per cent
Muriel Barton, Liberal Alliance 14,994 = 25.8 per cent
Christine Collette, Labour 9733 = 16.7 per cent

Electorate 75,284, Turnout 77 per cent (75 per cent in 1983) Conservative Majority 18,464 (12,712 in 1983) swing from Liberal to Labour 4 per cent.

Unfortunately the invitation to Neil Kinnock's house party at number 10, Downing Street, for 12 June was null and void.

My mother frequently asked me why I was fighting this election as I would certainly loose, and I am not sure that my answer held well. Why did I not choose Luton, Coventry or West Hertfordshire, where I might have had a chance of winning? I wanted, as always, to express my political opinions, to champion the causes of socialism and feminism, to take my share in a political battle. In fact, as indicated, it was Labour Party policy I championed and where my own politics differed, I could only add footnotes, apart from extraordinary meetings such as that with Gerald Kaufmann. I could make some attempt to bring a feminist perspective by virtue of being a woman candidate, still a fairly rare occurrence in 1987, by insisting that women's conference had to be respected by party organizers in Swindon, in free discussion at the Labour Heritage meeting, by not turning into a banking-model clone, by supporting the constituency's affiliation to the Labour Women's Action Group. Neil Kinnock had promised a Minister for Women and the literature issued under his name does show an awareness of contemporary feminist ideas. As a feminist and socialist I did not want to be perceived as a 'leader/heroine' but as just a member of a group. As the chair rotated at the Swindon miners' support group, so it should not matter who was candidate. However, I became 'the candidate'. At a public meeting on 4 June, Sue Stewart and I both celebrated our fortieth birthdays and were presented with huge bunches of red roses. A generous gesture, but one that underlined how difficult it was to make personal politics tell.

Conclusion

The initial questions of this study were (i) whether the idea that women have something special to offer in achieving social revolution could be put into practice through the mechanism of the Labour Party, and (ii) whether Labour Party men, by shutting their eyes and their ears to women's special gifts, impeded social change. Both these questions of course take it for granted that there is a special contribution women can make. Theory about women as a group and their different goals over time has here been called feminism, and described in its various stages. A third question has been posed, whether Labour women were influenced by and contributed to feminist theory and practice. Also recognized has been the importance of external influences affecting women's Labour Party participation, notably war and economic change.

From Mary Fenton Macpherson, through to Margaret MacDonald, Ada Salter, Marion Phillips, Mary Sutherland and Mrs Shailes, in the biographies and autobiographies, the women featured make a successive claim that women do have something special to offer. For instance, when women were first enfranchised, Marion Phillips wrote:

> ... it is felt that women are so newly come into political life that their development will be hindered and forced along the ordinary lines of political thought amongst men, thus losing the value of women's rich experience, if the whole of the work is conducted in organisations including both sexes.[1]

She thus envisaged a broadening of politics, the expression of new lines of political thought, through the agency of women, working together in separate organizations; using her own considerable gifts she achieved the affiliation of the Labour Party to the Women's Standing Joint Committee. Indeed, taking her case we can see that one woman, 'brilliant as diamonds', does count and can make a difference. In harnessing 'women's rich experience', the SJC/NJC was important in uniting political, trades union and consumer women. As Chief Women's Officer, the SJC/NJC secretary encouraged women into Labour Party women's sections, as did the Women's Labour League, which disbanded in their favour. Marion Phillips's 1918 and 1922 booklets of advice to women's sections were remarkably similar to the 1993 Labour Party booklet addressed to women members. The League and the SJC/NJC were channels for transporting feminist ideas into the Labour movement, about women's participation in politics and employment, and about their domestic life. Not least, these organizations gave an example of feminist practice by adopting a participative style and involving their affiliated membership. The 50,000 copies of the League leaflet 'What are the Chief Defects of your Home' were an early example and a prime case was the enquiry into the closing hours of shops at the end of the Second World War.[2] In later years feminist ideas were more rigorously theorized, but the basic claim of women's potential contribution remained much the same.

Yet was there a coherent call for action and did the Labour Party heed it? The evidence is in the affirmative; from the League onwards, the case was made that single and married women had a right to work, that their conditions should be good and that sweated labour should be outlawed. From the 1960s, to this was added the demand for good education and continued training for women, to improve their labour market position. When there were large-scale strikes, in 1911, 1926 and 1984/1985, women showed solidarity with the mostly male workforce involved. Labour women were constantly involved in international Labour movement organizations and were able to keep a dialogue going with women abroad, even in times of war. On welfare, school meals, health, poverty and housing constant pressure was applied and gains were made. These demands were heeded by the Labour Party; the SJC/NJC was asked to give evidence to government committees and to comment on White Papers. Lobbying before legislation was finalized was particularly effective, for instance before the passage of the 1911 National Insurance Act, and before the equality legislation of the Wilson/Callaghan governments. Although the wait for equal pay legislation was long, this was finally enacted, together with a comprehensive set of measures to outlaw sex discrimination. On other issues the Labour Party paid small attention to women's claims, notably issues around sexuality. The Women's

Labour League affiliated to the Association for Moral and Social Hygiene and campaigned against brothels in France; the SJC had its birth control committee, although this was not particularly active; the NJC supported the abortion campaign, all of which the Labour Party virtually ignored.

However, there is a difficulty with the above analysis, in that it treats 'the Labour Party' as an actor, a single agency, when both its cohesion and its capacity should be problematized. Much of the first phase of Labour Party historiography was devoted to understanding the variety of Labour's theory and practice although, as discussed in the introduction, it was flawed by its concentration on leading male figures and theorists, failing to address the fact that a good half of the individual membership was female.[3] It is true that the Labour Party men, refusing before the First World War to receive memoranda on affiliation from groups that were not affiliated, dominating constituency parties because of their trades union numbers between the wars, did present as a monolithic group; but we have seen that more recent studies have started to crack this perception. We need to ask how far Labour men wanted social change; how far they wanted to retain their social world, to replicate it in the wider community. What remains unwritten is a full appreciation of Labour as a social community, male and female. The disputes in the Women's Labour League that Katharine Bruce Glasier referred to, the two separate households of women at loggerheads, is interesting here. A full account should include the factor of sexuality; semi-covert, intimate relationships could prevent branch meetings being held in family homes.

When assessing its capacity to act and its cohesion, it should be remembered that, as Part I explains, the Labour Party started life in 1900 as the Labour Representation Committee, an agency for affiliated organizations. Labour became a political party in 1906 but there were very few periods throughout the twentieth centuries in which there was a Labour government with a sizeable majority. We should also remember that the Labour Party has always been devoted to parliamentarianism, not revolution. From its inception the Labour Party avoided the label 'socialist', although it had socialist parties amongst its affiliates, the largest being the Independent Labour Party which was present at the birth of the Labour Party and remained something of a socialist godmother until it disaffiliated in 1932. Between the wars the Labour and Socialist International was so called to allow the affiliation of the non-socialist Labour Party. War was instrumental in affecting Labour Party ideas and it was in 1918 that the Labour Party adopted a new, constituency-based organization and a constitution which included the following phrase, later known as Clause 4:

> To secure for the workers by hand or by brain the full fruits of their industry and the most equitable distribution therefor[e] that may be possible upon the basis of the common ownership of the means of production, distribution and exchange and the best obtainable system of popular administration and control in each industry and service.

This statement of socialism was far from fully reflected in Labour Party practice apart from the similarly eschatological period that followed the Second World War. In the 1980s it was hotly disputed until it was finally rejected under Tony Blair's premiership.

Heading a Labour government from 1997, Blair described his 'New Labour' style as epitomizing a 'third way' in British politics, signifying an end to the polarity of political appeal by social class, in favour of the social inclusion of all sections of society. By implication, the Labour Party would thus, to its benefit, rid itself of its (false, as I argue above) blue collar, male, white image. Efforts had been made to expand not only the occupation but also the gender and ethnic image of the party under Blair's predecessors, Neil Kinnock and John Smith, in Labour's long period of opposition to the Conservative governments of the late twentieth century. Now, while it would appear that reflecting Britain's multiculturalism remains a difficult task for Labour, its identity as primarily a worker's party has been greatly weakened. An unparalleled number of women Labour Members of Parliament changed the gender balance of the House of Commons; there are women cabinet ministers and women trades union leaders. Equally, heterosexuality is no longer assumed to be universal amongst Labour's leading figures. There is as yet no evidence that Gordon Brown's premiership will evoke great change; but it is wonderful to have a Home Secretary named Jacqui Smith.

However, the identity of New Labour is disputed; it is as diverse as the Party has always been.[4] Much of the commentary on New Labour ignores questions of gender and feminist influence. Some commentators argue that, women MPs notwithstanding, New Labour also remains as male-dominated overall as its predecessor,[5] while the élite group around Tony Blair's leadership was formed of young, male, white graduates. Some female writers have argued that New Labour is anti-feminist, because the policy of social inclusion leaves no room for feminist agitation:

> ...while feminist thinking provides part of the political imagery and vocabulary on which Labour drew, the need for a continued feminist politics was explicitly rejected...The image of modernity which was one in which old conflicts are assumed to have been settled.[6]

Others write that the results are mixed; some measures such as child tax credits are welcomed, but the pay gap between men and women continues.[7] Anna Coote reflects on these mixed results, asking 'What is it about New Labour and the "Third Way" that makes it both a positive force for women and deeply antipathetic to the women's cause'?[8] She welcomes welfare-to-work, child care measures and the minimum wage, but is of the opinion that repudiating redistribution makes pay equality impossible; time and political power ought, in her opinion, to be redistributed in addition to wealth and earnings. Coote also questions Labour's commitment to Christian influenced family values, because these tend to imply a domestic role for women. In a strange little pamphlet written in 2001, which illustrates the discomforts of life as New Labour women MPs, Harriet Harman and Deborah Mattison asked for women's support for Labour while also urging their Party on to more reform in women's interests. They refer to women's 'growing impatience that Labour should deliver on the areas of their key concerns: health, education and helping them manage their complex lives'. As did Mary MacArthur in 1918, they call for trades union delegations to reflect the numbers of women in their ranks and for two deputy leaders, one female.[9] Harriet Harman later succeeded in wining the deputy leadership election when Gordon Brown became Prime Minister in 2007.

Feminist theory indeed makes a problem of a policy of social inclusion by problematizing the nature of citizenship.[10] The Labour movement goal is full social, political and industrial citizenship for working people, but citizenship is both a gendered and an ethnicized project. It derives from a Western, male tradition of political philosophy that justified male privilege by attributing to men the qualities necessary for political activity. Thus Ruth Lister, who headed campaigns against poverty before theorizing welfare and society as an academic, wrote that the search to discover a citizen revealed: '...a definitely male citizen, and a white, heterosexual, non-disabled one at that'.[11] Interest in ethnicity and sexuality has refocused ideas about what it means to be a citizen, to belong to a nation state, challenging the existence of the hegemony presumed by social inclusion.

It is the great paradox for the left that, while the vision of socialism is the international unity of working people, Western parties operate within nation states, perceiving these states as both the route to welfare and defence against oppression. Indeed, the development of class-consciousness and the struggle to represent workers helped to achieve the formation of nation states. In Britain, the founding of the Labour Representation Committee in 1900 and the naming of the Labour Party in 1906 institutionalized the quest for working peoples' citizenship. Within the decade, the Labour Party's identification as a national party was fully illustrated, in common with that of other European social democratic parties, when they voted for the First World War estimates and joined coalition governments. This was a logical outcome of perceiving the state as one's chief line of defence against aggression. Similarly, far from being pacifist, the British Labour Party, as early as 1934, admitted the possible necessity of arming the National government against fascism.[12] The Labour Party is caught on the horns of its historical, but unacknowledged dilemma: how to balance national interest and the interests of the mass of the people, currently expressed as social inclusion. Labour thus took a belligerent and interventionist stance in the wars of the late twentieth and early twenty-first centuries, which themselves are part of the continued redetermination of nation states. Yet the rhetoric of (male) warrior intervening to aid (female) victim reinforces gender stereotypes. As Eleanor Barton wrote in 1934, 'Years ago, when we were struggling...[for the] vote, we were told that women did not bear arms, and, consequently, should not have the vote as she did not fight for her country'.[13] Citizenship is further problematized for women during war as they are sometimes the victims of sexual abuse, not only by enemy troops but also by their own military. The biggest single challenge to the policies of Tony Blair's governments was over British intervention in Iraq; but historical precedent was on his side. Meanwhile, an emphasis on cultural homogeneity continually creates new territorial boundaries, as can be seen in the developments of the Scottish Parliament and Welsh Assembly.

Debate on such dilemmas is eased by a postmodernist approach that unpicks the ideas of subjects holding rights, hierarchies and the possession of power. It also challenges political practice that rests on common identities and goals. Feminism's third wave drew from postmodernism and was a progression from the anti-essentialist recognition of difference that the NJC had recognized in the1980s. Here there could perhaps be room for the 'third way'. Third wave feminism in one sense turned full circle to the preoccupations of first wave feminism, in that it again questioned the construction of women's citizenship. Yet if this subject itself was deconstructed, the metanarrative or all-embracing explanatory theory of gender fell along with the metanarrative of the nation state; and, of course, that of class.

Third wave feminism differed from previous phases in that while theory expanded, it was no longer supported by a strong women's movement or distinct feminist activity. On the one hand, there was a backlash against feminism, while on the other many of the goals of the women's movement appeared to have been met. The pay gap had narrowed, jobs were more open to women, parental leave was established and there was more debate on the responsibilities of fatherhood. These gains were patchy and fragile and were largely enjoyed by younger women. Meanwhile, feminist theory had successfully challenged traditional disciplines in that gender had become a factor of debate. The short-lived growth of Women's Studies had propelled a new wave of feminist theory so that feminism was said to have moved from the street into the university. One might see a parallel here with the Labour movement, its graduate advisors and academics in government. John Prescott's role, as deputy leader to Tony Blair, might be considered as that of preserving and presenting a version of the former labouring-man image.

As it dealt with difference, a post-modernist approach was a useful tool for feminist theory, enabling it to address the fragmentation of second wave sisterhood by offering a philosophical vocabulary to discuss difference and the technique of deconstruction to explore subjecthood. It showed how language constructed meaning and offered the space to theorize the complexities of concepts such as gender and gendered sexualities. It also moved forward the debate on rights, casting these not as reflections of all-time values, but as negotiated interim settlements. Again, there were parallels within the Labour Party. One might see Cherie Blair's continual renegotiation of her role and status as examples, or Tony Blair's post-premiership conversion to Roman Catholicism, or his claiming for himself the right to leave office when and how he chose. Claire Short and Harriet Harman were stars of the feminist-socialist late second wave but failed to renegotiate their positions and suffered accordingly. Margaret Becket, however, proved adept at quiet self-reinvention.

Post-modernism was not without its detractors. Those feminists who wished to continue to value the idea of women's solidarity, to continue to prioritize women as the subject of their discourse, and who perceived the often obscure language of postmodernism as undermining women's attempts to theorize their own position in society rejected a post-modernist approach. They could point to the decline of the feminist movement as evidence of the harm done. Similarly, Labour movement traditionalists mourned the acceptance of difference as the herald of the decline of class solidarity. Acceptance of feminism was, in itself, recognition of a factor of difference within social class. However, as we have seen, the Labour Party always recognized feminism and made changing relationships through time with changing expressions of feminism. The answer given to the detractors of post-modernism was that the second wave feminism – or traditional Labour movement – they continued to promote was in itself a metanarrative, which had outlived its use and should be discarded as over-simplistic.

Third wave feminism did not lose sight of the second wave claim that the personal was political and its interest in sexuality. However, it went beyond the idea of social construction of sexuality, now seen as both inadequate to explain why it was women who were socialized into subordination and unable to deal with alternative sexualities. The umbrella heading 'Queer Theory' was used to describe thinking about sexuality, which destabilized gender categories while challenging the polarities of 'good/natural/healthy' and 'bad/unnatural' sexual behaviour. The main charge against Queer Theory was that it failed to deal with the reality of power. A post-modernist approach challenged the identification of a subject by sexual orientation or by a collective role. Judith Butler, one of the first to express these ideas, wrote: 'The prospect of *being* anything, even for pay, has always produce in me a certain anxiety, for to "be" gay, to "be" lesbian seems to me to be more than a simple injunction to become who or what I already am'.[14] Just so I was uncomfortable at 'being' the Candidate. Similarly, Labour's perception of women changed with the course of the Second World War, so that Soviet Army heroines were praised when women were needed to make armaments.

Theory then gives us tools for thinking about women and politics. Nevertheless, one must not cease to acknowledge that factors external to the Labour or feminist project have enormous effect. In different time periods, Labour Party/feminist relationships changed. The great movement for enfranchisement brought about the birth of the Labour Party and of the Women's Labour League; and women's representation in parliament was bound to be an issue these bodies addressed. An international perception was important in resisting fascism and the experience of the First and Second World Wars affected women's labour movement organization. As these wars illustrated, women's workforce position is paramount in determining their position in the Labour movement. In the period of second wave feminism, the economic position of women changed greatly and equal pay and sex discrimination became matters of debate and legislation by Labour governments. One is dealing with not just a relationship between the Labour Party and women, but with the economic, social and political position of women in society at any given time and the success or failure of contemporary Labour politicians. The relationship is triangular. In a sense, this book is a history of social change and how it is reflected in political thought.

Finally, I am writing my own history. Perhaps we always do. In this book especially I am using my own archives, memory and experience as a trades unionist, Labour Party member and feminist academic. I am also using my own past as a historian. I have met and debated not only with many of the people in the book, but many of the academics I cite. I offer a reflection on this past. However, I am left with a fundamental problem. If the 'Newer Eve' is ever to appear, and if her voice is to be heard, I cannot envisage that she will be anything but a socialist Eve. Surely a conservative Newer Eve is an impossibility. She will be faced with the response of Margaret Thatcher to the NJC in 1974, that politics must reflect, not change society. Yet without the disruption of society, there will be no space for my Eve. Over a century, the parliamentary road to socialism failed to provide sufficient space. Now, the quest as led successively by the Women's Labour League, the SJC and the NJC, to further the conditions of working women, relying on the Labour Party to provide the political clout, is an impossibility. These autonomous organizations, founded in 1906, ceased to exist in 1993. There is no Chief Woman's Officer for the Labour Party. The Labour movement, in the form that it took during these years, survives as a pale reflection. This history of affiliations is ended. The current history of the Labour Party is no longer being recorded, as it was from the time of James Middleton's assistant secretaryship to the Labour Representation Committee in 1902, in indexed conference reports (I have his copy) that contain the report of the National Executive Committee. Time to move on.

Notes

Introduction

1. For one of the few commentaries that does problemitize 'the complexities of feminism and Labour's response', see Martin Francis, 'Labour and Gender', in Duncan Tanner, Pat Thane and Nick Tiratsoo (eds), *Labour's First Century* (Cambridge University Press, 2000).
2. Matthew Worley, 'Building the Labour Party: Labour Party Activities in Five British Counties between the Wars', *Labour History Review*, 70 (1), 2005, p. 78. Worley's opinion is that continuing male dominance prevented success in other areas. Martin Francis, 'Labour and Gender' op. cit. asks why women succeeded in the field of welfare but not that of equal pay.
3. Worley, op. cit., p. 75. Cf. Steven Fielding and Duncan Tanner, 'The "rise of the Left" Revisited: Labour Party Culture in Post-War Manchester and Salford', *Labour History Review*, 7 (3) 2006, p. 215; 'Labour was a very masculine organisation, with many local parties being managed by male cliques'.
4. 'Is there a Future for Labour History?' *Labour History Review*, 62 (3) 1997, pp. 253–257.
5. Henry Pelling, *The Origins of the Labour Party* (Oxford University Press, 1963).
6. Lucy Middleton (ed.), *Women in the Labour Movement* (Medwood Burn, 1977).
7. Joni Lovenduski and Pippa Norris (eds), *Gender and Party Politics* (Sage, 1993); Pippa Norris and Joni Lovenduski, *Political Recruitment: Gender Race and Class in the British Parliament* (Cambridge University Press, 1995); Pippa Norris 'Gender Difference in Political Recruitment in Britain', *Government and Opposition*, 26 (1), Winter 1991.
8. Neil Evans and Dot Jones, ' "To help forward the work of humanity": Women in the Labour Party', in Duncan Tanner, Chris Williams and Deian Hopkins (eds), *The Labour Party in Wales* (University of Wales Press, 2000).
9. Ibid., p. 238.
10. Christine Collette, 'The International Faith: Rituals and Liturgies of British Labour Movement Internationalism, 1918–1939', in Berthold Unfried and Christine Schindler (eds), *Riten, Mythen und Symbole–Die Arbeiter-bewegung zwischen 'Zivilreligion' und Volksskultur* (Akademische Verlaggansanstalt, 1999).
11. Florence Davy 'From Zeppelins to Jets', *Labour Heritage Women's Research Committee Bulletin*, (2) 1987. Joan Davis, 'A Life in the Labour Movement', ibid. Many Labour Heritage women echoed these sentiments at conferences around Britain in the 1980s.
12. Sarah Perrigo, 'Women, Change and the Labour Party', *Parliamentary Affairs*, 49 (1) January 1996, p. 119.
13. See introduction to Fiona Montgomery and Christine Collette, *The European Women's History Reader* (Routledge, 2002) and Joanna Bornat and Hannah Diamed, 'Women's History and Oral History: developments and debates', *Women's History Review*, 16 (1) 2007.

14. Sarah Perrigo, op. cit., pp. 116–129.
15. Irene Wagner, 'Socialist London at War', *Labour Heritage Women's Research Committee Bulletin*, (2) Labour Heritage, 1987.
16. Dan Weinbren was instrumental in recording Labour Heritage members. See also Dan Weinbren, *Generating Socialism: Recollections of Life in the Labour Party* (Sutton, 1997), passim.
17. 'Doing History', *Labour Heritage Women's Research Committee Bulletin*, (3) 1990.
18. Steven Fielding and Duncan Tanner, 'The "Rise of the Left" ' op. cit. p. 211.

I.   Representation: the Women's Labour League

1. For the suffrage campaign, see special double issue of *Women's History Review* 14(3) and (4), 2005.
2. Women's Labour League secretarial correspondence (WLL) and related papers Labour Party archives and study centre, John Rylands library, Manchester University, Conference Report, 1906. These sections draw on Christine Collette, *For Labour and for Women: the Women's Labour League 1906–1918* (Manchester University Press, 1989).
3. League correspondence, WLL/3.
4. Ibid., WLL/90.
5. Ibid., WLL/89.
6. J.R. MacDonald and M.E. MacDonald papers, Public Records Office, London, PRO 30/69/1378, letter about Preston branch 29 October 1906.
7. Labour Party General Correspondence, Labour Party archives, 13/283, 13/285.
8. Ibid., 14/385.
9. Ibid., 14/342.
10. Ibid., 21/208.
11. League Correspondence, Lisbeth Simm's letters to Margaret MacDonald.
12. Ibid.
13. League Correspondence, executive committee 27 January 1909.
14. Annot Robinson papers (the property of Mrs H Wilson, Altrincham) Manchester Central Library, Misc 718.
15. League Correspondence, WLL/64.
16. Ibid., WLL/42,65.
17. The Gertrude Tuckwell Collection, 1890–1920, Trades Union Congress Library, London, 45/1.
18. League Correspondence, WLL/66.
19. MacDonald papers, PRO/69, 1373.
20. Ibid., PRO 30/69, 1373, 13 July 1906, 15 July 1906.
21. See Steven King, ' "We are to be trusted": Female Poor Law Guardians and the Development of the New Poor Law: The Case of England, 1880–1906', *International Review of Social History*, 49 (1) 2004, for a good review of the historiography on female guardians; he concludes that despite the hostility of male guardians, women achieved useful work.
22. Sheila Blackburn, 'Between the Devil of Cheap Labour Competition and the Devil of Family Poverty', *Labour History Review*, 71 (2) 2006, points out

that 'sweating' is a term bearing various interpretations and can be applied to men and women, working at home and in factories. Here it is women workers, in either location, that are considered.

23. MacDonald papers, 1373, 30 July 1906.
24. MacDonald papers, 1374, 13 November 1907.
25. Correspondence to and from Mr Cohen is divided between the League Correspondence, WLL/51-56 and MacDonald papers, 1366 and 1375.
26. League Correspondence, WLL/98.
27. MacDonald papers, 1374, 11 May 107 and 1375, 7 April 1908. For an account of the Women's Industrial Council and its approach to Trade Boards see Ellen Mappen, introduction to Clementina Black, *Married Women's Work* (Virago, 1984) and Ellen Mappen, 'Strategies for Change: Social Feminist Approaches to the Problem of Women's Work', in Angela John (ed.) *Unequal Opportunities: Women's Employment in England 1800–1914* (Blackwell, 1986).
28. Theresa Billington Greig, *The Consumer in Revolt* (London, c. 1912).
29. For Marion Phillips, see Marian Goronwy-Roberts, *A Life of Marion Phillips, MP* (Bridge Books, Wrexham, 2000).
30. Mary Agnes Hamilton, *Margaret Bondfield* (London, 1924), p. 110.
31. Sylvia E. Pankhurst, *The Suffragette Movement: An Intimate Account of Persons and Ideals* (London, 1931), pp.117–118.
32. Sir H.N. Bunbury (ed.), *Lloyd George's Ambulance Wagon: the Memoirs of A. J. Braithwaite* (Metheuen, 1957) p. 235.
33. J.R. MacDonald and M.E. MacDonald papers, Public Records Office, London, PRO 30/69, 1156, letter from Margaret Bondfield.
34. Ibid., 1157, Katherine Bruce Glasier to Ramsay MacDonald.
35. Ibid.
36. Ibid., 1158.
37. See Section 3 for brief biography of Clarice McNab.
38. The records of the negotiations are in the Labour Party Subject Files, Labour Party archives and study centre, LP/WLL/08/31-66; League Executive Committee Minutes 1914–18.
39. *Labour Woman*, July 1913.
40. M.E. Buckley, *The Feeding of Schoolchildren* (London, 1914) p. xii.
41. Margaret MacMillan, 'Citizens of Tommorow', *The Book of the Labour Party: Its History, Growth, Policy and Leaders*, vol. ii (Labour Publishing Co., London, 1925).
42. League Correspondence WLL/44, 39,35, 47.
43. For League work in South Wales see Neil Evans and Dot Jones, ' "To Help Forward the Great Work of Humanity": Women in the Labour Party in Wales', in Duncan Tanner, Chris Williams and Deain Hopin (eds), *The Labour Party in Wales, 1900–2000* (University of Wales Press, Cardiff, 2000).
44. League Correspondence, Lisbeth Simm's letters, WLL/135.
45. Enid Stacy's work for the Independent Labour Party is recorded in the ILP National Administration Committee Minutes, Labour Party Archives. See also the article by her niece, Angela Tuckett Gradwell, *North West Labour History Society Bulletin* 7, 1980–1981.
46. See subsequent notes on Marion Barry.
47. Enid Stacy, 'A Century of Women's Rights', in Edward Carpenter (ed.), *Some Forecasts for the Coming Century* (London, 1897).

48. I was privileged to work with Angela Tuckett Gradwell in the 1984–1985 miners' strike, where her political knowledge and not least, her accordion, were of great use in street collections.
49. 'Marion Barry' by Christine Collete from 'Oxford Dictionary of National Biography' (2004). By permission of Oxford University Press.
50. For Pete Curran's election campaign see James and Lucy Middleton papers, Ruskin College, Oxford, MID 138.
51. *Women's Trade Union Review*, April 1910.
52. First published in Elizabeth Ewan, Sue Innes, Siän Reynolds and Rose Piper (eds), *Biographical Dictionary of Scottish Women* (Edinburgh University Press, Edinburgh, 2006).

II.   War: the Standing Joint Committee

1. See Collette, *The International Faith: Labour's Attitudes to European Socialism, 1918–1939* (Ashgate, 1998), Chapter 6.
2. Cheryl Law, *Suffrage and Power: The Women's Movement 1918–1928* (London, 1997); see also Collette, 'Women and Politics' in Chris Wrigley (ed) *Early Twentieth Century Britain* (Blackwell, 2003).
3. The Gertrude Tuckwell Collection, Trades Union Congress Library, London 345/79. This is a *Daily Telegraph* report; the speech as reported in the League's annual report is less revolutionary.
4. Ibid. 353/6. 'Mary Longman, Women and Internationalism', in Marion Phillips (ed), *Women and the Labour Party* (Headley Bros., London, n.d.).
5. *Labour Leader*, 3 September 1914.
6. For Averil Sanderson Furniss's comments see Averil Sanderson Furniss, 'Citizenship of Women', *The Book of the Labour Party* (London, 1925), p. 254 and Sanderson Furniss and Marion Phillips, *The Working Woman's House* (London, 1920), pp. 10, 49.
7. Labour Party Subject Files, LP/WLL/108/44.
8. Ibid.
9. Standing Joint Committee papers, Labour Party archives and study centre, John Rylands Library, Manchester University, *Minute Book*, 20 June 1916, *Women's Emancipation, A Bill, 9 & 10 GEO.5*.
10. See Collette, 'Questions of Gender: Labour and Women', in Brian Brivati and Richard Heffernan (eds), *The Labour Party: A Centenary History* (MacMillan, Press Ltd., 2000), reproduced with permission of Palgrave MacMillan. Labour Party affiliation, Standing Joint Committee archives (SJC), Labour Party archives, Mary Sutherland to Dear Mr Gaitskell, 12 January 1949.
11. Matthew Worley, 'Building the Labour Party: Labour Party Activism in Five British Counties between the Wars', *Labour History Review*, 70 (1) 2005, p. 7 writes that membership of women's councils might exceed that of their male counterpart but were 'dwarfed by the affiliated membership of the trades unions'.
12. Marion Phillips, *Women and the Labour Party* (Headley Bros., London, n.d., no page nos.).
13. Marion Phillips and Grace Taverner, *Women's Work in the Labour Party: Notes for Speakers and Workers' Classes with Charts and Useful Forms* (Labour Party,

n.d.) and, cited, Marion Phillips, DSc (Econ.), JP, *Organisation of Women within the Labour Party: A Handbook for Officers and Members of Women's Sections* (Labour Party, 1921), p. 2. These are remarkably similar to the 1993 Labour Party pamphlet, *Women in the Labour Party.*

14. SJC, Marion Phillips to Dear Madam 7 June 1918, reissued June 1920.
15. SJC, General Purposes Committee minutes, 12 February 1925; 10 and 12 December 1925, SJC minutes 14 March 1929, 11 July 1929.
16. For Ellen Wilkinson's early political career, see below Section 8.
17. SJC report January to October, 1923.
18. SJC, memorandum to Committee on Design of Dwellings, June 1943.
19. SJC, Economics in Education sub-committee 1932; deputation to Board of Education, November 1932; R.F. Young, secretary to Board of Education Consultative Committee, 6 February 1932; memo to Board of Education Consultative Committee, July 1934.
20. SJC, 'What's wrong with domestic service', n.d.; 'First steps towards a domestic workers' charter', June 1930; House of Commons (anon.) to Dr Phillips, 6 June 1931; deputation document, 2 July 1931; TUC to SJC, 23 March 1932; Margaret Bondfield to Michael Brooks, n.d.
21. International Federation of Trades Union papers, IISG, Amsterdam, International Committee of Women Trades Unionists Conference, 1927, IFTU 127–129. Heimarbeit, IFTU 128. Translated from the German original by Marion Jones, Edge Hill University.
22. SJC, Statement to be placed before the Home Secretary on Government's Proposed Factory Bill 1929; League of Nations to SJC, 25 October 1925; SJC to League of Nations, Miss Gabrielle Radziwill, 12 September 1932, 27 October 1932; in 12 September letter Mary Sutherland states: 'on being appointed Labour Women's Officer of the party...I was also appointed secretary of the SJC'.
23. SJC, deputation to London County Council, 1934; Eleanor Barton, *Married Women and Paid Positions: A Plea for Solidarity Amongst Women* (Co-operative Guild, 1934); TUC and Labour Party, Employment of Married Women, n.d.
24. SJC, report of sub-committee, January–October 1923.
25. Margaret Sanger papers, IISG Amsterdam, vol. 20, Witcop to Sanger 4 March 1924, 6 April 1924, 8 August 1924. Sanger refusing to assist the couple with the fine.
26. First printed in Labour Heritage Women's Research Committee *Bulletin* 1, Spring 1986. See Sue Bruley, 'The Politics of Food: Gender, Family, Community and Collective Feeding in the General Strike and Miners' Lockout of 1926', *Twentieth Century British History*, 18 (1) 2007 which includes interviews with some of the women involved.
27. First published in Elizabeth Ewan, Sue Innes, Siän Reynolds and Rose Piper (eds), *Biographical Dictionary of Scottish Women* (Edinburgh University Press, Edinburgh, 2006). Mary Sutherland's papers are kept in the Labour Party Archives and Study Centre, John Rylands Library, Manchester University, but her personal papers were destroyed by her nephew after her death.
28. First appeared in Davis, Joan, *Labour Heritage Women's Research Committee Bulletin* 2, Spring 1987.
29. For IFWW see International Federation of Trades Union papers op. cit. IFTU 124, 1920.

30. Marion Phillips, *Labour Magazine*, ii (3) July 1922.
31. *Soviet Russia: An Investigation by Women Trades Unionists* (London, 1925).
32. International Federation of Trades Union papers op. cit._IFTU 130, resolutions from women's conference.
33. Ibid., IFTU 132, women's conference resolutions.
34. Ibid., IFTU 134.
35. Labour Party Conference Report, 1923.
36. Sozialistische Arbeiter–Internationale papers, IISG, Amsterdam, SAI 4333, notice of International Women's Conference August 1925.
37. Ibid, SAI 4359, Adler to all affiliates 10 March 1926.
38. Labour Party International Sub Committee Minutes, 8 October 1926.
39. SJC, SJC to League of Nations, Miss Gabrielle Radiziwell, 12 September 1922, 27 October 1922, Mary Hamilton, draft memorandum, 9 May 1932.
40. Sozialistische Arbeiter – Internationale papers op. cit., SAI 4336, Edith Kemiss, provisional agenda for conference, 23 July 1928.
41. Ibid., SAI 4345, William Gillies (Labour Party International Secretary) to Adler, 3 July 1931.
42. Helen Boak, 'Women in Weimar Politics', *European History Quarterly* 20 (3) July 1990.
43. Sara Huysmans, 'Women's Suffrage in Belgium', *Labour Magazine*, iii (7) November 1927.
44. Soialistische Arbeiter – Internationale papers, op. cit., SA1 4360, Alice Pels to Dear Comrade, 14 December 1941.
45. 'International Women', Labour Party Archives, Study Week Report 1936.
46. Soialistische Arbeiter – Internationale papers, op. cit., SA1 4367, Mary Sutherland for Women's Committee, August 1936.
47. Sozialistiche Arbeiter – Internationale papers, op. cit., SA1 4367, International Women's Committee Report 1937.
48. See Collette article on The Jarrow March on the BBC website, which contains a brief account of Ellen Wilkinson.
49. Labour Party conference report 1933.
50. Trades Union conference report 1933.
51. First produced in *Labour Heritage Women's Research Committee* Bulletins 1 and 2.
52. Of the people mentioned, Hugh Dalton had favoured armed resistance at the time of the Invasion of Czechoslovakia, a country he knew well; he became Minister of Economic Warfare in 1940 and set up the Special Operations Executive for subversion, sabotage and resistance in occupied countries. The Daltons mourned a daughter who, had she lived would have been about Irene Wagner's age. Margaret Cole, G.D.H. Cole and Harold Laski favoured popular front action against fascism and were founder members of the Socialist League in 1932, which dissolved itself in 1937 rather than be proscribed by the Labour Party. Harold Laski was a tutor of the London School of Economics and G.D.H. Cole at Nuffield College; the latter was conducting a Ministry of Labour inquiry in 1940. The Coles and Laski were prolific writers; Margaret and G.D.H. Cole wrote detective stories together.
53. Section 9 is based on my chapter first published as ' "Daughter of the Newer Eve": The Labour Movement and Women', *Labour's Promised Land? Culture*

and Society in Labour Britain 1945–51 Jim Fyrth (ed.) (Lawrence and Wishart, London, 1995).

54. James and Lucy Middleton papers, Ruskin College, Oxford, Middleton to Mrs Andrews for conference of women's advisory councils, 12 June 1941.
55. Leff, Ann, 'My Brilliant Career in War Work', *Labour Heritage Women's Research Committee* Bulletin 5, 1996.
56. Labour Research Department *Fact Service* no. 169, 1942.
57. *Fact Service* no. 77, 1941.
58. *Fact Service* nos. 44, 1940, nos. 77, 99, 140, 1941.
59. *Fact Service* nos. 17, 20, 22, 24, 1940, no. 121, 1942.
60. *Labour Monthly*, 'The war comes first', 1943.
61. General Secretary's papers, Morgan Phillips, Labour Party archives, box 15, Women's Matters, annual report SJC January – December 1945.
62. SJC Housing sub committee minutes 14 July 1942, 6 August 1942, 29 October 1942, 26 January 1943; memorandum to the Ministry of Health committee on Design of Houses and Flats, January 1943.
63. SJC, memorandum on evacuation, October 1939.
64. SJC, R.C. Wynn-Williams, Home Office to SJC, 27 February 1946; NUDAW memorandum; SJC questionnaire April 1946; SJC memorandum to Home Office, May 1946.
65. SJC note, February 1943.
66. Report of the 23rd National Conference of Labour Women 1945. Dame Anne Loughlin (National Union of Tailors and Garments Workers and SJC), 80th Annual Conference of the Labour Party Report 1951.
67. Joan Davis 'A life in the Labour Movement', *Labour Heritage Women's Research Bulletin* no.2 (1987); Bertha Elliot and others contributing to Labour Heritage Conference, 18 July 1992.
68. Annual conference of the Labour Party reports 1947, 1949, 1950.
69. Resolutions for Labour Party Women's Conference 1948, 1949,1950.
70. Report of the 45th Annual Conference of the Labour Party, 1945.
71. National Labour Women's Advisory Committee Minutes, 1951–57, Labour Party archives, minutes 6 December 1951; Morgan Phillips to Mary Sutherland, 11 January 1951; Mary Sutherland to Morgan Phillips, 16 February 1951.
72. Trades Union Congress 78th Annual Report 1946, *Labour Party Year Book 1946–7* (London, 1947).
73. *Labour Party Year Book* op. cit p.16, 10,876 women were recruited.
74. 47th Annual Conference of the Labour Party Report 1948.
75. Amabel Williams-Ellis, 'Is Women's Place in the Home' *Labour Discussion Series* no.9 (London 1947) p. 3, 9.
76. Trades Union Congress, 78th Annual Report 1946; *Resolutions for the National Conference of Labour Women, 1946*; 'seven resolutions submitted on nursery schools and day nurseries', pp.5–6: 24th Labour Women[s] Conference Report 1946, composite resolution carried unanimously ; 'Resolutions' op. cit. 1947; 25th Labour Women's Conference Report 1947 resolution lost; 'Resolutions' op. cit. 1948; 26th Labour Women's Conference Report 1948, previous questions moved.

77. 23rd Labour Women's Conference Report 1945. The SJC was preferred to press for 'the rate of the job' rather than 'equal pay'; trying to establish work of equal value has bedevilled claims under the current equal pay legislation.
78. Trades Union Congress, 77th Annual Report 1945.
79. Trades Union Congress, 79th Annual Report 1947; 80th Annual Report 1948; 81st Annual Report 1949; General Council line supported 3,835,000 to 1,765,000; 82nd Annual Report 1950; Voting 4,490,000 for immediate action on equal pay, 2,367,000 against; 83rd Annual Report 1951.
80. 48th Annual Conference of the Labour Party Report 1947.
81. Amabel Williams-Ellis, op. cit. pp. 4–6.

III.   The second wave: the National Joint Committee

1. Amy Black and Stephen Brooke, 'The Labour Party, Women and the Problem of Gender, 1951 to 1966', *Journal of British Studies* 36 (October 1997), p. 424.
2. I was acting full-time as a lay official for the National and Local Government Officers' Association and found this legislation beneficial both to membership morale and to negotiating stances.
3. Sheila Rowbotham, Lynne Segal, and Hilary Wainwright (London, Merlin, 1979).
4. Sarah Perrigo, Labour Party activist and historian, was one of the first to put this view forward. Perrigo, Sarah, 'Women, Change and the Labour Party', *Parliamentary Affairs*, 1996.
5. Amy Black and Stephen Brook, op. cit., pp. 430–431 record that women made up 42 per cent of the Labour Party membership from 1951 to 1970.
6. Hilda Smith papers (hereafter HS)HS6, NJC 4/2/67 n.d.
7. HS4 report of NJC 1965 & 1966 and HS6 op.cit.
8. Ibid.
9. HS16 NJC 11/6/67 Draft Declaration of Elimination of Discrimination Against Women.
10. HS4 report of NJC 1965 & 1966 and HS6 op.cit.
11. HS4 op.cit.
12. Ibid.
13. Ibid.
14. Ibid.
15. Ibid. and *H* 5 NJC 11/6/66 Committee on Local Authority and Allied Personal Social Services, Statement for Presentation to Seebohm Committee.
16. HS19 NJC 15/9/70 Evidence to Finer Committee on One Parent Families.
17. HS9 Evidence to the Royal Commission on the NHS and HS18 NJC 7/5/70 Notes on Future Structure of the NHS.
18. Ibid.
19. HS33 NJC 9/1/77 Draft Evidence on Health Care for Women.
20. HS40 NJC BM 7/1/79 Report for 1978 (?1977) and 1978.
21. HS24 NJC 24/10/74/R Comments on the Government White paper 'Equality for Women'.
22. HS34 NJC 12/2/79 Discussion document on the system of quota representation.

23. HS35 NJC 13/2/77Background paper on legislative protection for women and HS36 NJC 13/3/77 Protective legislation – evidence to EOC.
24. HS39 NJC – retirement ages – labelled by hand 1978.
25. HS37 NJC 1/1/78 Report of first meeting of working group on women and the law.
26. HS10 NJC 21/9/1971.
27. HS15, progress report on campaign, undated.
28. HS13 NJC campaign notes 'Women's and Girls Career and Employment Opportunities', January 1972.
29. HS11 copy reply from Right Honourable Margaret Thatcher, Secretary of State for Education and Science, 16/2/72.
30. HS15 progress report on campaign, undated.
31. HS14 NJC 19/7/71 copy of reply received from Mr C.A. Larsen, Central Training Council, Department of Training and Productivity, 13/7/71.
32. HS15 op.cit.
33. HS20.
34. HS21 op.cit.
35. HS22 NJC 41/7/23.
36. HS7 National Campaign for Nursery Education: Nursery Education and Equal Opportunities for Women (n.d.).
37. HS23 NJC 17/17/74 Elaboration of points raised by the Deputation.
38. HS26 NJC 11.1.75 'The Interrelationship of Education and Employment Opportunities'.
39. HS27 NJCWWO Report of Open Forum on the Interrelationship of Education and Employment Opportunities.
40. HS28 NJC 32/8/75 Curricula Differences for Girls and Boys: Education survey, HMSO, 1975.
41. HS32 NJC 37/8/76 Report of meeting NJC/John Tisdall.
42. HS44, NJC circular, Discrimination against Women in the Media, 1976.
43. HS41, Future role of the NJC, 10 July 1979.
44. HS50, NJC BM 5/1/81, NJC report for 2 years, 1979–1980.
45. HS51, NJC 2/1/82, NAD /W/5/1/82, report.
46. HS63, NJC 26/1/83, report for two years, 1981–1982.
47. HS63, op.cit.
48. HS77, NJC statement on social policy, 1985.
49. HS45, NJC 6/4/80, evidence to the Department of Health and Social Security.
50. HS48, Primary Health Care: an agenda for discussion. Response of the NJC.
51. HS58, JJC 17/10/82 NEC 25/10/82, Minutes of NJC 12/10/82.
52. Ibid: *HS 60*, NJC 19/12/82, report of delegation.
53. HS47, NJC 16/6/81, 'Women's Employment'.
54. HS50, op.cit.
55. HS63, op.cit.
56. Ibid., from *Spare Rib* October 1978.
57. Ibid.
58. HS56, NAD/W/5/1/82 NJC 2/1/82.
59. HS67, NJC/21/2/83.
60. Ibid.

61. Perrigo, Sarah, 'Women, Change and the Labour Party', *Parliamentary Affairs*, 1996.
62. HS83, minutes 14 August 1986, Peter Mandelsohn spoke on the Freedom and Fairness campaign.
63. HS73, minutes 15 October 1984. It was Hilda Smith who drew the issue to the committee's attention.
64. HS57, Report of the Working Party, n.d.
65. HS75, NJC 1/1/85, report for the two years 1983–1984. The Fawcett Society, named after Millicent Fawcett of the NUWSS, operates as a women's archive and study centre and carries out investigations.
66. Ibid.
67. Ibid.
68. Ibid.
69. HS56, NJC 51/4/84, report on retirement.
70. HS77, NJC statement on social policy, 1985.
71. Ibid.
72. HS75, op.cit.
73. HS77, op.cit.
74. Ibid.
75. Ibid.
76. Ibid.
77. HS83, NEC 24/9/86, minutes of NJC 14/8/86.
78. HS81, NJC, *A Monthly Journal for Working Women* 1987.
79. Perrigo op.cit. and Short, Claire, 'Women and the Labour Party', *Parliamentary Affairs*, 49 (1) 1996.
80. HS86, NJC, Future Programme of Work, 1987.
81. HS87, NJC 12/1/89.
82. A brief version of the campaign was given in Collette 'Questions of Gender: Labour and Women', in Brian Brivati and Richard Heffernan (eds), *The Labour Party: A Centenary History* (MacMillan Press Ltd, 2000), here reproduced with permission of Palgrave MacMillan.
83. Steven Fielding and Duncan Tanner, ' The "Rise of the Left" revisited', *Labour History Review* 71 (3) 2006, p. 217.
84. Pam Tatlow, 'Rights for Labour Women', in Sue Sturgeon and John Hurley (eds), *Reforming Labour: Reclaiming the People's Party* (Polemic Books, 2001), p. 116.
85. The niece of Enid Stacy, see Part I, Section 3.
86. See Part II, Section 6 for Florence Davy.
87. This, and the leaflets reproduced, are from the author's own papers.

Conclusion

1. Marion Phillips, *Women and the Labour Party* (Headley Bros., London, n.d., no page nos.).
2. It is notable that when Labour governments from 1997 sought to find out people's opinions, they had no such ready-made system available and resorted to less satisfactory methods such as open meetings and caravan tours.

3. José Harris, 'Labour's Political and Social Thought', in Duncan Tanner, Pat Thane and Nick Tiratsoo (eds), *Labour's First Century* (Cambridge University Press, 2000) is a good overview of changes in theory.
4. There is a good discussion of the different meanings of New Labour in Steven Driver and Steve Martell, *New Labour* (Polity, 2006).
5. Patrick Seyd and Paul Whitely, *New Labour's Grassroots: The Transformation of the Labour Party Membership* (Palgrave MacMillan, 2002) records that 6 out of every 10 members are male.
6. Janet Newman, *Modernising Governance: New Labour, Policy and Society* (Sage, 2001), p. 177. See also Pam Tatlow, 'Rights for Labour Women', in Sue Sturgeon and John Hurley (eds), *Reforming Labour: Reclaiming the People's Party* (Polemic Books, 2001).
7. Polly Toynbee and David Walker, *Better or Worse: Has Labour Delivered?* (Blomsbury Publishing, 2005).
8. Anna Coote, 'Feminism and the Third Way: A Call for Dialogue', in Stuart White (ed.), *New Labour:the Progressive Future* (Palgrave, 2001).
9. Harriet Harman and Deborah Mattison, *Winning for Women* (Fabian Pamphlet 596, 2001).
10. The feminist argument about citizenship as most accessibly put in Jan Jindy Pettman, *Worlding Women: A Feminist International Politics* (Routledge, 1996). See also Julia Kristeva, 'Women's Time', *Signs*, 7 (1) 1981.
11. Ruth Lister, *Citizenship: Feminist Perspectives* (Routledge, 1997), p. 66.
12. Collette, Christine, *The International Faith: Labour's Attitudes to European Socialism, 1918–1939* (Ashgate, 1998).
13. Mrs Barton, *Married Women and Paid Positions: A Plea for Solidarity Amongst Women* (Co-operative Women's Guild 1934).
14. Judith Butler, *Bodies that Matter* (New York, 1993), p. 30.

Bibliography

Manuscript sources

Hilda Smith Papers, at present with Baroness Gould.

Labour Party Archives, John Rylands University Library, National Museum of Labour History, Manchester

Standing Joint Committee papers.
Labour Party General correspondence.
Labour Party Subject files.
International Women.
Women's Labour League secretarial correspondence and related papers.

International Institute of Social History, Amsterdam

International Committee of Women Trades Unionists Conference reports, 1927, 1933, 1936.
International Federation of Trades Union papers.
Sozialistische Arbeiter-Internationale papers.
Margaret Sanger papers.

Ruskin College, Oxford

James and Lucy Middleton Papers.
Pete Curran's election campaign.

Public Record Office, London

Ramsay and Margaret MacDonald papers.
ILP National Administration Committee minutes.

Printed sources

Primary

Mrs Barton, *Married Women and Paid Positions: A Plea for Solidarity Amongst Women* (Co-operative Women's Guild, 1934).
Buckley, M.E., *The Feeding of Schoolchildren* (London, 1914).
Bunbury Sir, H.N. (ed.) *Lloyd George's Ambulance Wagon: The Memoirs of A.J. Braithwaite* (Methuen, 1957).

Ford, Isabella, *Women and Socialism* (London, 1904).
Furniss, S., and Marion Phillips, *The Working Woman's House* (London, 1920).
———, 'Citizenship of Women', *The Book of the Labour Party: its History, Growth, Policy and Leaders*, vol. ii (Labour Publishing Co., London 1925).
Greig, Theresa Billington, *The Consumer in Revolt* (London, c. 1912).
Hamilton, Mary Agnes, *Margaret Bondfield* (London, 1924).
MacMillan, Margaret, 'Citizens of Tomorrow', *The Book of the Labour Party: Its History, Growth, Policy and Leaders*, vol. ii (Labour Publishing Co., London, 1925).
Pankhurst Sylvia, E.,*The Suffragette Movement: An Intimate Account of Persons and Ideals* (London, 1931).
Phillips, Marion, *Organisation of Women in the Labour Party: A Handbook for Officers and Members of Women's Sections* (Labour Party, 1921).
——— and Taverner, Grace, *Women's Work in the Labour Party: Notes for Speakers and Workers Classes with Charts and Useful Forms* (Labour Party, n.d.).
——— (ed.), *Women and the Labour Party* (Headley Bros., n.d.).
Snowden, Ethel, *The Feminist Movement* (London, 1914).

Reports

Labour Party Conference Reports.
Soviet Russia: An Investigation by Women Trades Unionists (London, 1924).
Trades Union Congress Reports.

Newspapers and periodicals

Women's Trade Union Review.
Feminist Review.
Labour Woman.
Labour Leader.

Secondary

Alberti, Johanna, *Beyond Suffrage: Feminism in War and Peace 1914–1928* (Macmillan, 1985).
———, 'British Feminists and Anti-Fascism in the 1930s', in Oldfield, Sybil (ed.), *This Working Day World* (Taylor & Francis, 1994).
Bland, Lucy and Doan, Laura (eds), *Sexology in Culture* (Polity, 1998).
Butler, Judith, 'Imitation and Gender Subordination', in Ann Garry and Marilyn Pearsall (eds),*Women, Knowledge and Reality* (Routledge, 1996).
Coates, David and Lawler, Peter (eds), *New Labour in Power* (Manchester University Press, 2000).
Collette, Christine, *For Labour and for Women: The Women's Labour League 1906–1918* (Manchester University Press, 1989).
———, 'Daughter of the Newer Eve', in Jim Fyrth (ed.), *Labour's Promised Land* (Lawrence and Wishart, 1995).
———, *The International Faith: Labour's Attitudes to European Socialism, 1918–1939* (Ashgate, 1998).

———, 'The International Faith: Rituals and Liturgies of British Labour Movement Internationalism, 1918–1939', in Berthold Unfreid and Christine Schindler (eds), *Riten, Mythen und Symbole-Die Arbeiterbewegung zwischen "Zivil-religion" und Volkskultur* (Akademische Velagsanstalt, 1999).

———, 'Questions of Gender', in Brian Brivati and Richard Hefferman (eds), *The Labour Party: A Centenary History* (Macmillan, 2000).

Coote, Anna, 'Feminism and the Third Way: A Call for Dialogue', in Stuart White (ed.), *New Labour: The Progressive Future?* (Palgrave, 2001).

Francis, Martin, *Ideas and Policies under Labour, 1945–51* (Manchester University Press, 1997).

Goronwy-Roberts, Marian, *A Life of Marion Phillips, MP* (Bridge Books, 2000).

Graves, Pamela, *Labour Women: Women in British Working Class Politics 1918–1939* (Cambridge University Press, 1994).

Harman, Harriet and Mattison, Deborah, *Winning for Women* (Fabian Pamphlet 596, 2000).

Harrison, Brian, *Prudent Revolutionaries* (Oxford University Press, 1987).

Lister, Ruth, *Citizenship: Feminist Perspectives* (Routledge, 1997).

———, ' "She has Other Duties': Women, Citizenship and Social Security', in Sally Baldwin and Jane Falkenham (eds), *Social Security and Social Change: Challenges to the Beveridge Model* (Harvester Wheatsheaf, 1994).

Lockwood, Annie, *A Celebration of Pioneering Labour Women* (North Tyneside Fabians, 1995).

Lovenduski, Joni and Pippa Norris (eds), *Gender and Party Politics* (London, Sage, 1993).

Lunn, Kenneth (ed.), *Race and Labour in Britain in the Twentieth Century* (London, Frank Cass, 1985).

Mappen, Ellen, 'Introduction', to Clementina Black, *Married Women's Work* (Virago, 1984).

———, 'Strategies for Change: Social Feminist Approaches to the Problem of Women's Work', in Angela John (ed.), *Unequal Opportunities: Women's Employment in England, 1800–1914* (Blackwell, 1985).

Newman, Janet, *Modernising Government: New Labour Policy and Society* (Sage, 2001).

Norris, Pippa and Lovenduski, Joni, *Political Recruitment: Gender, Race and Class in the British Parliament* (Cambridge University Press, 1995).

Pettman, Jan Jindy, *Worlding Women: A Feminist International Politics* (Routledge, 1996).

Rowbotham, Sheila, Segal, Lynne and Wainwright, Hilary, *Beyond the Fragments* (Merlin, 1979).

Sturgeon, Sue and Hurley, John (eds), *Reforming Labour: Reclaiming the People's Party* (Polemic Books, 2001).

Seyd, Patrick and Whitely, Paul (eds.), *New Labour's Grassroots: The Transformation of the Labour Party Membership* (Palgrave Macmillan, 2002).

Tanner, Duncan, Williams, Chris and Hopkin, Deian (eds), *The Labour Party in Wales, 1900–2000* (University of Wales Press, 2000).

———, Thane, Pat and Tiratsoo, Nick (eds), *Labour's First Century* (Cambridge University Press, 2000).

Thane, Pat, 'The Feminism of Women in the British Labour Party', in Smith, H. (ed.), *Twentieth Century British Feminism* (Elgar Press, 1990).

Toynbee, Polly and Walker, David, *Better or Worse? Has Labour Delivered?* (Bloomsbury Publishing, 2005).
Voet, Rian, *Feminism and Citizenship* (Sage, 1998).
Wainwright, Hilary, 'New Forces of Democracy for Socialist Renewal', in David McLellan and Sayers, Sean (ed.), *Socialism and Democracy* (London, Macmillan, 1991).
Walby, Sylvia, *Gender Transformations* (Routledge, 1997).
Weinbren, Dan, *Generating Socialism: Recollections of Life in the Labour Party* (Sutton, 1997).

Journals

Black, Amy and Brooke, Stephen, 'The Labour Party, Women and the Problem of Gender 1951–66', *Journal of British Studies*, 36, 1997.
Blackburn Sheila, 'Between the Devil of Cheap Labour Competition and the Deep Sea of Family Poverty: Sweated Labour in Time and Place, 1840–1914', *Labour History Review*, 71 (2) 2006.
Bornat, Joanne and Diamond, Hanna, 'Women's History and Oral History: Developments and Debates, *Women's History Review*, 16 (1) 2007.
Bruley, Sue, 'The Politics of Food: Gender, Family, Community and Collective Feeding in South Wales in the General Strike and Miners' Lockout of 1926', *Twentieth Century British History*, 18 (1) 2007.
Cain, Harriet and Nina Yuval Davis, 'The Equal Opportunities Community' and the Anti-Racist Struggle', *Critical Social Policy* 29 vol.10 (2) Autumn 1990.
Collette, Christine 'Socialism and Scandal', *History Workshop Journal*, 23, 1987.
———, 'New Realism, Old Traditions', *Labour History Review*, 56 (1) 1991.
Davis, Joan, 'A Life in the Labour Movement', *Labour Heritage Women's Research Committee*, Bulletin no. 2, 1987.
Davy, Florence, 'From Zeppelins to Jets', *Labour Heritage Women's Research Committee*, Bulletin no. 2, 1987.
Fielding, Steven and Tanner, Duncan, 'The "Rise of the Left" Revisited: Labour Party Culture in Post-War Manchester and Salford', *Labour History Review*, 7 (3) 2006.
Gradwell, Angela Tuckett, 'Enid Stacy', *North West Labour History Society*, 7. 1980–1981.
Humphrey, Jill C., 'To Queer or not to Queer a Lesbian and Gay Group? Sexual and Gendered Politics at the Turn of the Century', *Sexualities*, 2 (2) May 1999.
King, Steven, ' "We are to be trusted": Female Poor Law Guardians and the Development of the New Poor Law: The Case of Bolton, England', *International Review of Social History*, 49 (1) 2004.
Kristeva, Julia, 'Women's Time', *Signs*, 7 (1) Autumn 1981.
Leff, Ann, 'My Brilliant Career in War Work', *Labour Heritage Women's Research Committee*, Bulletin no. 5, 1996.
Perrigo, Sarah, 'Women, Change and the Labour Party', *Parliamentary Affairs*, 1996.
Rock, Dorothy, 'The Best University', *Labour Heritage Women's Research Committee*, Bulletin no. 3, 1990.

Roe, Elisabeth, 'The Women from the Ministry', *Feminist Review*, 63, Autumn 1999.

Rose, Sonia, 'Gender and Labour History', *International Review of Social History*, 38 (Supplement 1) 1993.

Short, Clare, 'Women and the Labour Party', *Parliamentary Affairs*, 49 (1) 1996.

Thane, Pat, 'Women and Labour Politics', *Labour History Review*, 55 (3) 1990.

Tobin, Ann, 'Lesbianism and the Labour Party', *Feminist Review*, 34, Spring 1990.

Walter, Natasha, 'Women are Fed Up under New Labour', *Independent* 21 January 2000.

Worley, Matthew, 'Building the Labour Party: Labour Party Activism in Five British Counties between the Wars', *Labour History Review*, 70 (1) 2005.

Index

Note: in general, job titles refer to position currently held when referred to, eg Ernest Bevin, Minister of Labour, which was his current title. When an individual is mentioned several times over a long career, the highest position reached is given, eg Margaret Bondfield, Minister of Labour, a position she did not reach until 1929.